"Up! Flee! Out into broad and open land!
And this book full of mystery,
From **NOSTRADAMUS'** own very hand,
Is it not sufficient company?
The stars' course then you'll understand
And Nature, teaching you, will then expand
The power of your soul, as when
One **SPIRIT** to another **SPEAKS.**"

Faust, act 1, scene 1.

ONLY KNOWN AUTHENTIC PORTRAIT OF NOSTRADAMUS
PAINTED FROM LIFE BY HIS SON CAESAR

A rare item from the Henry C. Roberts Collection.

THE
COMPLETE
PROPHECIES OF
NOSTRADAMUS

Translated, Edited and Interpreted

BY

HENRY C. ROBERTS

Published by

NOSTRADAMUS, INC.

380 CANAL STREET, N. Y. C. 13, N. Y.

Fourteenth Printing
1966

PRINTED IN THE UNITED STATES OF AMERICA
AMERICAN BOOK-STRATFORD PRESS, INC., NEW YORK

INTRODUCTION

Nearly everyone, at one time or another, has heard or read something about Nostradamus and his prophecies. Yet, the astonishing fact is that not since 1672 has there been printed an English edition of his complete quatrains. As a bookseller, I was struck by this lack because of the great number of people, interested in predictions and other phenomena of this nature, who had come to me over a period of years, inquiring for the complete works of Nostradamus in English. As a student of the occult, always seeking materials on the subject, I too was anxious to procure the unabridged work of the man who is acknowledged as one of the greatest seers in the history of occult science.

Spurred on by these incentives, I began to search the field for all books, old and new, pertaining to Nostradamus. The reward was scanty. The current available books on Nostradamus dealt with but a few of his more noted quatrains, discussing them at length, but making no attempt to bring to light more than a few hundred out of the thousand he had purportedly written.

At long last I obtained, at an almost prohibitive price, a copy of the afore-mentioned 1672 edition: *The True Prophecies or Prognostications of Michael Nostradamus*, translated and annotated by Theophilus de Garencieres. I had perused but a few pages when I was struck by the sense of familiarity that these verses seemed to hold for me. Words that the author claimed held no significance for him, took on for me a definite meaning, became clearly focused into patterns of events—past, present and future. Here, I felt, was my book.

Such being the case, I determined to start the long and arduous task of making available, a new complete edition of Nostradamus, using all the materials at hand, bringing to them new interpretations in the light of recent events, taking as much as possible the same position as if Nostradamus were alive today—speaking with both our voices.

Avoiding the hitherto lengthy explanations that, I felt, bewildered rather than enlightened the reader, I have tried to make the interpretations concise and simple; I have also, as much as was feasible, tried to preserve the spirit and cadence of the original quatrains. The present text is the result, and I believe it to be clean and true. At all times, where there were discrepancies or ambiguities in the French text, I have accepted the oldest versions, especially considering Garencieres' book as the most authoritative.

From the time of the Delphic Sibyl it has been the characteristic of occult prophecies and utterances, often to seem unintelligible and garbled to the uninitiate. The strange, broken, and often incoherent nature of the quatrains, both in French and English, is the hallmark of prophetic media.

Nevertheless, at this point, I feel that a few words of explanation are necessary with regard to certain questions that may arise in the reader's mind. Primarily, we must clear up the fact that the word "prophecy" does not, in its literal sense, apply to every one of these quatrains. A good number of the verses have reference to events of the days before and during the time of Nostradamus—events that distressed, pleased, or shocked him, and which he considered important enough to record for posterity. But the bulk of his work was based upon his awesome gift of prognostication, and it is this that we are mainly concerned with. Even after deep study and wide consultation of occult materials, it was not always possible to assign these predictions to definite places or people. It would have been an easy matter to lightly attribute certain doings to certain people, but that would have taken on the nature of "guessing," and we say, in closing, that we prefer to leave that to the reader; for he will inevitably attempt to do so, and we urge him so to do—with "our" blessing.

HENRY C. ROBERTS

New York, N. Y.
November, 1946

INTRODUCTION TO SECOND EDITION

Beyond a shadow of doubt, the methods employed and results obtained by Nostradamus in looking into the future were outside of the physical framework.

What to the contemporary critics of his day, for want of a better term they chose to call magic or occult, we today now recognize as the operation of certain tenuous and imponderable laws that permeate the entire Cosmos. These intangible but all pervading forces we group today under the general title of "Extra Sensory Perception."

Such startling and apparently miraculous phenomena as mediumism, telepathy, telekinesis, etc., are today the serious subject of study by such accredited scientists as Dr. Rhine of Duke University and Prof. Gardner Murphy of New York University. An entirely new line of investigation is in progress in this new science of "Para-psychology" which promises rich rewards for mankind.

Who knows? Perhaps some day this new line of scientific activity may be developed to a point where it will have a practical application to our every day life and make possible a revolutionary concept of nature's forces.

HENRY C. ROBERTS

New York, N. Y.
March 2, 1949

PREFACE TO FIRST EDITION

A Letter of Dedication to his son, Caesar Nostradamus

Thy late coming, Caesar Nostradamus, my son, hath caused me to bestow much time in continual and nocturnal watchings, that I might leave a memorial of me after my death, to the common benefit of mankind, concerning the things which the Divine Essence hath revealed to me by astronomical revolutions. Since it hath pleased the immortal God that thou art come late into this world, and canst say that thy years are but few, and thy months incapable to receive into thy weak understanding what I am forced to define of futurity; since it is not possible to leave thee in writing what might be obliterated by the injury of time, for the hereditary gift of occult prediction shall be locked up in my breast; considering also that events are definitely uncertain, and that all is governed by the power of God who inspired us not by a Bacchic fury nor yet by Lymphatic motion, but by astronomical effects—"*Soli numine divino afflati praesagiunt et spirito prophetico particularia.*" *

Although I have often foretold long before what hath afterwards come to pass, and in particular regions, acknowledging all to have been done by divine virtue and inspiration, I was willing to hold my peace by reason of the injury—not only of the present time, but also of the future—because to put them in writing, the Kingdoms, Sects, and Regions shall be so diametrically opposed, that if I should relate what shall happen hereafter, those of the present Reign, Sect, Religion and Faith, would find it so disagreeing with their fancies, that they would condemn that which future ages shall find and know to be true. Consider also the saying of our Saviour, "*Nolite sanctum dare canibus neque mittatis margaritas vestras ante porcos, ne forte conculcent eas pedibus suis, et conversi dirumpant vos.*" (Matt. vii. 6)

For this reason I have withheld my tongue from the vulgar, and my pen from paper. But, afterwards, I was willing for the common good to enlarge myself in dark and abstruse sentences, declaring the future events, chiefly the most urgent and those which I foresaw (whatever human mutation happened) would not offend the hearers, all under dark figures

---

* "Such alone as are inspired by the divine power can predict particular events in a spirit of prophecy."

more than prophetical. Although "*Abscondidisti hoec à sapientibus, et prudentibus, id est, potentibus et regibus, et enucleasti ea exiguis et tenuibus.*" * The prophets, by means only of the immortal God and good Angels, have received the spirit of vaticination, by which they foresee things, and foretell future events. For nothing is perfect without Him, whose power and goodness are so great to His creatures, that though they are but men, nevertheless by the likeness of their good genius to the Angels, this heat and prophetical power draws near us, as do the rays of the sun, which cast their influence alike upon bodies that are elementary and non-elementary. As for us, who are but men, we cannot attain anything by our natural knowledge, of the secrets of God our Creator. "*Quia non est nostrum noscere tempora, nec momenta,*" etc. (Acts i. 7)

There are, or may come some persons, to whom God Almighty will reveal by impressions made on their understanding some secrets of the future, according to judicial astrology, as it hath happened in former times, when a certain power and voluntary faculty possessed them as a flame of fire. So by His inspiration, they were able to judge of divine and human things, for the divine works that are absolutely necessary, God will complete.

But, my son, I speak to thee a little too obscurely. There are secrets that are received by the subtle spirit of fire, by which the understanding is moved to contemplate the highest celestial bodies, being active and vigilant to the very pronunciation without fear or any shameful loquacity; all of which proceeded from the divine power of the Eternal God, from whom all goodness flows.

Now, my son, although I have inserted the name of prophet here, I will not attribute to myself so sublime a title, for "*Propheta dicitur hodie, olim vocabatur videns,*" ** and prophets are those properly, my son, that see things remote from the natural knowledge of mankind. Or, to put the case, the prophets, by the means of the perfect light of prophecy, may see divine things as well as human (which cannot but be seeing the effects of future predictions) and do extend a great distance, for the secrets of God are incomprehensible, and their efficient power is far remote from the natural knowledge, taking their origin in the free will, causing those things to appear which otherwise could not be known, neither by human auguries nor by any hidden knowledge or secret virtue under Heaven. Only by the means of some indivisible eternal being, and by Herculean agitation the causes come to be known by the celestial motion.

I say, therefore, my son, that you may not understand me well, because

* Thou hast hidden these things from the wise and prudent and hast revealed them to the small and weak."
** "He who is called prophet now, once was called seer."

the knowledge of this matter cannot yet be imprinted in thy weak brain. Future causes afar off are subject to the knowledge of human creatures, if (notwithstanding the Creator) things present and future were neither obscure nor hidden from the intellectual seal; but the perfect knowledge of the cause of things cannot be acquired without the divine inspiration, seeing that all prophetical inspiration received hath its original principle from God the Creator, next, from good luck, and afterwards from nature. Therefore, causes, independently produced or not produced, the prophecy partly happens where it hath been foretold, for the understanding being intellectually created cannot see occult things, unless it be by the voice coming from the limbo, by the means of the thin flame, to which the knowledge of future causes is inclined. And, also, my son, I entreat thee not to bestow thy understanding on such fopperies which dry up the body and damn the soul, and bring vexation to the senses. Chiefly abhor the vanity of the execrable magic forbidden by the Sacred Scriptures and by the Canons of the Church; except from this judicial astrology by which, and by the means of divine inspiration, with continual calculations, we have put in writing, our prophecies.

Although this occult philosophy was not forbidden, I could never be persuaded to meddle with it, although many volumes concerning that art, which hath been concealed a great while, were presented to me. But fearing what might happen, after I had read them, I presented them to Vulcan and, while he was devouring them, the flame mixed with the air, there was an unwonted light more bright than the usual flame and it was as if there were lightning, shining all the house over, as if it had been all in a flame. Therefore, that henceforth you might not be abused in the search of the perfect transformation, as much lunar as solar, and to seek in the waters uncorruptible metal, I have burnt them all to ashes. But as to the judgment which cometh to be perfected by the help of the celestial judgment, that I will manifest to you that you may have knowledge of future things; rejecting the fantastic imaginations that may arise, and limiting the particularity of places which were arrived at by divine and supernatural inspiration, according to the celestial figures, by an occult property, and by a divine virtue, power and faculty—in the presence of which the three aspects of time are comprehended by eternity, an evolution that ties into one the cause that is past, present, and future; "quia omnia sunt nuda et aperta. . ." *

Therefore, my son, thou mayst, notwithstanding thy tender brain, comprehend things that shall happen hereafter, and may be foretold by celestial natural lights, and by the spirit of prophecy, not that I will attribute to myself the name of a prophet, but as a mortal man, being no

* "For all things are naked and open."

farther from Heaven by my sense than I am from Earth by my feet.
"*Possum non errare, falli, decipi,*" * (albeit) I am the greatest sinner
of the world subject to all human afflictions. But being surprised sometimes by a prophetical mood, and by a long calculation, pleasing myself
in my study, I have made Books of Prophecies, each one containing a
hundred Astronomical Stanzas, which I have joined obscurely, and are
perpetual prophecies from this year to the year 3797, at which some perhaps will frown, seeing so large an extension of time, and that I treat of
everything under the Moon. If thou livest the natural age of a man thou
shalt see in thy climate, and under the Heaven of thy nativity, the future
things that have been foretold.

God only knoweth the eternity of the light proceeding from Himself,
and I say freely to those to whom His incomprehensible greatness hath by
a long melancholic inspiration revealed, that by the means of this occult
cause, divinely manifested, chiefly by two principal causes, there is compre-
hension and understanding in him that is inspired and prophetic. One is
that which cleareth the supernatural light and foretelleth by the doctrine of the planets, and the other forecasts by inspired revelation, which
is a kind of participation in the divine eternity, by means of Him, of God
the Creator. And by these means he knows that what is predicted is true,
and hath taken its original from above, and such light and small flame is
of all efficacy and sublimity, no less than the natural light makes the
philosophers so secure, that by the means of the principles of the first
cause, they have attained the greatest depth of the profoundest sciences.

But I must not wander too far, my son, from the capacity of thy sense.
I find that learning shall be at a great loss, and that before the universal
conflagration shall happen so many great inundations, that there shall
scarce be any land that shall not be covered with water, and this shall last
so long, that except for Ethnographies and Topographies all shall perish.
Before and after these inundations in many countries there shall be such
scarcity of rain and such a great deal of fire, and burning stones shall fall
from Heaven, that nothing unconsumed shall be left. All this shall happen
a little while before the great conflagration.

Although the planet Mars makes an end of his course, and is come
to the end of his last period, nevertheless he shall begin it again. Some
shall be gathered in Aquarius for many years, others in Cancer also for
many years. Now we are governed by the Moon, under the power of
Almighty God; which Moon before she hath finished her circuit, the Sun
shall come, and then Saturn. According to the celestial signs, the reign
of Saturn shall come again, so that all being calculated, the world draws
near to its anaragonic revolution (death-dealing).

* "I am able not to err, be deceived nor fail."

From this present time that I write this, before 177 years, three months, eleven days, through pestilence, famine, war, and for the most part, inundations, the world between this and that prefixed time, before and after, for several times shall be so diminished, and the people shall be so few, that they shall not find enough to till the ground, so that they shall remain fallow as long as they had once been tilled. We are now in the seventh millenary, which ends all and brings us near the eighth, where the firmament of the eighth sphere is, which, in a latitudinary dimension, is the place where the Great God shall make an end of this revolution, where the celestial bodies shall move again, and the superior motion that maketh the Earth firm and stable, "*non inclinabitur in seculum seculorum*," * unless His will be accomplished and not otherwise.

Although by ambiguous opinions exceeding all natural reasons by Mahometical dreams, also sometimes God the Creator by the ministers of His messengers of fire and flame, shows to our external senses, and chiefly to our eyes, the causes of future predictions, signifying the future event, that will manifest to him that prophesies. For the prophecy that is made by the internal light, comes to judge of the thing partly with and by the means of external light, although the part which seemeth to come by the eye of understanding, comes only from the lesion of its imaginative sense. The reason is evident why what he foretelleth comes by divine inspiration, or by the means of an angelical spirit, inspired into the prophetic person, anointing him with vaticinations, moving the fore part of his fancy, by divers nocturnal apparitions, so that by astronomical administrations, he prophesies with a divine certitude, joined to the holy prediction of the future, having no other regard than to the freedom of his mind.

Come now, my son, and understand that I find by my revelations (astrological), which agree with the divine inspiration, that the swords draw near to us now, and the plague and the war more horrid than hath been seen in the life of three men before, and also famine, which shall return often, for the stars agree with the revolution, "*Visitabo in virga ferrea iniquitates eorum, et in verberibus percutiam eos.*" ** For the mercies of God shall not be spread for a while, my son, before most of my prophecies shall come to pass, thus oftentimes shall happen sinister storms. "*Conteram ego, et confringam,*" (said the Lord) "*et non miserebor.*" † And a thousand other accidents shall happen by waters and continual rains, as I have more fully at large declared in my other Prophecies, written *in soluta oratione*, limiting the places, times and prefixed terms, that men coming after, may

---

* "Whence it shall not deviate from age to age."
** "I will visit their iniquities with a rod of iron, and with blows will strike them."
† "I will trample them and break them, and not show pity."

see and know that those accidents are certainly come to pass, as we have marked in other places, speaking more clearly, although the explication be involved in obscurity: *"Sed quando submoventa erit ignorantia"*; * the case shall be made more clear. Making an end here, my son, accept this gift of thy father, Michael Nostradamus, hoping to expound to thee every prophecy of these quatrains, praying to the Immortal God that he will grant thee a long life in felicity.

* "When the time arrives for the removal of ignorance."

From Salon, this 1st of March, 1555.

1

Estant assis, de nuit secrette estude,
Seul, repose sur la selle d'airain,
Flambe exigue, sortant de solitude,
Fait proferer qui n'est a croire vain.

Seated at night in my secret study,
Alone, reposing over the brass tripod,
A slender flame leaps out of the solitude,
Making me pronounce that which is not in vain.

Nostradamus clearly shows his method of preparing for a nocturnal visitation from divine sources, from which he shall gain the knowledge of future events for the benefit of Posterity.

2

La verge en main, mise au milieu des branches,
De l'onae je mouille & le limbe & le pied,
En peur j'escris fremissant par les manches;
Splendeur Divine; le Divine prez s'assied.

With divining rod in hand, I wet the limb and foot,
Set in the middle of the branches.
Fearsome awe trembles my hand, I await,
Heavenly Splendor! The Divine Genius sitteth by.

Evidently our author employed an instrument similar to the present forked, divining rod, now used for locating water. In a large brass bowl filled with water, various segments were marked off and, as the rod dipped to the proper significant areas, messages would emanate.

3

Quand la littiere du tourbillon versee,
Et seront faces de leurs manteaux couvers,
La Republique par gens nouveaux vexee,
Lors blancs & rouges jugeront a L'envers.

When the litter shall be overthrown by a gust of wind,
And faces shall be covered with cloaks,
The Republic shall be vexed by new people,
Then shall White and Red judge wrongly.

During a period of transition, a temporary group, which will be neither Red nor White, shall be in power over the Republic.

4

Par l'Univers sera fait un Monarque,
Qu'en paix & vie ne sera longuement,
Lors se perdra la Piscature Barque,
Sera regie en plus grand detriment.

In the world shall be a Monarch,
Who will not leave peace, nor be long alive,
Then will be lost the Fishing Boat,
And shall be governed to its great detriment.

The Roman Catholic Church is often compared to a ship or boat, by Nostradamus. At a time when a Temporal Ruler shall reign over the entire earth, the Church shall be conspicuous by its absence.

5

Chassez seront sans faire long combat,
Par le pais seront plus fort grevez,
Bourg & Cite auront plus grand debat,
Carcas, Narbonne auront coeurs esprouvez.

They shall be driven away without great fighting,
Those of the country shall be greatly grieved,
Town and City shall have a mighty debate,
Carcassone, Narbonne shall prove their heart.

Here is nothing mysterious. It must be borne in mind that Nostradamus was a devout Catholic, and in keeping with the then current struggle between the Protestants and Catholics for power, he foretells a fraternal melee, centering about Carcassone and Narbonne in Languedoc.

6

L'oeil de Ravenne sera destitue,
Quand a ses pieds les aisles sailli-
ront;
Les deux de Bresse auront consti-
tue,
Turin, Verceil, que Gaulois foule-
ront.

The eye of Ravenna shall be desti-
tute,
When the wings shall rise at his
feet.
The two of Brescia shall have established Turin and Venice,
Which the French shall have trod
upon.

One who lives in Ravenna shall not find time for the pursuit of riches
when the wings of inspiration arise.
The French shall ultimately have sovereignty.

7

Tard arrive, l'execution faite,
Le vent contrare, lettres au che-
min prinses,
Les conjurez quatorze d'une secte,
Par le Rousseau seront les entre-
prinses.

One arriving too late, the execution will take place,
The wind being contrary, and letters intercepted on the way.
The conspirators fourteen of a
separate body,
By the Red One, the enterprise
shall be undertaken.

The Red One will be the leader of a conspiracy involving fourteen
members, terminating in an execution, previously delayed.

8

Combien de fois prinse cite solaire,
Seras, changeant les loix barbares
& vaines,
Ton mal s'approche, plus seras tributaire,
Le grand Adrie recouvrira tes
veines.

How often taken, O city of the Sun
shall thou be?
Changing thy vain and barbarous
laws,
Thy Evil groweth nigh, Thou shalt
be more tributary,
The great Venice shall recover thy
veins.

Heliopolis, or Baalbec, an ancient city in Syria near Damascus, famous
for its ruins, is used symbolically by Nostradamus to indicate the growing
evil in the world.

9

De l'Orient viendra le coeur punique,
Fascher Adrie, & les hoirs Romu-
lides,
Accompagne de la classe Libique
Trembler Melites, & proches Isles
vuides.

From the East of Africa shall come
the Lion-Heart,
To vex Venice and the heirs of
Romulus,
Accompanied by the Libian Tribe,
Malta shall tremble and the neigh-
boring islands shall be empty.

A remarkably prophetic description of the role of Emperor Haile
Selassie, in World War II, who reconquered Ethiopia, in East Africa,
and sent an expedition to aid the Allied Cause, eventually defeating the
Fascists of Italy, self-styled "Heirs of Romulus."

10

Sergens transmis dans la Cage de
Fer,
Ou les enfans septains du Roy
sont pris,
Les vieux & peres sortiront bas
d'enfer,
Ains mourir voir de son fruit mort
& cris.

Sergeants sent into the Cage of
Iron,
Where the seven children of the
King are,
The old men and fathers shall see
the death and cries of their first
fruit,
And before they die, shall go
through Hell.

A description of the incidents that came to pass during the "Reign of
Terror" in the French Revolution. The daily roll calls of those proscribed
for the guillotine are graphically portrayed.

11

Le mouvement de sens, coeur,
pieds, & mains,
Seront d'accord, Naples, Leon, Si-
cile,
Glaives, Feux, Eaux, puis au Noble
Romains,
Plongez, Tuez, Morts, par cerveau
debile.

Naples, Spain and Sicily shall agree
To the movement with heart, feet
hands and sense,
Swords, Fires, Water, then to the
Noble Romans,
Plunged into death by a weak
brain.

The active cooperation of Fascist Italy and Falangist Spain is foretold,
predicting dire results to both Mussolini and his cohorts.

12

Dans peu ira fauce brute fragile,
De bas en haut ensleve prompte-
ment,
Puis en estant desloyal & labile,
Qui de Verone aura gouvernment.

In a little while a treacherous brute
shall be raised,
Quickly from a low to high estate,
Unfaithfully and swiftly,
He shall have the government of
Italy.

A continuation of the previous quatrain, this depicts the rise of Mussolini from an insignificant rabble rouser to Duce, or Leader of the Italian
State.

13

Les exiles, par ire, haine intestine,
Feront au Roy grand conjuration,
Secret mettront ennemis par la
mine,
Et les vieux siens, contre eux sedi-
tion.

The exiles, by anger, shall spread
internal strife,
And make against the King a great
conspiracy,
Secret enemies shall they put in
the mine,
And raise the old ones against
them by sedition.

The progress of the Italian conspiracy is indicated—the rise of a fifth
column rife with internal dissensions, culminating with a plot against
King Victor Emmanuel.

14

De gens esclave, chansons, chants,
& requestes,
Captifs par Princes, & Seigneurs
aux prisons,
A l'aduenir par idiots sans testes,
Seront receus par divins oraisons.

Being kept prisoners, by Princes
and Lords,
The slavish people petition for
songs and books,
For the future, idiots without
heads
Shall be received by divine prayers.

The forecast of a revolution in Russia. The Russian, or Slavonic,
people, held in subjection by their rulers, will seek enlightenment and
surcease from oppression.

15

Mars nous menace par la force bellique,
Septante fois fera le sang respandre,
Auge & ruine de l'Ecclesiastique,
Et par ceux qui d'eux rien ne voudront entendre.

Mars threatens us with a warlike
force,
Seventy times he shall cause blood
to be shed,
Causing the ruin of the Clergy
And those who will hear nothing
from them.

The Damoclean Sword of War shall hang over Humanity for a period
of Seventy Great Wars, eventually causing a debacle among the heedless
mortals as well as the Church.

*CENTURY 10
72 page 336*

16

Faux a l'Estang, joint vers la Sagit-
taire,
En son haut auge de l'exaltation,
Peste, Famine, Mort de main mili-
taire,
Le Siecle approcher de renovation.

When a fish pond that was a
meadow shall be mowed,
Sagittarius being in the ascendant,
Plague, Famine, Death by the mili-
tary hand,
The Century approaches renewal.

In 1999, as the old century is about to expire, between November 23rd
and December 21st, the climactic War of Wars shall be unleashed.

17

Par quarante ans l'Iris n'apparoistra,
Par quarante ans tous les jours sera
veu,
La Terre aride en siccite croistra,
Et grand deluge quand sera ap-
parceu.

For forty years the rainbow shall
not appear,
For forty years it shall be seen every
day,
The parched earth shall wax drier
and drier,
And a great flood when it shall
appear.

A continuation of the preceding stanza—the prediction depicts conditions during the Armageddon.

18

Par la discorde, negligence Gauloise,	Through the discord and negligence of the French,
Sera passage a Mahomet ouvert,	A passage shall be opened to Mahomet,
De sang trempe la terre & mer Senoise,	The land and sea of Italy shall be bloody,
Le Port Phocen de voiles & nefs couvert.	And the harbor of Marseilles shall be covered with sails and ships.

The Arab Mohammedan Confederacy, dominated by the Mohammedan Church, shall find an entering wedge into geo-politics largely through French aid.

19

Lors que serpens viendront circuir l'air,	When the serpents shall come to encompass the air,
Le sang Troien verse par les Espagnes,	The French blood shall be angered by Spain,
Par eux; grand nombre en sera fait tare,	By them, a great number shall perish,
Chef fuit, cache aux marets dans les saignes.	The chief flies, and hides in the rushes of the marshes.

At the beginning of World War II, the air superiority of the Nazis was clearly demonstrated much to the chagrin of the French, who, threatened by Spain, were forced to maintain a strong force at their border. Eventually, the French President and his entourage were forced to fly from Paris.

20

Tours, Orleans, Blois, Angers, Renes & Nantes,	Tours, Orleans, Blois, Angers, Reims and Nantes,
Cites vexees par soudain changement,	Cities vexed by sudden change,
Par langues estranges seront tendues tentes,	By strange languages tents shall be set up,
Fleuves, Darts, Rennes, Terre & Mer tremblement.	Rivers, Darts, Rennes, Land and Sea shall tremble.

The German Invasion continues, and the above-named cities are quickly changed over to Nazi rule. The strange German language becomes the official speech, and the rest of France trembles under bombardment from the air.

21

Profonde argile blanche nourrit
 rocher,
Qui d'un abysme istra l'acticineuse,
En vain troublez ne l'seront
 toucher,
Ignorant estre au fond terre argi-
 leuse.

A deep white clay a rock supports,
Which shall break out of the deep
 like milk,
In vain people shall be troubled,
 not daring to touch it,
Being ignorant that in the bottom
 there is a milky clay.

A prediction of a new and as yet undiscovered method of utilization
of Nature's resources, producing powerful actinic properties.

22

Ce qui vivra & n'aura aucen sens,
Viendra le fer a mort son artifice,
Autun, Chalons, Langres, & les
 deux Sens,
La guerre & la glasse fera grand
 malefice.

That which shall live shall leave
 no direction,
Its destruction and death will come
 by stratagem,
Autun, Chalons, Langres, and from
 both sides,
The war and ice shall do great
 harm.

A forecast of the use of supersonic weapons, traveling in the near absolute zero temperature above the stratosphere.

23

Au mois troisiesme se levant le So-
 leil,
Sanglier, Leopard, aux champs
 Mars pour combatre,
Leopard lasse au Ciel esttena son
 oeil,
Un Aigle autour du Soleil voit
 sesbatre.

In the third month at the rising of
 the sun,
The Wild Boar and Leopard in
 the fields of Mars battle,
The Leopard weary, lifts his eyes
 to Heaven
And seeth an eagle playing about
 the Sun.

The English Lion, or Leopard, doggedly holds off the German Boar,
as the American Eagle gains altitude for his fateful swoop.

24

A Cite Nevue pensif pour condamner,	In the New City, to condemn an idea,
Loisel de Proie au ciel se vient offrir,	The Bird of Prey shall offer himself to the sky,
Apres Victoire a captifs pardonner	After Victory the prisoners shall be forgiven,
Cremone & Mantoue grands maux auront ouffert.	After Cremona and Mantua have suffered much.

After many cities have received severe damage, and victory is achieved, a trial shall be held in New City (Nu-Rem-Burg). Most of the prisoners shall be given light sentences.

25

Perdu, trouve cache de si long siecle	Lost, found again, hidden so great a while,
Sera Pasteur demy-Dieu honore,	A Pasteur as Demi-God shall be honored,
Ains que la Lune acheve son grand Siecle,	But before the moon her great cycle ends,
Par autre vents fera dishonore.	By other ancient ones shall be dishonored.

Louis Pasteur, the great French physician, is shown here to be worshipped almost as a demi-god for his discoveries, until a resurgence of an older school.

26

Le grande du Fondre tomb d'heure diurne,	The great man falleth by lightning in the day,
Mal & predit par porteur populaire,	An evil foretold by the postulant one,
Suivant presage tombe d'heure nocturne,	According to the forecast, another falls in hours of the night,
Conflict Rheims, Londres, Etrusque, Pestifere.	A conflict at Rheims and London, and a plague in Tuscany.

The taking over of Czechoslovakia by Hitler, the resignation of President Benes, the dissensions over the matter between France and England, and the dire warning of the consequences of this betrayal, are all remarkably outlined in this prophecy.

27

Des soubs le chesne Guyen du ciel frappe,
Non loin de la est cache le thresor,
Qui par long siecles avoir este grappe,
Trouve mourra, l'oeil creve de ressor.

Underneath the cord, Guien struck from the sky,
Near where is hid a great treasure,
Which has been many years a gathering,
Being found, he shall die, the eye put out by a spring.

Paratroopers alight near the Nazi's plunder hoard and, captured, they are executed.

28

La Tour de Bouk craindra fuste barbare,
Un temps, long temps apres barque Hesperique,
Bestial, gens, meubles tous deux feront grand tare,
Taurus & Libra quelle mortelle pique.

The Tower of Bouk shall be in awe of barbarous musty odor,
For a while, and a long time after afraid of Spanish craft,
Cattle, people and goods, both shall receive a great damage,
Taurus and Libra, oh, what a deadly feud!

The Tower of Bouk is a fortified place at the mouth of the Rhone. It shall be attacked by gas, discharged from craft flying the Spanish flag, sometime in April or October.

29

Quand le poisson, terrestre & aquatique,
Par forte vague au gravier sera mis,
Sa forme estrange suave & horrifique,
Par mer aux murs bien tost enemies.

When the fish, that is both terrestrial and aquatic,
By a strong wave shall be cast upon the shore,
With his strange, fearful, horrid form,
Soon after the enemy shall come to the walls by the sea.

A clear account of the D-Day Invasion of the Normandy beaches, with an exact description of the amphibious tanks and ducks employed by the Allies.

30

La Nef estrange par le tourment
Marin,
Abordera pres le port incognu,
Nonobstant signs due remeau pal-
merin.
Apres mort, pille, bon advis tard
venu.

The strange ship by the Seas torment,
Shall come near the unknown port,
Notwithstanding the signs given
to it of the bows and palms,
It shall die, be plundered, a good
advice come too late.

A prophetic description of France in the days preceding the War,
when the Ship of State was sabotaged and plundered by avaricious, selfish,
factional disputes.

31

Tant d'ans les guerras, en Gaule
dureont,
Outre la course du Castulon Mon-
arque,
Victoire incerte trois grands cou-
roneront,
Aigle, Coq, Lune, Lion Soleil en
Marque.

So many years the wars shall last in
France,
Beyond the course of the Castil-
lian monarch,
An uncertain victory three great
ones shall crown
The Eagle, the Cock, the Moon,
the Lion leaving the sun in its
mark.

At the conclusion of the war, an insecure truce is declared between
the victors—United States, France, China, and England—all of whom
will exact a penalty from the Land of the Rising Sun, or Japan.

32

La grand Empire sera tost translate,
En lieu petit qui bien tost viendra
coistre,
Lieu bien infime d'exigue comte,
Ou au milieu viendra poser son
scepter.

The great Empire shall soon be
translated
Which shall grow soon into an inferior place of small account,
In the middle of which he shall
come,
To lay down his scepter.

A continuation of the previous stanza. Great Japan will degenerate
into a minor power, with the Emperor abdicating the throne.

33

Pres d'un grand pont de plaine spa-
cieuse,
Le grand Lion par force, Cesarees,
Fera abatre hors cite, rigoureuse,
Par effroy portes luy seront reser-
rees.

At a great bridge, near a spacious
plain,
The great Lion, by Caesarous
forces,
Shall come to be pulled down before the rigorous city,
The gates which shall be shut to
him.

Winston Churchill will re-enter English politics to save the Tory
Party from Labor, but, by a coalition, shall be defeated.

34

L'oiseau de proye volant a la fenestre,
Avant conflict, fait au Francois
parure,
L'un bon prendra, l'autre ambigue
sinistre,
La partie foible tiendra pour bonne
augure.

The bird of prey flying to the win-
dow,
Before battle shall appear to the
French,
One shall take good omen of it, the
other, an ambiguous one,
The weaker party shall hold it a
good sign.

A foreign Demagogue will cause intrigue by dividing the various
parties, and the faction weakest in numbers will be spurred to action.

35

Le Lion jeune le vieux surmontera,
En champ bellique par singulier
duelle,
Dans cage d'or loeil il lui crevera,
Deux plays une puis mourir mort
cruelle.

The young Lion shall overcome
the old one
In martial field by a single duel,
In a golden cage he shall put out
his eye,
Two wounds from one, then he
shall die a cruel death.

One of the most famous of Nostradamus' prophecies:—The Young
Lion, a Scottish Knight, in a tournament with King Henry II, the Old Lion,
accidentally pierced his golden helmet with a splinter of his wooden lance,
putting out his eye and penetrating his brain, causing the King to die "a
cruel death."

36

Tard le Monarque se viendra re-
    pentir.
De navior mis a mort son adver-
    saire,
Mais viendra bien a plus haut con-
    sentir,
Que tout son sang par mort fera
    deffaire.

The Monarch shall repent too late,
That he has not put his adversary
    to death,
But he shall give his consent to a
    greater thing than that,
Which is, to kill all his adversary's
    kindred.

Toussaint L'Overture, the great leader of the Negroes of Haiti, and his connection with Napoleon I, is here foreseen. Despite his fight on the side of the French, L'Overture was eventually deposed as Governor of Haiti by Napoleon, and brought to France where he died in prison.

37

Un peu devant que le Soleil saba-
    conse
Conflict donne, grand peuple du-
    bieux,
Profligez, port-marin ne fait re-
    sponce,
Pont & sepulchre en deux es-
    tranges lieux.

A little before the sun sets,
A battle shall be given, a great peo-
    ple shall be doubtful,
Of being foiled, the sea port makes
    no answer,
A bridge and sepulchre shall be in
    two strange places.

One of the numerous prophecies that refer to the events in the great Armageddon.

38

Le sol & l'aigle victeur parois-
    stront,
Response vain au vaincu lon as-
    seure,
Par Cor ne cris, harnois n'arreste-
    ront,
Vindicte paix, par mort lacheve a
    l'heure.

The sun and eagle shall appear to
    be victorious,
A vain answer shall be made good
    to the vanquished,
By no means, arms shall not be
    stopped,
Peace, prosecuted by death, it shall
    be achieved.

A movement shall arise for the suppression of armament and wars. War in itself will become so terrible that nations will achieve peace through fear of Universal Death.

39

De nuit le lit le supresme estrange,
Pour avoir trop suborne blonde
esleu,
Partrois l'Empire subroge exancle,
A mort metra, carte ne pacquet
leu.

By night, in the bed, the chief one
shall be strangled,
For having corrupted too much the
fair elect,
By three the Empire subrogate
exancle.
He, devoted to death, reading
neither card nor packet.

The author purposely obscured this prophecy in the third line, because the persons concerned were then alive, viz., King Phillip II of Spain, who caused his only son, Don Carlos, to be strangled in bed, for suspicion of being intimate with his wife, Elizabeth of France and daughter of Henry II.

40

La tourbe fausse dissimilant folie
Fera Bizance un changement de
loix,
Istra d'Egypt qui veus que l'on de-
slie,
Edict, changant monnoys & alloys.

The false troupe dissembling their
folly,
Shall make in Constantinople, a
change of laws,
One shall come out of Egypt who
will have untied the edict,
Changing the money and the
standards.

At a convention held in the Near East, the Nations will attempt to draw up an economic and financial formula for the free flow of world trade.

41

Siege a cite & de nuit assaille,
Peu eschapez non loing de Mer
conflict,
Femme de joys, retour fils, de fail-
lie
Poison & lettres cache dedans le
plic.

A siege laid to a city, and assaulted
by night,
A few shall escape to fight not far
from the sea,
A woman swoons for joy to see her
son returned,
A poison hidden in the fold of
letters.

A local incident which meant much to contemporary Provençals, but which now, from our distant point of view, has lost its importance.

42

Les dix Calendes d'Avril de fait
Gothique,
Rescuscite encor par gens malins,
Le feu estaint, assemblee diabo-
lique,
Cherchand les os de d'amant &
Psellin.

The tenth of the Calends of April,
Gothic account,
Raised up again by malicious per-
sons,
The light put out, a diabolical as-
sembly,
Seek for the bones of the lovers
and Psellus.

An account of a witches' assembly, on the twenty-third of April, old
style—evil persons assemble and various diabolical acts are performed in
the dark, all according to Psellus, a famed Byzantine writer on Black Magic.

43

Avant qu'avien le changement
d'Empire,
Ill adviendra un cas bien merveilleux,
Le champ mue, le pilier de Por-
phyre,
Mis, translate sur le Rocher Noi-
leux.

Before the change of Empire
comes,
There shall be a strange accident,
A field shall be changed, and a
pillar of Porphyry
Shall be transported upon the
chalky cliffs.

England will change its course of Empire, when upon the chalky cliffs
of Dover, shall appear a pillar, or adherent, of Porphyry (a famous anti-
Christian philosopher of ancient Rome, A.D. 233–305).

44

En bref seront de retour sacrifices,
Contrevenans seront mis a martyre,
Plus ne seront moins, abbez ne
novices,
Le miel sera beaucoup plus cher
que cire.

In a short time sacrifices shall return again,
Opposers shall be put to martyrdom,
There shall be no more monks,
abbots, nor novices,
Honey shall be dearer than wax.

A period of persecution against the Catholic Church is foretold, when
Protestants will forbid the use of wax candles used in the Catholic ritual.

45

Secteur de Sectes, grand paine au delateur,
Beste en theatre, dresse le jeu scenique,
Du fait antique ennobly l'inventeur,
Par sectes, monde confus & schismatique.

Followers of Sects, great pains to the informer,
A beast on the stage prepares the scenes,
The inventor of that iniquitous fact shall be famous,
By sects the world shall be confused and schismatic.

Nostradamus, a confirmed Catholic, and a believer in the infallibility of the Church, releases a blast of condemnation at Martin Luther, whose appearance divided the Christian World into innumerable Sects.

46

Tout aupres d'Auch, de Lectoure & Mirande,
Grande feu du ciel en trois nuits tombera,
Chose adviendra bien stupende & mirande,
Bien peu apres al terre tremblera.

Near Auch, Lectoure and Mirande,
A great fire shall from the sky for three nights fall,
A thing shall happen stupendous and wonderful,
And shortly after the ground shall quake.

Auch, Lectoure, and Mirande are towns in Guyenne, a Province of France, in the vicinity of Bordeaux. This area, Nostradamus informs us, will bear watching.

47

Du Lac Lemans les sermons fascheront,
Des jours seront reduit par des sepmains,
Puis mois, puis an, puis tous dafalliront,
Les Magistrats damneront leurs Loix vaines.

The sermons of the Leman Lake shall be troublesome,
Some of the days shall be extended weeks,
Then into months, then into years, when they shall fail,
The magistrates shall condemn their own inept laws.

Lake Leman is the ancient name for Geneva. Here is clearly foretold the efforts and final failure of the League of Nations.

cen7aey 10 336
74 page

48

Vingt ans du regne de la lune passez,
Sept mil ans autre tiendra sa monarchie,
Quand le soleil prendra ses jours laissez,
Lors accomplit a fine ma Prophecie.

Twenty years of the reign of the moon having passed,
Seven thousand years another shall hold his monarchy,
When the sun shall resume his days past,
Then is fulfilled and ends my prophecy.

The end of the world is here explicitly prophesied by Nostradamus. In the year 7000 the Sun will destroy the Earth and again resume its undisputed sway.

49

Beaucoup, beaucoup avant telles menees,
Ceux d'Orient par la vertu Lunaire,
L'An mil sept cens feront grands emmenees,
Subjugant presque le coin Aquilonaire.

Much, very much before these doings happen,
Those of the East by virtue of the Moon,
In the year 1700, shall carry away great multitudes,
And shall subdue almost the whole northern section.

In the year 2025, by ritual, China, having completed her industrial and economic expansions, will absorb almost the whole of Northern Russia and Scandinavia.

centary 10 335
71 page

50

De l'aquatique triplicite naistra,
Un qui fera Feudy pour sa feste,
Son bruit, loz, regne & puissance croistra,
Par Terre & Mer, aux Orients tempeste.

From the aquatic triplicity shall be born,
One who shall make Thursday his holiday,
His fame, praise, rule, and power shall grow,
By Land and Sea to become a tempest to the east.

A triple alliance shall bring forth one who is a follower of Thor, God of Thunder, bringing much grief to the East.

51

Chef d'Aries, Jupiter and Saturn,	Heads of Aries, Jupiter and Saturn,
Dieu Eternal quelles mutations!	O Eternal God, What changes
Puis apres long siecle son malin	there shall be!
temps retourne,	After an era his evil time returns,
Gaule & Italy quelles emotions!	Gaule and Italy, what commotion!

A period of unrest in Italy shall culminate in the intervention of the French and a complete change in the social order.

52

Les deux malin de Scorpion con-joint,	The two evils of Scorpion being joined,
Le Grand Seigneur meurtry dedans sa salle,	The Grand Seignior murdered in his hall,
Peste a l'Eglise par le nouveau Roy jonts,	Plague to the Church by a King joined to it,
L'Europe basse & Septentrioanle.	Europe in the depths and dismembered.

The Church, as well as all Europe, is to be cut up by one born a member of the Catholic Church.

53

Las qu'on verra grand peuple tourmente,	Alas, how a great people shall be tormented
Et la Loy Saincte en totale ruyne,	And the Holy Laws in total ruin,
Par autres loix toute la Chrestiente,	By other laws, all Christianity troubled,
Quand d'or, d'argent trouve nouvelle mine.	When new mines of gold and silver will be found.

The industrial revolution, the discovery of gold mines in Africa, Australia, etc., the rise of the God of Mammon, shall bring grief to all of Christendom.

54

Deux revolts faits du malin falci-gere	Two revolts shall be made by the evil torch bearer,
De regne & siecles fait permutation	Which shall make a change of the reign and age,
Le mobil signe en son endroit s'in-gere,	The mobile sign to right shall meddle,
Aux deux esgaux & d'inclination.	And shall have an inclination to the two equals.

The evil genius of the age shall instigate two revolts, in the name of enlightenment; the Swastika shall make concessions to the right and to both leaders.

55

Soubz l'opposite climat Babylo-nique,	In the climate opposite to the Babylonian,
Grande sera de sang effusion,	There shall be a great effusion of blood,
Que terre & mer, air. ciel sera inique,	So that the land and sea, air and heaven shall seem unjust,
Sectes, faim, regnes, pestes, confu-sion.	Sects and famine shall rule over plague and confusion.

Cataclysmic destruction, with great loss of life, is promised to the land of the Pacific, far in the East (the antipodes of the Near East or Babylonia).

56

Vous verrez tost & tard faire grand change	Sooner or later, you shall see great changes,
Horreurs extresmes & vindications,	Extreme horrors and persecutions,
Que si la lune conduite par son ange,	The moon led by her angel,
Le ciel s'approche des inclinations.	The heaven draws near its inclination.

This quatrain reflects, as do so many of Nostradamus' prophecies, his repeated prophetical conviction of the great changes to take place in the future, most of which will lead to strife among humans and the ultimate destruction of the Earth.

57

Par grand discord la trombe tremblera,	By great discord, the trumpet shall vibrate,
Accord rompu, dressant la teste au ciel,	Agreement broken, lifting the head to heaven,
Bouche sanglante dans le sang nagera,	A bloody mouth shall swim in blood,
Au sol sa face oingte de laict & miel.	The face turned to the sun anointed with milk and honey.

A clear and forthright prediction. Japan will treacherously break her agreement with the United States and, plunging into the bloody war, she will embark on her East Asia Co-Prosperity scheme, promising a future land of milk and honey to her cohorts.

58

Trenche le ventre, naistra avec deux testes	Slit in the belly, it shall be born with two heads,
Et quatre bras, quelques ans entiers viura,	And four arms, and shall live a few years,
Jour qui Aquilare celebrera ses festes,	The day that Aquila shall celebrate his feasts,
Foussan, Thurin, chef Ferrare suyura.	Fossan, Turin, the chief of Ferrara shall run away.

A monstrous thing shall be brought into being, but shall not exist long. When Aquila (a Jewish Proselyte who literally translated the Hebrew Scriptures into Greek) celebrates his feast, the Italians shall have much sorrow.

59

Les exilez deportez dans les Isles,	The exiles that were carried into the Isles,
Au changement d'un plus cruel Monarque,	At the whim of a most cruel monarch,
Seront meurtris, & mis deux des scintilles	Shall be murdered, and put in the sparks of fire,
Qui de parler ne seront este parques.	Because they had not been sparing of their tongues.

Hitler's wholesale extermination of the Jews and Poles, followed by the infamous cremation of their bodies, is indicated in this quatrain.

60

Un Empereur naistra pres d'Italie,
Qui a l'Empire sera vendu bien
   cher,
Diront avec quels gens il se ralie
Qu'on trouvera moins Prince que
   boucher.

An Emperor shall be born in Italy.
Who shall cost the Empire dear,
They shall say, with what peoples
   he keeps company!
He shall be found less a Prince
   than a butcher.

A presage of the coming of Napoleon, born in Corsica (then an Italian possession), and the subsequent wars and destruction he will bring to Europe.

61

La republique miserable infelice,
Sera vastee du nouveau Magistrat,
Leur grand amas de l'exil malefice,
Fera Sueve ravir leur grand con-
   tract.

The miserable and unhappy republic
Shall be wasted by the new Magistrate,
Their great number of broken refu-
   gees,
Shall cause Sweden to break her
   contract.

This refers to the dissipation of the resources of France, and the repudiation by Sweden of her treaty with France in favor of a Russian alliance, on December 3, 1804.

62

La grande perte las! que feront les
   lettres
Avant le cicle de laton a parfaict,
Feu, grand deluge, plus par ignares
   sceptres
Que de long siecle ne se verra re-
   faict.

Alas, what a great loss shall learning suffer
Before the cycle of the moon is
   accomplished,
By fire, great flood, and ignorant
   scepters,
More than can be made good again
   in a long age.

The cycle of the moon shall end when, on the last cataclysmic day, it shall fall on the earth; until then much misery shall happen due to the ignorance of men.

century 10
89 63 page 341

Les fleaux passees diminue le monde,	The scourge being past, the world shall be made smaller,
Long-temps la paix, terres inhabitees,	Peace for a long time, lands inhabited,
Seur marchera par le ceil, terre, mer & Onde,	Everyone safe shall go by air, land and sea,
Puis de nouveau les guerres suscitees.	And then the wars shall begin anew.

In the period after the great influenza epidemic, that followed World War I, great progress was made in air travel, etc.; then after a brief time, World War was renewed.

64

De nuict soleil penseront auoir veu,	They shall think to have seen the sun in the night,
Quand le porceau demy homme on verra,	When the hog half a man shall be seen,
Bruit, chant, bataille au Ciel battre apperceu	Noise, singing, battles in the sky shall be perceived,
Et bestes brutes a parler on orra.	And brute beasts shall be heard to speak.

This presages modern mechanized warfare: searchlights, baby tanks, whistling bombs, dog fights in the air, and radio equipment.

65

Enfant sans mains, jamais veu si grand foudre	A child without hands, lightning never so great was seen,
L'enfant Royal au jeu d'esteuf blesse,	The Royal child, wounded at the tennis court,
Au puy brisez, fulgures allant moudre,	Bruised at the well, lightning going to the ground,
Trois sur le chaines par le milieu trousse.	Three in the midst of the field shall be struck thereby.

An allegorical attempt to show that when the "Oath of the Tennis Court" was taken by the French Revolutionists, the Royal Three were irretrievably struck down, viz; Louis XVI, Marie Antoinette, and the Dauphin.

66

Celuy qui lors portera les nouvel-
les,
Apres un peu il viendra respirer,
Vivers, Tournon, Montferrant &
Pradelles,
Gresle & tempeste, les fera sous-
pirer.

He that then shall carry the news,
A little while after shall draw his
breath,
Viviers, Tournon, Montserrant,
and Pradelles,
Hail and storm shall make them
sigh.

A continuation of the preceding quatrain—the mounting storm of the Revolution rolls over all France.

67

La grand famine que je sens approcher,
Aouvent tourner puis estre univer-
selle,
Si grande & longue qu'on viendra
arracher,
Du bois racine, & l'enfant de ma-
melle.

The great famine do I see drawing
near,
Turning from one way to another
and then becoming universal,
So great and long, that they shall
come to pluck
The root from the wood and the
child from the breast.

The French Revolution continues and a period of famine and exhaustion follows.

68

O quel horrible & malheureux
tourment!
Trois innocens qu'on viendra a
livrer,
Poison suspecte, mal garde tradi-
ment
Mis en horreur par bourreaux eny-
vrez.

O what a horrid and sad torment
Shall be put to three innocents,
Poison shall be suspected, evil
guards shall betray them.
They shall be put to horror by
drunken executioners.

Three innocent persons shall be suspected of a poison plot, and they shall be tortured and put to death by drunken executioners.

69

La grand montagne ronde de sept estades,
Apres paix, guerre, faim, inondation,
Roulera loing, abysmant grand contades,
Mesmes antiques, & grand fondation.

The great mountain encompasses seven stadia,
After peace, war, famine, and inundation,
Shall tumble a great way, sinking great countries,
Even ancient houses and their great foundations.

Great institutions, after surviving the vicissitudes of war, etc., shall go down, carrying with them the long established order and the ruling castes.

70

Pluys, faim, guerre, en Perse non cessee,
La foy trop grande trahira le Monarque,
Par la finie en Gaule commencee,
Secret augure pour a un estre parque.

Rain, famine, war in Persia having not ceased,
Too great credulity shall betray the Monarch,
Being ended there, it shall commence in France,
A secret omen to one that he shall die.

The weak, vacillating policy of Louis XVI, and his too great faith in advisers, bring France to the brink of disaster, and an unheeded omen to the King himself.

71

La tour marins trois fois prinse & reprinse
Par Espagnols, Barbares, Ligurins,
Marseille & Aix, Arles par ceux de Pise
Vast, feu, fer, pille, Avignon des Thurins.

The sea tower three times taken and retaken,
By Spaniards, Barbarians, and Italians,
Marseilles, and Aix, Arles by those of Pisa,
Waste, fire, iron, pillage, Avignon by Piedmont.

Confirmation of Quatrain 28, Century One—wherein France is attacked by the Axis.

72

Du tout Marseille des habitans changee
Course & pour fuitte jusques pres de Lyon,
Narbon, Tholoze par Bordeaux outragee,
Tuez, captifs, presque d'un million.

Marseilles shall wholly change her inhabitants,
These shall run and be pursued as far as Lyons,
Narbonne, Toulouse shall wrong Bordeaux,
Killed and prisoners shall be almost a million.

The Vichy Regime of Marshal Petain occupied the territory of Toulouse, Lyons, and Narbonne. German troops entered Paris (June 14, 1940) and the government fled to Bordeaux.

73

France a cinq parts par neglect assaillie
Tunys, Argiels esmeuz par Persiens,
Leon, Seville, Barcelone faillie
N'aura la classe par les Venitiens.

France by neglect shall be assaulted by five sides,
Tunis and Algiers shall be stirred by the Persians,
Leon, Seville, Barcelona shall be missed,
And not be pursued by the Venetians.

By the pettiness of her political parties, France will be invaded, and in French Africa the Italians will cause unrest, while the cities of Spain remain untouched.

74

Apres sejourne vogueront en Epire
Le grand secours viendra vers Antioche,
Le noir poil crespe tendra fort a l'Empire,
Barbe d'airain le rostira en broche.

After a stay, they shall sail toward Epirus,
The great aids shall come toward Antioch.
The black hair curled, shall aim much to the Empire,
The brazen beard shall be roasted on a spit.

An Axis expedition will be sent to Epirus (Greece) and the Mediterranean. Mussolini, the Black One, will aim at expansion of the Italian Empire.

75

Le tyran Siene occupera Savone,
Le fort gaigne tiendra classe ma-
   rine,
Les deux armees par la marque
   d'Ancone
Par effrayeur le chef s'en examine.

The tyrant of Sienna shall occupy
   Savone,
The fort being won, shall hold a
   fleet,
The two armies shall go by the
   way of Ancona,
Where by fear the chief shall be
   examined.

The tyrant of Italy shall occupy French Savoy, thereby tying up the
British fleet on the coast. Two Italian armies will proceed east, past
Ancona, on the Adriatic Sea. Marshal Balbo will be executed.

76

D'un nom farouche tel profere sera,
Que les trois soeurs auront fato le
   Nom
Puis grand peuple par langue & fait
   dira,
Plus que nul autre aura bruit &
   renom.

By a wild name one shall be called,
So that three sisters shall have the
   name of Fate
Afterward a great people by tongue
   and deeds shall say,
He shall have fame and renown
   more than any other.

One of the more obscure of Nostradamus' stanzas. Quite evidently it
refers to the Three Fates and their influence upon the lives of men; but a
specific explication cannot be gathered from it.

77

Entre deux mers dressera promontoire
Que puis mourra par le mords du
   cheval,
Le sien Neptune pliera voille noire,
Par Calpre & classe supres de Rocheval.

Between two seas shall a promontory be raised,
By him, who shall die by the biting
   of the horse,
The proud Neptune shall fold the
   black sail,
Through Calpre, and a fleet shall
   be near Rocheval.

In Greek legend, according to the history of Theseus, the Greeks, in
order to please the Minotaur, sent him a tribute of Athenian children in a
ship with black sails.

78

D'un chef vieillard naistra sens he-
 bete,
Degenerant par scavoir & par
 armes,
Le chef de France par sa soeur re-
 doute,
Champs divisez, concedez aux gens
 L'armes.

An old head shall beget an idiot,
Who shall degenerate in learning
 and in arms,
The head of France shall be feared
 by his sister,
The fields divided and granted to
 the people's army.

An explication that the corrupt oligarchy of France will so degenerate
that the social and economic order will collapse of its own weight.

79

Bazax, Lectore, Condon, Ausch,
 Agine,
Esmeus par loix, querelles & mono-
 pole,
Car Bourd, Tholouse, Bay mettra
 en ruyne,
Renouveller voulant leur tauropole.

Bazax, Lectore, Condon, Auch,
 Agine,
Being moved by laws, quarrels and
 monopoly,
They shall put to ruin Bordeaux,
 Toulouse, Bayonne,
Going about to renew their Tauro-
 pole.

The Northern industrial districts of France will try to exploit the
agricultural regions.

80

De la sixiesme claire splendeur ce-
 leste,
Viendra tonner si fort eu la Bour-
 gongne,
Puis naistra monstre de tres-hy-
 deuse beste,
Mars, Avril, May, Juin grand char-
 pin & rongne.

From the sixth bright celestial
 splendor,
Shall come very great lightning to
 Burgundy,
After which shall be born a monster of a most hideous beast,
In March, April, May and June
 shall be great quarrelling and
 muttering.

The sixth planet from the Sun, or Saturn, shall shed a clear light on
horrifi＿ events to occur in the above-named months.

81

D'humain troupeau neuf seront
  mis a part;
De jugement & conseil separees,
Leur sort sera divise en depart,
Kappa, Theta, Lambda, morts,
  bannis, egarez.

Of the human flock, nine shall be
  set aside,
Being divided in judgment and
  counsel,
Their destiny shall be to be divided,
Kappa, Theta, Lambda, dead, banished, scattered.

The Supreme Court of the United States, consisting of nine members,
is here indicated.

82

Quand les colomnes de bois grande
  tremblee,
D'auster conduicte couverte de rubriche,
Tant vuidera dehors une grand
  assemblee,
Trembler Vienne & le pays d'Aus-
  triche.

When the wooden columns shall
  be shaken
By the stern wind and covered by
  a ruby hue,
Then shall go out a great assembly,
And Vienna and the land of Austria shall tremble.

The weak foundations are shaken by the rising Red Storm, which will
make strong progress in Austria.

83

La gent estrange divisera butins
Saturne & Mars son regard furieux,
Horrible estrange aux Toscans &
  Latins,
Grec qui seront a frapper curieux.

The alien agent shall divide boo-
  ties,
Saturn and Mars shall have his
  aspect furious,
Horrid and strange to the Tuscans
  and Latins,
The Grecians shall be curious to
  strike.

Enemy alien agents shall loot occupied countries to feed the ravenous
maw of the military octopus, to the horror of the easy-going Latins, who
are about to be attacked by the Greeks.

84

Lune obscur cie aux profondes te-
  nebres,
Son frere passe de couleur ferrigine;
Le grand cache long temps soubs
  les tenebres,
Tiendra fer dans la pluie sanguine.

The moon shall be obscured in the
  deepest darkness,
Her brother shall pass being of a
  ferruginous colour;
The great one long hidden under
  shadows,
Shall make his iron lukewarm in
  the bloody rain.

At a time when vision is obscured, the Sun shall take on a tinge of red, or iron rust, and this will be the signal for the great one to rise and whet his sword.

85

Par la response de dame, roy
  trouble,
Ambassadeurs mespriseront leur
  vie,
Les grand ses freres contrefera double,
Par deux mourront ire, hain envie.

A king shall be troubled by the
  answer of a lady,
Ambassadors shall despise their
  lives,
The great one being undecided,
  shall counterfeit his brothers,
They shall die by two, anger,
  hatred, and envy.

Another of Nostradamus' obscure quatrains and, according to his own interpretation, merely denoting "there shall be anger, hatred and envy."

86

Le grande Royne quand se verra
  vaincue
Fera excez de masculin courage;
Sur cheval fleuve passera toute nue,
Suitte par fer, a foy fera outrage.

When the queen shall see herself
  vanquished,
She shall do a deed of masculine
  courage,
Upon a horse, she shall pass over
  the river naked,
Followed by iron she shall do
  wrong to her faith.

Marie Antoinette, seeing herself vanquished, flees imprisonment stripped naked of all wealth, and denies her identity to her captors.

87

Ennosigee, feu du centre de terre,
Fera trembler autour de Cite Neu-
fue;
Deux grands rocher long temps
ferot la guerre,
Puis Arethusa rougira nouveau
Fleuve.

Ennosigee, fire of the center of the
earth,
Shall make an earthquake of the
New City,
Two great rocks shall long time
war against each other,
After that, Arethusa shall color red
the fresh river.

A terrific fire, of the same nature as that at the center of the earth,
shall make a shambles of "New ——— City." (Arethusa was an everflow-
ing classic spring.)

88

Le divin mal surprendra le grand
Prince,
Un peu devant aura femme es-
pousee;
Son puy & credit a un coup viendra
mince,
Conseil mourra pour la teste rasee.

The divine sickness shall surprise
a great prince,
A little while after he hath married
a woman,
His support and credit shall at
once become slender,
Council shall die for the shaven
head.

Napoleon's desire to found an empire led to his marriage to Marie
Louise, who bore him an heir. His quarrels with the Pope are also indicated here.

89

Tous ceux de Ilerde seront dedans
Moselle
Mettans a mort tous ceux de Loyre
& Seine,
Secours marin viendra pres d'haute
velle.
Quand l'Espagnol ouvrira toute
viene.

All those of l'Isle shall be in the
Moselle,
Putting to death all those of Loire
and Seine,
The sea chase shall come near the
high city
When the Spaniard shall open all
veins.

Quarrels and warfare among the provinces of France are here referred
to.

90

Bourdeaux, Poitiers, au son de la campane,	Bordeaux, Poitiers, at the sound of the bell,
A grand classe ira jusques a l'Angon,	With a great navy shall go as far as Langon,
Contre Gaulois sera leur tramontane,	Against the French shall their Tramontane be,
Quand monstre hideux naistra pres d'Orgon.	When a hideous monster shall be born near Orgon.

Tramontane, in Italian, is the North Wind; Orgon is a town in Gascony.—An implication that France will be pitted against Northern adversaries and native quislings.

91

Les Dieux feront aux humains apparence,	The Gods shall make it appear to mankind,
Ce qu'ile seront autheurs de grand conflit.	That they are the authors of a great war,
Avant ciel veu serain, espee & lance,	The sky that was serene shall show sword and lance,
Que vers main gauche sera plus grand affliction.	On the left hand the affliction shall be greater.

Predestined by the Gods, war shall make its appearance without warning, largely in the air.

92

Sous un la paix par tout sera clemence	Under one shall be peace, and everywhere clemency,
Mais non long temps, pille & rebellion	But not for a long while, then shall be plundering and rebellion,
Par refus, ville, terre & mer entammee,	By a denial shall town, land and sea be assaulted,
Morts & captifs, le tiers d'un million.	Dead and taken prisoner shall be the third part of a million.

The sneak attack on Pearl Harbor, by the Japanese, ushered the United States into World War II, resulting in 350,000 American casualties.

93

Terre Italique pres des monts trem-
blera,
Lyon & Coq, non trop confererez,
En lieu de peur, l'un l'autre s'ai-
dera,
Seul Castulon & Celtes moderez.

The Italian land of the mountains
shall tremble,
The Lion and the Cock shall not
agree very well together,
And for fear shall help one another,
Only Spain and the Celts shall be
neutral.

The old animosities between the French and the English will be wiped
out during their mutual engagement in a war of world-wide proportions.
The neutrality of Spain and Ireland during this conflict is indicated.

94

Au port Selim le tryan mis a mort
La liberte non pourtant recouvree
Le nouveau Mars par vindicte &
remort.
Dame par force de frayeur hon-
oree.

In the port, Selim the tyrant shall
be put to death,
And yet, liberty shall not be recovered,
The new War by vengeance and
remorse begun,
A lady by force of fear shall be
honored.

The reference here is to Selim II of Turkey, under whose leadership the
great naval battle of Lepanto was fought.

95

Devant Moustier trouve enfant
besson
D'heroicq sang de moyne vestu-
tisque,
Son bruit par secte, langue & Puissance son,
Qu'on dira soit efleue le Vospique.

Before the monastery shall one
twin be found
From heroic blood of a monk and
ancient,
His fame by sect, tongue and power
shall be founded,
So that they shall say, Vopisk is
highly raised.

One of a pair of illegitimate twins, found deserted in a church, shall
rise to great heights.

96

Celuy qu'aura la charge de destruire
Temples & sectes changees par fan-
tasie,
Plus aux rochers qu'aux vivans
viendra nuyre,
Par langue ornee d'oreilles ressai-
sies.

He that shall be in charge to destroy
Churches and sects changed by fan-
tasy,
Shall do more harm to the stones
than to the living,
By a smooth tongue filling up the
ears.

One shall undertake a campaign to destroy the Churches, but will not succeed, due to the firmness of the faithful, more durable than stone.

97

Ce que fer, flamme, n'a sceu para-
cheuer,
La douce langue au conseil viendra
faire
Par repos, songe, le roy fera resuer,
Plus l'ennemy en feu, sang militaire.

What neither iron nor fire could
achieve,
Shall be done by a smooth tongue
in a council,
In sleep a dream shall make the
king to think,
The more the enemy in fire and
military blood.

The propaganda and infiltration tactics of native traitors shall accomplish as much for the enemy as actual military operations.

98

Le chef qu'aura conduit peuple infiny
Loing de son ciel, de moeurs &
langue estrange,
Cinq mil en, Crete, & Thessale
finy,
Le chef fuyant sauve en la marine
grange.

The leader who shall lead an infinite number of people,
Far from their country to one of
strange manners and language,
Five thousand in Candia and Thessaly finished,
The leader escaping, shall be safe
in a barn on the sea.

The Axis fiasco in attempting to invade on all fronts is foretold, as well as the escape of the chief criminal, Hitler, in a submarine.

99

Le Grand Monarque qui fera compagnie,
Avec deux Roys unis par amitie,
O quel souspir sera la grande mesnie,
Enfant Narbon a l'entour quel
pitie.

Le Grand Monarque shall keep
company,
With two kings united in friendship,
Oh what fights shall be made by
their followers,
Children, O what a pity about Narbonne,

Le Grand Monarque refers to Louis XIV. He exhausted France by his
desires of conquest, preparing the way for the Revolution.

100

Long temps au ciel veu gris oyseau,
Aupres de Dole & de Tosquane
terre,
Tenant au bec un verdoyant rameau
Mourra tost grand, & finira la
guerre.

For a long while shall be seen in
the air a gray bird,
Near Dola and the Tuscan land,
Holding in his beak a green bough,
Then a great one shall die and the
war be finished.

The role of Franklin D. Roosevelt is here clearly prophesied, indicating
his untimely and tragic death just a few weeks before the close of the
war in Europe.

CENTURY II

1

Vers Aquitaine par insuls Britan-
iques
Et par aux mesmes grandes incur-
sions
Pluyes, gelees feront terroir iniques
Port Selyn fortes fera invasions.

Towards Gascony by English as-
saults
By the same shall be made great
incursions,
Rains, frosts shall make the ground
unrighteous,
Port Selyn shall make strong invasions.

The English shall invade Gascony at a time of rain and frost and the
Turks shall make a great incursion.

2

La teste bleue fera la teste blanche,
Autant de mal que France a fait
leur bien,
Mort a l'anthenne, grande pendu
sur la branche
Quand des prins siens le Roy dira
combien.

The blue law shall do the white
law
As much harm, as France has done
it good,
Dead on the antenna, a great one
hanged on a branch,
When a king taken by his own
shall say "How much?"

The one wearing the blue beret shall prevail over the aged white one,
and a ruler shall be held for ransom as the radio remains silent.

3

Pour la chaleur solaire sur la mer
De Negrepont les poissons demy
  cuits,
Les habitans les viendront entemer
Quand Rhod & Gennes leur faudra
  le biscuit.

By the heat of the sun upon the
  sea,
At Black Bridge, the fishes shall be
  half broiled,
The inhabitants shall come to cut
  them up,
When Rhodes and Genoa shall
  want biscuits.

A terrific heat will be engendered in the sea, destroying marine life,
and the lands near the Mediterranean shall lack luxuries.

4

Depuis Monach jusqu'au pres de
  Sicile,
Toute la plage demourra desolee
Il n'y aura faux-bourgs, cite, ne
  ville,
Que par Barbares, pille soit & vol-
  lee.

From Monaco as far as Sicily,
All the sea coast shall be left desolate,
There shall not be suburbs, cities
  nor towns,
Which shall not be pillaged and
  plundered by Barbarians.

The western Italian Sea Coast from Monaco to Sicily will be invaded
and sacked by barbarians.

5

Quand dans poissin fer & lettre
  enfermee
Hors sortira qui pis fera la guerre,
Aura par mer sa classe bien ramee,
Apparoissant pres de Latine terre.

When in an iron fish, a letter shall
  be shut up,
He shall go out, that shall afterwards make war,
He shall have his fleet by the sea
  well provided,
Appearing by the Roman Land.

In a submarine, one bearing an important letter and military secrets
shall land and afterwards lead a nation to victory. Gen. Clark's daring feat
—culminating in the North African campaign—is clearly foreshadowed.

6

Aupres des portes & dedans deux citez	Near the gates and within two cities,
Seront deux fleaux onc n'apperceu yn tel,	Shall be two scourges, I never saw the like,
Faim dedans peste, de fer hors gens boutez,	Famine, within plague, people thrust out by the sword,
Crier secours au grand Dieu immortel.	Shall cry for help to the great God immortal.

This prognosticates conditions in Budapest, one of the Axis satellites, in the closing days of the War.

7

Entre plusieurs aux iles deportes	Among many that shall be transported into the islands,
L'un estre nay a deux dents en la gorge	One shall be born with two teeth in his mouth,
Mourront de faim, les arbres esbroutez.	They shall die of hunger, the trees shall be eaten,
Pour eux neuf Roy nouvel edict leur forge.	They shall have a new king, who shall make new laws for them.

The Australian Islands, after much travail, shall produce a strong leader, under whose leadership independence shall be achieved.

8

Temples sacrez prime facon Romaine,	Temples consecrated and the early Roman way,
Reietteront les goffes fondemens,	Shall reject the tottering foundations,
Prenant leurs loix premieres & humaines	Sticking to their first humane laws,
Chassant, non tout, des saincts les cultemens.	Expelling, but not altogether, the worshipping of saints.

The rise of the Reformation and split from the Catholic Church is here predicted; and the retaining in Protestant litany of only a few of the Saints.

9

Neuf ans le regne le maigre en paix tiendra	Nine years shall the lean one keep the kingdom in peace,
Puis il cherra en soif si sanguinaire	Then he will fall into such a bloody thirst,
Pour luy grand peuple sans foy & loy mourra,	That a great people shall die without faith or law,
Tue par un beaucoup plus debonnaire.	He shall be killed by one much wilder than himself.

The references here point to the reign of Louis XVI—the short period of peace at the start of his kingship, the bloody and lawless revolution, and his eventual execution before the eyes of the roaring mobs of Paris.

10

Avant long temps le tout sera range	Before long, all shall be arranged,
Nous esperons un siecle bien senestre	We look for an era most sinister,
L'estat des masques & des seule bien change,	The state of the masks and they alone shall be changed,
Peu trouveront qu'a son rang vueille estre.	They shall find few that will keep their rank.

A continuation of the preceding prophecy, describing the chaotic conditions to prevail during the Revolution.

11

Le prochain, fils de l'asnier paruiendra	The eldest son of L'Aisnier shall prosper,
Tant esleve jusques au regne des forts	Being raised to the degree for the great ones,
Son aspre gloire un chacun la eraindra,	Everyone shall fear his high glory,
Mais ses enfans du regne jettez hors.	But his children shall be cast out.

This is the famous prediction Nostradamus sent to the Lord of L'Aisnier, who had written him to know of his children's future.

12

Yeux clos ouverts d'antique fantasie	Eyes shut, shall be opened by an antique fancy,
L'habit des seules seront mis a neant;	The clothes of the solitary shall be brought to nothing,
Le grand monarque chastira leur frenaisie,	The great monarch shall punish their frenzy,
Ravir des temples le thresor par devant.	For having ravished the treasure of the temple before.

The Goddess of Justice, with blindfolded eyes, will be resurrected, and shall mete out punishment to the ravishers of the people and the temple.

13

Le corps sans ame plus n'estre en sacrifice,	The body without soul shall be no more admitted in sacrifice,
Jour de la mort mis en nativite,	The day of death placed on the birthday,
L'esprit divin fera l'ame felice	The divine spirit shall make the soul happy,
Voyant le verbe en son eternite.	By seeing the voice in its eternity.

A prophecy of the reformation of the ceremony of the Mass, and the Sacrament of the Lord's Supper.

14

A Tours, Gien, garde gande seront yeux penetrans,	At Tours, Gienn, on guard shall be piercing eyes,
Descouvriront de loing la grand' sireine,	Who shall discover before long the great queen,
Elle & sa suitte au port seront entrans,	She and her suite shall enter into the port,
Combats poussez, puissance souveraine.	By the fight shall be thrust out the reigning power.

The Goddess of Reason, installed to replace supernatural religion, approaches the centers of Culture.

15

Un peu devant monarque trucide,
Castor, Pollux, en nef, astre crai-
nite,
L'Arain public, par terre & mer
vuide,
Pise, Ast, Ferrare, Turin, terre in-
terdicte.

A little before a monarch is killed,
Castor, Pollux, and a Comet in
the sky appears,
The public Brass, by land and sea
shall be emptied,
Pisa, Asti, Ferra, Turin shall be
forbidden countries.

A time of unrest is prophesied—great disturbances in Castor and Pollux,
the constellations of the Twins or Gemini. Toward the Ship or Argonauts,
a Comet will appear.

16

Naples, Palerme, Sicile, Syracuse,
Nouveaux Tyrans, Fulgures, faex
celestes,
Force de Londres, Gand, Bruxelles
& Suise
Grand hecatombe, triomph, faire
festes.

Naples, Palermo, Sicily, Syracuse,
New tyrants, Lightnings, Celestial
Fires,
An Army from London, Ghent,
Brussels,
And Switzerland, a sacrifice, tri-
umph and feasts.

The British army will invade Europe, and meanwhile Switzerland, untouched, will benefit thereby.

17

Le camp du temple de la vierge
vestale,
Non esloigne d'Ethene & monts
Pyrenees;
Le grand conduit est cache dans
la male,
North, getez, fleuves, & vigues mas-
tinees.

The camp of the temple of the
vestal virgin,
Not far from Ethene and the Pyrenees Mountains,
The great passage is driven in the
wall,
Rivers overflow in the North and
the vines spoiled.

At Tivoli, the site of the antique temple of the Vestal Virgin, a great
passage cuts through, and there will be a great flood.

18

Nouvelle pluie subite, impetueuse	A new rain, sudden, impetuous,
Empeschera subit deux excertites,	Shall suddenly hinder two armies,
Pierre, ciel, feux, faire la mer pier-reuse	Stone, heaven, fire, shall make the sea strong,
La mort de sept, terre & marin subites.	The death of seven shall be sudden upon land and sea.

At the D-Day Invasion of the Normandy Coast, the rain of missiles fired from new type rocket guns was most intense, also concrete floating docks were sunk at the beaches to form breakwaters and rallying points for the attack.

19

Nouveaux venus, lieu basty sans defence	Newcomers shall build a place without a fence,
Occuper place par lors inhabitable,	And shall occupy a place that was not then habitable,
Prez, maisons, champs villes prendre a plaissance,	They shall at their pleasure take fields, houses and towns,
Faime, peste, guerre, arpent long labourable.	There shall be famine, plague, war, and a long arable field.

Continuing the preceding stanza, the allied invaders occupy the unin-habited fortified coast and advance successfully inward.

20

Freres & Soeurs en plusieurs lieux captifs,	Brothers and sisters shall be slaves in various places,
Se trouveront passer pres du Mon-arque	And shall pass before the monarch,
Les contempler ses Deux yeux en-tentifs,	Who shall look upon them with attentive eyes,
Des plaisant voir, meton, frond, nez les marques.	They shall go in heaviness, witness their chin, forehead and nose.

The brutal enslavement of entire populations by the Nazis is explicitly foreshadowed.

21

L'Ambassadeur envoye par Birmes,	The ambassador that was sent in
A my-chemin d'incogneus repous-	the small ship,
sez,	In the middle of the way, shall be
De Sel renfort viendront quartre	repulsed by unknown men,
triremes,	And from the salt, to his rescue
Cordes & chaines en Negrepont	shall come four great ships,
troussez.	Ropes and chains shall be carried
	to the Black Bridge.

Rudolph Hess, personal aide to the German Fuehrer, flew solo to England to contact influential British leaders with his unofficial peace terms which were rejected in a closed session of Parliament.

22

Le Camp Ascop d'Europe partira,	The Camp Ascop shall go from
S'adioignant proche de l'isle sub-	Europe,
mergee,	And shall come near the sub-
D'Arton classe phalange pliera	merged Island,
Nombril du monde plus grand voix	From Arton shall a phalange go
subrogee.	by sea and land
	By the navel of the world, a greater
	voice shall be subrogated.

Apparently a reference to the submerged continent of Atlantis, originally the Navel, which nourished all ancient human culture.

23

Palais oyseaux, par oyseau dechasse,	Palace birds, driven away by a bird,
Bien tost apres le Prince parvenu,	Soon after that, the Prince is come
Combien qu' hors fleuve ennemy	to his own,
repousse.	Although the enemy be driven be-
Dehors saisi, trait d'oyseau sous-	yond the river,
tenu.	He shall be seized without, by a
	trick of the bird.

Parasitic hangers-on will be expelled from the government, by one who is an Eagle, and a master of stratagem.

24

Bestes farouches de faim fleuves
tranner,
Plus part du camp encontre Ister
sera,
En cage de fer le grand sera tra-
isner,
Quand rien enfant Germain ob-
servera.

Wild beasts for hunger shall swim
over the rivers,
Most of the field shall be near the
Ister, *Austrian & Italy, Pola*
Into an iron cage he shall cause the
great one to be drawn,
When the child of Germany shall
observe nothing.

The country about the Danube—Ister—shall be desolated and famine-
stricken, as the great one of Germany shall be exhibited in an iron cage
and German children shall be blind.

25

La garde estrange trahyra for ter-
esse,
Espoir & ombre du plus haut mariage,
Garde deceue, fort prins dans la
presse,
Loire, Saone, Rhone, Gar a mort
outragez.

The garrison of strangers shall betray the fort,
Under the game of hope of a
higher union.
The garrison shall be deceived, and
the fort taken quickly
Loire, Saone, Rhone, Gardone, out-
raged by death.

Fifth columnists working for a united Fascistic world shall be active,
while the rivers of France shall be desecrated.

26

Pour la faveur que la cite fera,
Au grand qui tost perdra champ de
bataille
Puis le sang Pau, Thesin versera
De sang, feux, morts, noyez de
coupe de taille.

Because of the favor, the city shall
show
To the great one, who soon shall
lose the battle,
The Thesin shall pour blood into
the River Po,
Of fire, blood, drowned, dead by
the edge.

Because of disputes, a town on the River Thesin, a river which empties
into the Po, shall see a great slaughter.

27

Le divin verbe sera du ciel frappe
Qui ne pourra proceder plus avant,
Du reserant le secret estoupe
Qu'on marchera par dessus & de-
vant.

The divine voice shall be struck by
heaven
So that he cannot proceed any
further,
The secret of close-mouthed one
shall be closed,
That people shall tread upon and
before it.

A voice, of celestial quality which will be perfection itself, shall appear, the secret of which will be inviolate.

28

Le penultiesme du surnom de
Prophete,
Prendra Diane pour son jour &
repos,
Loing vauera par frenitique teste,
Et delivrant vn grand peuple d'im-
posts.

The last but one, of the surname
of Prophet,
Shall take Diana for his day and
his rest,
He shall wander far by reason of
his raving head,
Delivering a great people from im-
positions.

This concerns a false Prophet, which is here called the last but one of that Surname, who shall make Diana (that is Monday, dedicated to Diana) his Sabbath day; and he shall wander about persuading many people to pay no taxes.

29

L'Oriental sortira se son siege,
Passer les monts Appenins, voir la
Gaule,
Transpassera le ciel, les eaux &
neige,
En un chacun frappera de sa gaule.

The Oriental shall come out of his
seat,
Shall pass over the Apennines
Mountains and see France,
Shall go over the air, the waters and
the snow,
And shall strike everyone with his
staff.

An invasion by an Eastern people shall strike France, by way of Italy, utilizing the air, the sea and snow.

30

Un qui les dieux d'Annibal infer-
naux
Fera renaistre, effrayeur des hu-
mains,
Oncq plus d'horreur, ne plus dire
journaux,
Qu'advint viendra par Babel aux
Romains.

One that shall cause the infernal
gods of Hannibal
To live again, the terror of mankind,
There never was more horror, not
to say ill days,
Did happen, or shall, to the Romans by Babel.

Horrors, worse than any unloosed by Hannibal, the then enemy of
civilization, shall be unloosed upon the modern world.

31

En Campania Cassilin fera tant
Qu'on ne verra que d'eau les
champs couverts
Devant, apres, la pluye de long
temps
Hors mis les arbres rien l'on temps.

In Campania, the Castilian shall
so behave himself,
That nothing shall be seen but the
fields covered,
Before and after, it shall not rain
for a long time,
Except the trees, no green shall be
seen.

In Campania, the Spaniard will strip the country of all wealth even
to the verdure of the fields.

32

Laict, sang, grenovilles escondre en
Dalmatie
Conflt donne, peste preste, de ba-
liene
Cry sera grand par toute Esclavo-
nie,
Lors naistra monstre pres & dedans
Ravenne.

Milk, blood, frogs shall rain in
Dalmatia,
A battle fought, the plague near
Basel,
A great cry shall be through all
Slovakia,
Then shall be born a monster, near
and within Ravenna.

Dalmatia shall be in unrest, and Basel (Switzerland) and Czechoslovakia shall be in fear of an Italian monster.

33

Dans le torrent qui descend de Veronne,	In the torrent which descends from Verona,
Par lors qu'au Pau guidera son entree,	About the place where it enters into the Po,
Un grand naufrage, & non moins en Garonne,	A great shipwreck, and no less in Garonne,
Quand ceux de Gennes marcheront leur contree.	When those of Genoa shall go into their country.

When the Italians of Genoa invade France, they are foredoomed to destruction and shipwreck.

34

L'ire insensee du combat furieux,	The mad anger of the furious fight,
Fera a table par freres le fer luyre,	Shall cause by brothers the iron to glisten at the table,
Les departir mort blesse curieux,	To part them, one mortally wounded, curious,
Le fier duelle viendra en France nuyre.	The fierce duel shall do harm after in France.

A quarrel between two allies shall be the cause of a misunderstanding that will do France much harm.

35

Dans deux logis de nuict le feu prendra,	The fire shall take by night in two houses,
Plusieurs dedans estouffez & rostis,	Many shall be stifled and burnt by it,
Pres de deux fleuves pour seur il adviendra,	Near two rivers it shall for certain happen
Sol, l'Arc & Caper, tous seront amortis.	Sun, Arc, Caper, they shall all be mortified.

In a town near two rivers, a momentous decision will be made, and many shall suffer by it—all this to happen when the Sun is in the signs of Arc (Sagittarius), and Caper (Capricorn).

36

Du grand prophete lettres seront prinses,
Entre les mains du tyran deviendront,
Frauder son roy seront les entreprinses,
Mais ses rapines bien tost le troubleront.

The letters of the great prophet shall be intercepted,
They shall fall into the hands of the tyrant,
His undertakings shall be to deceive his king,
But his extortions shall trouble him soon.

Before the great prophet shall triumph, his plans shall be betrayed by selfish, tyrannical interests.

37

De ce grand nombre que l'on envoyera
Pour secourir dans le fort assiegez,
Peste & famine tous les deux devorera,
Hors mis septante qui seront profligez.

Of the great number which shall be sent,
To relieve the besieged in the fort,
Plague and famine shall devour them all,
Except seventy that shall be beaten.

A warning that biological warfare and fearful destruction of both plant and animal life is imminent.

38

Des condamnez sera fait un grand nombre,
Quand les monarques seront conciliez;
Mais l'vn d'eux viendra si mal encombre,
Que guerre ensemble ne seront raliez.

There shall be a great number of condemned men,
When the monarchs shall be reconciled,
But one of them shall come to such a bad obstacle,
That their reconciliation shall not last long.

At the finish of a great war, the guilty ones will be condemned but one of the victors will be much dissatisfied.

39

Un an devant le conflit Italique,	One year before the Italian con-
Germain, Gaulois, Espagnols pour	flict,
le fort,	German, French, Spaniards for the
Cherra l'escole maison de republic,	fort,
Ou, hors mis peu, seront suffoquez	The schoolhouse of the republic
morts.	shall fall,
	Where except few, they shall be
	suffocated to death.

One year before Italy enters World War III, Paris will be overwhelmed by a terrific onslaught of atomic-powered rockets.

40

Un peu apres non point longue in-	A little while after, without any
tervalle,	great difference of time,
Par mer & terre sera fait grand	By land and sea shall a great tu-
tumulte,	mult be made,
Beaucoup plus grand sera pugne	The sea fight shall be much greater,
navalle,	Fire and beasts, which shall make
Feux, animaux, qui plus feront	great affront.
d'insulte.	

Shortly after the time mentioned in the previous stanza, tremendous naval and military activity shall ensue, and bombardment by incendiary bombs will cause havoc on land and sea.

41

La grand estoile par sept jours	The great star shall burn for the
bruslera,	space of seven days,
Nue fera deux soliels apparior,	A cloud shall make two suns ap-
Le gros mastin toute nuict hurlera,	pear,
Quand grand pontife changera de	The big mastiff shall howl all night,
terroir.	When a great Pope shall change
	his country.

In 1939, Pope Pius XII was installed. There also began a period of terrible sights for the world, amid the howling of the great Dogs of War.

42

Coq, chiens, & chats, de sang seront repeus,
Et de la playe du tyrant trouve
mort,
Au lict d'un autre jambes & bras
rompus,
Qui n'avoit pwu mourir de cruelle
mort.

A cock, dogs and cats shall be fed
with blood,
And with the wound of the tyrant
found dead,
In the bed of another with legs
and arms broken,
Who could not die before by a
cruel death.

The French Nation (the Cock), and the rabble of Paris (cats and dogs),
were satiated with the blood of the guillotine and the beheading of
Robespierre, the tyrant of the Revolution. He had been ordered seized by
the Convention, and in the struggle was dangerously wounded, tied on
a strange bed and executed the next morning.

43

Durant l'estoille cheuelue apparente,
Les trois grand princes seront faits
ennemys,
Frappez du ciel paix terre trembu-
lente,
Pau, Tymbre, Undans, serpens sur
le bord mis.

During the time when the hairy
star is apparent,
The three great princes shall be
made enemies,
Struck from heaven, place quaking
earth,
Arne, Tiber, full of surges, serpents
cast upon the shore.

The reappearance of Halley's Comet, due in 1985, will again presage
profound changes in human destiny.

44

L'aigle poussee entour des pavil-
lons,
Par autres oyseaux d'entour sera
chassee,
Quand bruit des cymbres, tubes et
sonnaillons
Rendront le sens de la Dame in-
sensee.

The eagle flying among the tents,
By other birds shall be driven away,
When the voice of cymbals, trum-
pets, and bells
Shall make sense to the lady who
was insane.

During the festivities of the marriage of Napoleon with Marie Louise
(sister of the Emperor of Austria), Josephine, his divorced wife, was insane
with jealousy.

45

Trop le ciel pleure l'Androgin pro-
cree
Pres de ciel sang human respandu,
Par mort trop tarde grand peuple
recree,
Tard & tost vient le secours attendu.

Heaven bemoaneth too much the
Androgyn born,
Near heaven human blood shall
be spent,
By death too late a great people
shall be diverted,
Late and soon cometh the help
expected.

The church shall bewail the birth of a Hermaphrodite who will cause
great shedding of blood of the Holy People. He shall not be disposed of
until he has done much harm.

46

Apres grand troche humain, plus
grand s'appreste.
Le grand moteur les siecles renou-
velle,
Pluye, sang, laict, famine, feu, &
pest;
Au ciel veu, courant longue estin-
celle.

After a great human change, another greater is near at hand.
The great motor, reneweth the
ages,
Rain, blood, milk, famine, sword,
plague,
In the heavens shall be seen a running fire with long sparks.

After the great industrial age of steam and electricity, another stupendous revolution will be near. A new type of motive power will accel-
erate all human progress, but before this happens, there will be seen awesome aerial projectiles causing much suffering.

47

L'ennemy grand vieil, dueil meurt
de poison,
Les souverains par infinis subju-
guez.
Pierres plouvoir cachez soubs la
toyson,
Par mort articles en vain sont alle-
guez.

The great and old enemy grieveth,
dieth by poison,
An infinite number of sovereigns
conquered.
It shall rain stones, they shall hide
under rocks,
In vain shall death assert articles.

The old enemy of mankind, war, shall no longer exist, nor will poverty
and the allied ills. All this will happen after a period of human suffering.

48

La grand coppie qui passera les monts,
Saturne en l'arc tournant du poisson Mars,
Venins chachez soubs testes de Saulmons,
Leurs chefs pendus a fil de polemars.

The great army shall pass over the mountains,
Saturn, Aries, Mars turning to the fishes,
Poisons hidden in the heads of Salmons,
Their captain hanged with a string of the polemars.

An invasion over the mountains is indicated, with melancholy results, as this force will be driven into the sea and the captain slain.

49

Les conseillers du premier monopole,
Les conquerans seduits par la Melite,
Rhodes, Bisance pour leur exposant pole
Terra faudra le pour suivants de suite.

The counselors of the first monopoly,
The conqueror being seduced by the Melite,
Rhodes, Bizance, for exposing their pole
The ground shall fail the followers of the runways.

In the Latin tongue, Melites are classified as the inhabitants of the Island of Malta. The sense seems to be that Malta will successfully oppose its would-be conquerors who shall not be able to land planes on its runways.

50

Quand ceux d'Hinault, de Gand & de Bruxelles
Verront a Langres le siege devant mis,
Derriere leurs flancs seront guerres cruelles,
La pluye antique, fera pis qu' ennemys.

When those of Hainault, of Gand and Brussels
Shall see the siege laid before Langres,
Behind their sides shall be cruel wars,
The old wound shall be worse than enemies.

War shall devastate various cities of Holland, Belgium and Northern France.

51

Le sang du juste a Londres sera faute,	The blood of the just shall be dry in London,
Bruslez par foudres de vingt trois les six,	Burnt by the fire of three times twenty and six,
La dame antique cherra de place haute,	The ancient dame shall fall from her high place,
De mesme secte plusieurs seront occis.	Of the same sect many shall be killed.

The great Fire of London, 1666, three times twenty and six, with the subsequent falling of the statue of the Virgin from St. Paul's Steeple, is exactly predicted and occurred as forecast.

52

Dans plusieurs nuicts la terre tremblera,	During many nights the earth shall quake,
Sur le printemps deux efforts feront suitte,	About the spring, two great earthquakes shall follow one another,
Corinthe, Ephese aux deux mers nagers,	Corinth, Ephesus shall swim in the twin seas,
Guerre s'esmeut par deux vailants de luitte.	War shall be moved by two great wrestlers.

An era of earth-shaking events will occur in the region of Greece, caused by the actions of two great powers.

53

La grand peste de cite maritime	The great plague of the maritime city,
Ne cessera que mort ne soit vengee;	Shall not cease until the death be revenged,
Du juste sang par pris damne sans crime,	Of the just blood by price condemned without crime,
De la grand' dame par fainte n'outrages.	Of the great dame not feigned abused.

The great plague of London, 1665, shall be inflicted on the populace, as a revenge for the execution of Charles I.

54

Par gent estrange, & de Romains loingtaine,	By a strange people and a remote nation,
Leur grand cite apres eau fort troublee;	The great city near the water shall be much troubled,
Fille sans main trop different domaine,	The girl without great difference for an estate,
Prins, chef terreure n'auoit este riblee.	The chief frightened, at not having been warned.

The great city, near the sea, shall be much troubled by a strange nation, and by a surprise attack.

55

Dans le conflit le grand qui peu valloit,	In the fight the great one, who was but little worth,
A son dernier fera cas merveilleux;	At his last endeavor shall do a wonderful thing,
Pendant qu'Hadrie verra ce qu'il falloit,	While Adria shall see what was wanting,
Dans le banquet pongnale l'orgueilleux.	In the banquet he shall stab the proud one.

The arch criminal seeing that the fight is lost shall go down in ruin, and drag his Italian fellow-conspirator with him.

56

Que peste & glaive n'a s'en definer,	He whom neither plague nor sword could destroy,
Mort dans le pluies sommet du ciel frappe,	Shall die in the rain being stricken by thunder,
L'abbe mourra quand verra ruyner	The abbot shall die when he shall see ruined
Ceux au naufrage, l'escueil voulant grapper.	Those in the shipwreck, striving to catch hold of the rock.

Continuation of the preceding stanza; the arch criminal shall escape from the area of conflict, and those left behind in the wreck shall not be saved.

57

Avant conflit le grand mur tombera,	Before the battle, the great wall shall fall,
Le grand a mort, mort trop subite & plainte,	The great one to death, too sudden and bewailed,
Nef imparfaict la plus part nagera,	The boat being imperfect the most part shall swim,
Aupres du fleuve de sang la terre tainte.	Near the river the earth shall be dyed with blood.

The great West Wall will fall, and the Great One and his cohorts, deserting the sinking ship, shall suffer heavy losses.

58

Sans pied ne main, dent aygue & forte	Without foot or hand, sharp and strong teeth,
Par globe au fort de port & l'aisne nay,	By a globe, in the middle of the port, and the first born,
Pres du portail desloyal se transporte,	Near the gate shall be transported by a traitor,
Seline luyt, petit grand emmene.	The moon shineth, the little great one carried away.

A kidnapping at night, by an alien, of an infant belonging to a great one, shall take place.

59

Classe Gauloise par appuy de grand' garde,	The French Fleet by the help of the great guards,
Du grand Neptune, & ses tridens soldats,	Of great Neptune, and his tridented soldiers,
Rongee Provence pour soustenir grand' bande,	Shall gnaw Provence by keeping great company,
Plus Mars, Narbon, par javelots & dards.	Also, Mars shall plague Narbonne by javelots and darts.

The French Fleet, with the aid of the British Navy, shall invade France, at the same time a heavy bombardment shall be kept up.

60

La Foy Punique en orient rompue,
Grand, Jud, & Rosne, Loyre &
  Tag, changeront,
Quand du mulet la faim sera re-
  peve
Classe espargie sang & corps na-
  geront.

The Punic Faith broken in the
  east,
Great Jud, and Rhone, Loire and
  Tagus shall be changed,
When the mule's hunger shall be
  satisfied,
The fleet scattered, blood and
  bodies shall swim.

The false faith broken in the East shall unleash a series of changes,
while the rivers shall be choked with bodies and the fields shall remain
uncultivated.

61

Agen, Tamins, Gironde & la Rochelle,
O sang Troien mort au port de la
  flesche,
Derriere le fleuve au fort mise l'es-
  chelle,
Pointes, feu, grand meurtre sus la
  breche.

Agen, Tomains, Gironde and Rochelle,
O Trojan blood, death is at the
  harbor of the arrow,
Beyond the river, the ladder shall
  be raised against the fort,
Points, fire, great murder upon the
  breach.

Civil Wars in France, between various cities, are predicted.

62

Mabus puis tost, alors mourra
  viendra,
De gens & bestes une horrible deffaite,
Puis tout a coup la vengeance on
  verra,
Sang, main, soif, faim, quand
  courra la comette.

Mabus shall come, and soon after
  shall die,
Of people and beasts shall be a
  horrible destruction,
Then on a sudden the vengeance
  shall be seen,
Blood, hand, thirst, famine, when
  the comet shall run.

The coming of the comet shall occur in the period of reconstruction,
and there will be vengeance for wrongs inflicted on humanity by selfish
interests.

63

Gauloise, Ausone, bien peu sub-
jugera,
Pau, Marne, & Seine fera perme
l'vrie,
Qui le grand mur contre eux dressera,
Du moindre au mur le grand perdra
la vie.

The French fleet shall a little subdue Ausonne,
Pau, Marne, and Seine shall make
permanent the truth,
Which shall raise a great wall
against them,
From the less to the wall the great
one shall lose his life.

Bordeaux is called Ausonne by Nostradamus because Ausonius, a Latin poet, was born there. During World War II part of the French fleet was sunk in the harbor of Bordeaux, thereby rendering it unfit for use by the Germans (creating a wall against them).

64

Seicher de faim, de soir gent Gene-
voise,
Espoir prochain viendra au defail-
lir,
Sur point tremblant sera loy Gehe-
noise,
Classe au grand port ne se peut
accueillir.

Those of Geneva shall be dried up
with hunger and thirst.
A near hope shall come when they
shall be fainting,
The Hellish law shall be upon a
quaking point,
The navy shall not be able to come
into port.

At Geneva men shall almost succeed in outlawing war and dismantling all navies, but those of Geneva shall have no support.

65

Le parc enclin grand calamite,
Par l'Hesperie & Insubre fera,
Le feu en nef, peste & captivite,
Mercure en l'arc, Saturne fenera.

The park inclineth to great calamity,
Which shall be through Hesperia
and Insubria,
The fire in the ship, plague and
captivity,
Mercury in Aries, Saturn shall
wither.

Spain and the House of Savoy (Italy) are due for a great calamity when the sun is in Mercury and Aries.

66

Par grand dangers le captif eschappe,	The prisoner escaped through great danger,
Peu de temps grand la fortune changee,	A little while after shall become great, his fortune being changed,
Cans le palais le peuple este attrape,	In the palace the people shall be caught,
Par bon augure la cite assiegee.	And by a good sign the city shall be besieged.

A reiteration of the escape and temporary ascendency of an ill-fated leader.

67

La blonde au nez forche viendra commettre	The fair one shall fight with the forked nose
Par le duelle & chassera dehors.	In duel, and expel him forth.
Les exilez dedans fera remettre,	The exiles shall be re-established,
Aux lieux marins commettant les plus forts.	Putting the stronger of them in maritime places.

La Belle France—the Fair One—shall expel the intruder, regaining peace and a strong navy.

68

De l'aquilon les efforts seront grande,	The endeavors of the north shall be great,
Sur l'ocean sera la porte ouverte,	Upon the ocean the gate shall be open,
Le regne en l'isle sera reintegrande,	The kingdom in the island shall be re-established,
Tremblera Londres par voile descouverte.	London shall quake, for fear of sails discovered.

A very remarkable prophecy. Charles II is re-established on the British throne; and the forays of the Dutch Fleet under Admiral Van Tromp against quaking London are predicted.

69

Le Roy Gaulois par la Celtique dextre	The French King, by the Celtic right hand,
Voyant discorde de la Grand Monarchie,	Seeing the discord of the Great Monarchy,
Sur les trois parts fera fleurir son sceptre,	Upon three parts of it, will make his scepter to flourish,
Contre la cappe de la grand Hierachie.	Against the cap of the great Hierarchy.

Henry II, King of France, seeing the discord in England under the Commonwealth, will aid in the restoration of Charles II.

70

Le dard du Ciel fera son estendue,	The dart of heaven shall make his circuit,
Morts en parlant grande execution,	Some die speaking, a great execution,
La pierre en l'arbre la fiere gent rendue,	The stone in the tree, the fierce people humbled,
Bruit humain monstre, purge expiation.	Human noise, a monster purged by expiation.

The blitz of London is herewith prophesied—blockbusters, scattering stones into trees, will cause instant death and terror, even to the mightiest.

71

Les exiles en Sicile viendront,	The banished persons shall come into Sicily,
Pour deliverer de la gent faim estrange,	To free the foreign nation from hunger,
Au point du jour les Celtes luy faudront,	In the dawning of the day the Celts shall fail them,
La vie demeure a raison Roy se range.	Their life shall be preserved, the King shall submit to reason.

The Jews, banished from Italy by the Fascists, shall return at the invasion of Sicily, under the leadership of a Jewish General. The King will rescind the oppressive laws and the Jews will rebuild the shattered industrial machine.

72

Armee Celtique en Italie vexee, De toutes parts conflit & grande perte, Romains fuis, o Gaule repousee, Pres du Thesin, Rubicon pugne incerte.	'The French Army shall be vexed in Italy, On all sides fighting, and a great loss, The Romans run away, and though France, repulsed Near the Ticino, by Rubicon the fight shall be doubtful.

A French Army will be routed from Italy. Two great battles will be fought, one by the river Ticino, and one by the Rubicon; but so great will be the slaughter that the victory will be a doubtful one.

73

Au Lac Fucin de Benacle rivage, Prins du Leman ou port de l'Origuion, Nay de trois bras predict belliq' image, Par trois couronnes au grand Endymion.	At the Fucin Lake of the Benacle shore, Near the Leman at the port of Lorguion, Born with three arms, a warlike image, By three crowns to the great Endymion.

Nostradamus confessed his inability to interpret this obscure stanza. In this later day it becomes clearer. Fascism had its birth near Lake Fucino, in Central Italy—the three-armed image indicates the strife and war that will follow.

74

De Sens, d'Autun viendront jusques au Rhosne Pour passer outre vers les monts Pyrenees, La gent sortir de la marque d'Auconne, Par terre & mer le suyvra a grands trainnees.	They shall come from Sens and Autun, as far as the Rhone, To go further to the Pyrenees Mountains, The nation shall come from the mark of Ancona, By land and sea shall follow speedily after.

Sens and Autun, two typical French towns, obviously represent the spirit of the Maquis during World War II. Harassed by the Nazis, the Maquis were forced to scatter, sometimes fleeing to the shelter of the Pyrenees Mountains. The import of the remainder of this quatrain indicates quite clearly the eventual re-birth of France as a united nation.

75

La voix ouye de l'insolit oiseau,
Sur le canon du respiral estage;
Si haut viendra de froment le bois-
    seau,
Que l'homme d'homme sera Antro-
    pophage.

The noise of the unwanted bird
    having been heard,
Upon the canon of the highest
    story,
The bushel of wheat shall rise so
    high,
That Man shall be a man-eater.

A period of great famine and high prices shall prevail, at the appearance of the bird of prey.

76

Foudre en Bourgogne fera cas por-
    tenteux,
Que par engin homme ne pourroit
    faire,
De leur senat, Sacrifiste fait boy-
    teux,
Fera scavoir aux ennemis l'affaire.

Lightning in Burgundy, with mar-
    velous portents,
Which never could have been done
    by art,
Of their senate, Sacriste being
    lamed,
Shall make known the business to
    the enemies.

The Sacriste, or clergy, shall betray the interests of the state to the
enemies at a time of stress.

77

Par arcs, feux, poix, & par feu re-
    poussez,
Crys, hurlemens sur la minuict
    ouys;
Dedans sont mis par les ramparts
    cassez,
Par cunicule les traditeurs fuis.

Being repulsed with bows, fires
    and pitch,
Cries and howlings shall be heard
    about midnight;
They shall get in through the
    broken walls,
The betrayers shall run away
    through the sewers.

By treason, some shall let in the enemy within the fortress, the betrayers themselves shall escape (the "fifth column" in Madrid).

78

Le grand Neptune du profond de la mer,
De gent Punique & sang Gaulois mesle,
Les isles a sang, pour le tardif ramer,
Pluy luy nuira que l'occult mal cele.

The great Neptune, in the deep of the sea,
Having joined African and French blood,
The islands shall be put to the sword and the slow rowing
Shall do them more harm than the concealed evil.

Great Britain in a joint invasion with France shall capture the Islands, the invaders suffering less from sunken mines than from tardiness in landing.

79

La barbe crespe & noire par engin,
Subjuguera la gent cruelle & fiere;
Le grand Chyren ostera du longin,
Tous les captifs par Seline baniere.

The frizzled and black beard by fighting
Shall overcome the fierce and cruel nation;
The great Henry shall free from bonds,
All the captives made by Selim's banner.

In 1571, five years after the death of Nostradamus, the Battle of Lepanto was fought. Don Juan of Austria, called the "Frizzled and Black Beard," defeated the Turks. Henry of France also redeemed many of the Christian slaves.

80

Apres conflit du leffe l'eloquence,
Par peu de temps se tramme saint, repos,
Point on n'admet les grands a delivrance,
Des ennemis sont remis a propos.

After the battle, the eloquence of the wounded man,
Within a little while shall procure a holy rest,
The great ones shall not be delivered,
But shall be left to their enemies' will.

A truce shall be proclaimed through the intercession of the church, but the agreement to parole the leaders shall be violated.

81

Par feu du ciel la cite pres qu'-
aduste,
Urna menace encor Deucalion,
Vexes Sardaigne par la Punique
fuste,
Apres qu Libra lairra son Phaeton.

By fire from heaven the city shall
be almost burnt,
The waters threaten another Deucalion,
Sardinia shall be vexed bv an African fleet,
After that Libra shall have left
her Phaeton.

Deucalion, a figure in Greek mythology, was the only human left after
the great flood.

A city shall be so destroyed from the air as to be nearly lifeless, all
this to occur when the sign of Libra has reached its last half.

82

Par faim la proye sera loup pris-
sonnier,
L'assaillant hors en extreme detresse;
Un nay ayant au devant le dernier,
Le grand n'eschappe au milieu de
la presse.

By hunger, the prey shall make the
wolf prisoner,
Assaulting him then in great distress;
The eldest having got before the
last,
The great one doth not escape in
the middle of the crowd.

The Wolf (Rome), being hungry, shall snatch at the prey offered to
it and become entrapped, while the greatest of all shall not escape the
vengeance of the mob.

83

Par le traffic du grand Lyon change,
Et la plus-part tourne en pristine
ruine,
Proye aux soldats par pille ven-
dange,
Par jura mont & Sueve bruine.

The great trade of the great Lion
altered,
The most part turns into pristine
ruin,
Shall become a prey to soldiers and
reaped by wound
In Mount Jura, and Suabia great
fogs.

The industrial supremacy of the British Lion shall be endangered. England shall become the scene of pillage and the home of wounded soldiers.
Mt. Jura and Suabia (Germany) shall have some relation to these events.

84

Entre Champagne, Sienne, Flora, Ostie	Between Campania, Sienna, Pisa and Ostia,
Six mois neuf jours ne pleuvera une goutte;	For six months and nine days there shall be no rain,
L'Estrange langue en terre Dalamtie,	The strange language in Dalmatian land,
Courira sus, gastant la terre toute.	Shall overrun, spoiling all the country.

Italy, suffering much from want, shall seek to despoil Dalmatia—Albania—by overrunning the country.

85

Vieux plains de barbe sous le statut severe,	The old plain beard, under the severe statue,
A Lyon fait dessus l'Aigle Celtique,	Made at Lyon upon the Celtic Eagle,
Le petit grand trop outre persevere,	The little great too far perseveres,
Bruit d'armes au ciel, mer rouge Lygustique.	Noise of arms in the sky, and the Ligurian sea made red.

The power of the German Air Force will for a time sustain the big and little Fuehrers (obviously Hitler and his satellites), and war will rage in the air and on the sea.

86

Naufrage a classe pres d'onde adriatique,	A fleet shall suffer a shipwreck near the Adriatic sea,
La terre esmeu sur l'air en terre mis;	The earthquakes, a motion of air comes upon the land;
Egypte tremble augment Mahommetique,	Egypt trembles for fear of the Mohammedan increase,
L'Heraut se rendre a crier est commis.	The Herald surrendering shall be commissioned to cry.

In the Mediterranean Seas a fleet will be wrecked, the earth will shake with the sound of terrible weapons, and the air will vibrate with a strange whirring. Mohammedan influence will increase to the detriment of the rulers of Egypt. The mouthpiece shall desert to the Victor and shall be commissioned under him.

87

Apres viendra des estremes contrees,
Prince Germain sur le throsne
dore.
En servitude & par eaux recontrees
La dame serve, son temps plus n'a
dore.

After that, shall come out of the
remote countries,
A German Prince upon a gilded
throne.
The slavery and waters shall meet,
The lady shall serve, her time no
more worshipped.

The accession of the Hanoverian Kings of England commencing with George I is here indicated.

88

Le circuit du grand fait ruyneux,
Au nom septiesme le cinqueiesme
sera;
D'un, tiers plus grand estrange bel-
liquex,
Mouton, Lutece, Aix garantira.

The circuit of the great deed
ruined,
The seventh name shall be that of
the fifth,
From a third person, one greater,
a warlike man,
Aries shall preserve Paris nor Aix.

The reference here is to the French league against Henry III and Henry IV, which numbers being joined together, make seven.

89

Un jour seront amis les deux grands
maistres,
Leur grand pouvoir se verra aug-
mente,
La terre nefue sera en ses hauts
estres,
Au sanguinaire, le nombre ra-
compte.

One day the two great masters
shall be friends,
Their great powers shall be in-
creased,
The new land shall be in a flourish-
ing condition,
The number shall be told to the
Bloody Person.

The new land of the United Americas shall enjoy great prosperity, due to its co-operation with the great land of the East, the United States of Europe, much to the displeasure of a cruel and bloody man.

90

Par vie & mort change regne d'-
  Hongrie,
La loy sera sera plus aspre que serv-
  ice,
Leur grand cite d'Urlemens, plaints
  & cris,
Castor and Pollux ennemis dans la
  lice.

By life and death the kingdom
  of Hungary shall be changed,
The law shall be more severe than
  the service,
Their great city shall be full of
  howling and crying.
Castor and Pollux shall be enemies
  in the lists.

Strict laws shall hamper the liberties of Hungary much to the detriment of their chief city. Brothers shall be enemies in the field.

91

Soleil levant un grand feu on verra,
Bruit & clarte vers Aquilon ten-
  dant;
Dedans le rond mort & cris on
  orra,
Par glaive, feu, faim, mort les at-
  tendans.

At the rising of the sun a great fire
  shall be seen
Noise and light tending to the
  north;
Within the round, death and cries
  shall be heard,
Death by sword, fire, hunger
  watching for them.

A great calamity shall occur, when the rising sun shall attack early in
the morning from a northerly direction.

92

Feu, couleur d'or de ciel en terre
  veu,
Frappe du haut n'ay, fait cas merveilleux;
Grand meurtre humain, prinse du
  grand veveu,
Morts d'expectacles, eschappe l'or-
  gueilleux.

Fire the color of gold, from
  heaven to earth shall be seen,
Stricken of the high born, a mar-
  velous event.
Great murder of mankind, great
  loss of infants,
Some dead looking, the proud one
  shall escape.

Continuation of the preceding stanza; the prophecy of an outstanding
event, the greatest destruction of human life by unknown forces.

93

Bien pres du Tymbre presse la Ly- bitine,	Near the Tiber, going towards Libia,
Un peu devant grand inondation;	A little before a great inundation,
Le chef du nef prins, mis en la sentine,	The master of the ship being taken shall be put into the well,
Chasteau, palais en conflagration.	And a castle and a palace shall be burnt.

An event to take place in Italy. The head of the Ship of State (Mussolini) will be degraded and the king (Victor Emmanuel) will be exiled.

94

Grand Pau, grand mal pour Gau- lois recevra,	Great Po shall receive great harm from the French,
Vain terreur au maritin Lyon,	A vain terror shall seize upon the maritime lion,
Peuple infiny par la mer passera,	Infinite people shall go beyond the sea,
Sans eschapper un quart d'vn mil- lion.	Which shall not escape even a quarter million.

Italian cities shall receive great harm from the French, resulting in an exodus of their inhabitants.

95

Les lieux peuplez seront inhabi- tables,	The populous places shall be deserted,
Pour champs avoir grand division;	A great division to obtain fields,
Regnes livrez a prudens incap- ables,	Kingdom given to prudent inca- pable
Entre les freres mort & dissention.	When the great brothers shall die by dissension.

Civil War will cause the populace to leave congested places and seek rural pursuits.

96

Flambeau ardant au ciel sera veu,
Pres de la fin & principe du
Rhone,
Famine, glaive, tarde le secours
poreu,
La Perse tourne envahir Mace-
doine.

A burning shall be seen by night in
Heaven,
Near the end and beginning of the
Rhone,
Famine, sword, too late help shall
be provided,
Persia shall come against Mace-
donia.

Incendiary attacks will strike along the Rhone River in France, at the same time that the war will continue in the East.

97

Romain Pontife garde de t'ap-
pocher,
De la cite qui deux fleuves arrouse;
Ton sang viendras aupres de la
cracher,
Toy & les tiens quand fleurira la
rose.

Roman Pontiff take heed to come
near,
To the city watered with two rivers,
Thou shall spit there thy blood,
Thou and thine when the rose
shall bloom.

The Pope is forewarned to stay close to Rome under penalty of death.

98

Celuy du sang resperse le visage,
De la victime proche sacrifice,
Venant en Leo augure presage,
Mais estre a mort lors pour la fi-
ancee.

He that shall have his face bloody,
With the blood of the victims near
to be sacrificed,
The sun coming into Leo shall be
an augury by presage,
That then he shall be put to death
for his confidence.

In the summer, one who is great oppressor of humanity shall be cut down by death, before his bloody plans fully mature.

99

Terroir Romain qu'interpretatoit augure,
Par gens Gauloise par trop sera vexee,
Mais nation Celtique craindra l'heure,
Boreas, classe trop loing l'avoir poussee.

The Roman country in which the augur did interpret,
Shall be too much vexed by the French nation,
But the Celtic nation shall fear the hour,
The North Wind had driven the navy in too far.

Rome, site of the ancient college of Augurs, shall be at cross swords with the nation of Celts (France).

100

Dedans le isles si horrible tumulte,
Rien on n'orra qu'une bellique brigue,
Tant grand sera des prediteurs l'insulte,
Qu'on se viendra ranger a la grand ligne.

In the islands shall be such horrible tumults,
That nothing shall be heard by a warlike surprise,
So great shall be the assault of the robbers,
That everyone shall shelter himself under the great line.

The London blitz, with all its horrid tumult due to the assault by the Nazis, is clearly foreshadowed even to the seeking of shelter by the populace in the London underground lines.

CENTURY III

1

A pres combat & bataille navale,	After the fight and sea battle,
Le grand Neptun a son plus haut beffroy,	The great Neptune in his highest steeple,
Rouge adversaire de peur deviendra pasle	The red adversary shall wax pale with fear,
Mettant le grand Ocean en effroy.	Putting the great Ocean in a fright.

After a war ending in a frightful sea battle, Great Britain shall rise to the heights of Empire, but not until her adversary shall first make the sea a frightful place for her mariners.

2

Le divin verbe pourra a la substance,	The divine word shall give to the substance
Comprins ciel, terre, or occult au fait mystique,	Heaven and earth, and gold hid in the mystic fact,
Corps, ame, esprit ayant tout puissance	Body, soul, spirit, having all power,
Tant soubs ses pieds comme au siege Celique.	As well under his feet, as in the Heavenly Seat.

A hermetic stanza, expounding the secret of the philosopher's stone, whereby medieval alchemists sought for a catalyst to convert base metals into gold.

3

Mars & Mercure & l'argent joint
ensemble
Vers le midy extreme siccite,
Au fond d'Asie on dit a terre tremble,
Corinthe, Ephese lors en perplex-
ite.

Mars, and Mercury and silver
joined together,
Towards the south a great drought,
In the bottom of Asia shall be a
great earthquake
Corinthe and Ephesus shall then
be in perplexity.

From India, the bottom of Asia, a great movement shall spread, much
to the perplexity of Christianity—II Corinthians 1–8 and Ephesians
3–3, "How that by revelations was made known to me the mystery, as
I wrote before, in a few words."

4

Quand seront proches le deffaut
des lunaires,
De l'un a l'autre ne distant grande-
ment,
Froid, sicite, danger vers les fron-
tieres,
Mesme ou l'oracle a prins com-
mencement.

When default of the luminaries
shall be near,
Not being far distant one from
another,
Cold, drought, danger towards the
frontiers,
Even where the oracle had his beginning.

When two great lights shall be nearly eclipsed, privations will be increased, even where the oracle (Nostradamus) was born.

5

Pres loing defaut de deux grand
luminaires,
Qui surviendra entre Avril & Mars,
O quel cherte! mais deux grande
debonnaires,
Par terre & sea secourront toutes
parts.

Near the eclipse of the two great
luminaries,
Which shall happen between April
and March,
O what a dearth! But two great
ones bountiful
By land and sea shall succour them
on all sides.

Verification of the preceding verse, naming the time of the event, and
also the rehabilitation and relief of the stricken areas by two bountiful
nations.

6

Dans temples clos le foudre y entrera,	In closed temples the lightning shall fall,
Les citadins dedans leurs forts grevez,	The citizens shall be distressed in their strength,
Chevaux, boeufs, hommes, l'onde leur touchera,	Horses, oxen, men, the water shall touch the wall,
Par faim, soif, soubs les plus foibles armez.	By hunger, thirst, down shall come the worst provided.

The temples of learning shall be destroyed, but the citizens will hold fast, even through much suffering and loss.

7

Les fugitifs feu du ciels aux les piques,	The fugitives, fire of heaven on the pikes,
Conflit prochain des corbeaux s'estatans;	A fight near at hand, the ravens croaking,
De terre on crie, aide secours celiques,	They cry from the land, Help, O heavenly powers,
Quand pres des murs seront les combatans.	When near the walls shall be the fighting men.

A prediction of the taking of the Bastille, when the inflamed populace of Paris, armed largely with pikes, assaulted the walls of the fortress.

8

Les Cimbres joints avec leurs voisins,	The Welsh, joined with their neighbors,
Depopuler viendront presque l'Espagne,	Shall come to depopulate most of Spain,
Gens amaffez Guienne & Limousins,	People gathered from French towns,
Seront en ligue & leur feront compagne.	Shall be in league with them, and keep them company.

Spain will be almost depopulated by the efforts of the British and French volunteers.

9

Bordeaux, Rouen, & la Rochelle
joints,
Tiendront autour de la grand mer
Oceane,
Anglois, Bretons, & les Flamens
conjoints,
Les chasseront jusques aupres de
Rouane.

Bordeaux, Rouen and Rochelle
joined together,
Will range about upon the great
ocean,
English, Bretons and Belgians,
joined together,
Shall drive them away as far as
Rouane.

The great fleet of France will be driven from the seas by the British
and Flemish fleets.

10

De sang & faim plus grand calamite,
Sept fois s'appreste a la marine
plage,
Monech de faim, lieu pris captivite,
Le grand mene, croc, enferree cage.

Of blood and famine, what a great
calamity,
Seven times is ready to come upon
the sea coast,
Monaco by hunger, the place taken
captivity,
The great one carried away, and
shut up in a cage.

Monte Carlo (Monaco) shall starve during a period of national
calamity, when the place is captured and the greatest one in France shall
be imprisoned.

11

Les armes battre au ciel longue sai-
son,
L'arbre au milieu de la cite tombe,
Vermine, rongue, glaive en face
tyfon,
Lors le Monarque d'Adrie suc-
combe.

Armies shall fight in the air a great
while,
The tree shall fall in the middle of
the city,
Vermin, scabs, sword, firebrand in
the face,
When the Monarch of Venice
shall fall.

A flaming tree shall fall in the middle of the city, spreading death and
firebrands; aerial combat shall be the order of the day and the Italians
shall be defeated.

12

Par la tumeur de Heb., Po, Tag.,
  Tibre de Rome,
Et par l'estang Leman & Aretin,
Les deux grands chefs & citez de
  Garonne,
Prins, morts, noyez, partir, humain
  butin.

By the swelling of Heb., Po, Tag.,
  Tiber of Rome,
And by Lake Leman, and cities of
  Garonne,
The two great leaders will be taken,
Dead, drowned, the human booty
  shall be divided.

Heb. is the river Hebrus in Thrace, the river Po is in Italy, and Tag. is the Tagus river in Portugal. Throughout Europe there will be a great disturbance, but the chief instigators will eventually meet violent deaths.

13

Par foudre en l'arche or & argent
  fondu,
Des deux captifs l'un l'autre, man-
  gera,
De la cite le plus grand estendu,
Quand submergee la classe nagera.

In the ark, lightning, gold and
  silver melted,
Of two prisoners, one shall eat up
  the other,
The greatest of the city shall be
  laid down,
When the navy that was drowned,
  shall swim.

When the ships that were sunk are afloat again, the greatest of the enemy's cities will be destroyed by a thunderbolt, leaving them with valueless money.

14

Par le rameau du vaillant person-
  nage,
De France infirme, par le pere infelice,
Honneurs, richesses, travail en son
  vieil age,
Pour avoir creu le conseil d'homme
  nice.

By the branch of the valiant personage,
Of weak France, by the unfortu-
  nate father,
Honours, riches, labour in his old
  age,
For having believed the counsel of
  a nice man.

Louis Philippe (whose father, descended from the brother of Louis XIV, was executed during the revolution) conspired with General Dumouriez and was exiled from Paris on the discovery of their plot to overthrow the Republic in 1793. Returning as King in 1830, he later enjoyed great riches and honors.

15

Coeur, vigueur, gloire, le Regne changera,	Heart, vigour and glory shall change the Kingdom,
De tous points, contre ayant son adversaire,	In all points, having an adversary against it,
Lors France enfance par mort sujugera,	Then shall France overcome childhood by death,
Le grand Regent sera lors plus contraire.	The great Regent shall then be most contrary to it.

The courage, vigor and glory of France were reanimated by Napoleon. His greatest adversary was the Pope, "Regent of St. Peter's Temporal Rule."

16

Le Prince Angloise Mars a son coeur de ciel,	The English Prince Mars has his heart from Heaven,
Voudre pour suyure sa fortune prospere;	Will follow his prosperous fortune;
Des deux duels l'vn percera le fiel,	Of two duels, one shall pierce the gall,
Hay de luy, bien ayme de sa mere.	Being hated of him, and beloved of his mother.

A martial English Prince will follow the dictates of his heart rather than his fortune, and his escapades shall cause much bitterness, but he shall still be beloved by the Queen.

17

Mont Aventine brusler nuict sera veu,	Mount Aventine shall be seen to burn in the night,
Le Ciel obscur tout a un coup en Flandres;	The Heavens shall be darkened upon a sudden in Flanders,
Quand le Monarque chassera son neveu,	When the Monarch shall expel his nephew,
Lors Gens d'eglise commettront les esclandres.	Then churchmen shall commit scandals.

The burning of Mount Aventine, one of the seven hills of Rome, is probably one of the many symbolizations used by Nostradamus to indicate war.

18

Apres la pluye laict, assez longuette,
En plusieurs lieux de Reims le ciel
  touche,
O quel conflit de sang pres d'eux
  s'appreste!
Peres & Fils, Roys n'oseront approche.

After a long rain of milk,
In many places of Rheims the
  lightning shall fall,
O what a bloody fight is making
  ready for them,
Father and Son, both Kings, shall
  not dare to come near.

After a period of peace and plenty, France shall be involved in a
bloody war.

19

En Luques sang & laict viendra
  pleuvoir,
Vn peu devant changement de pre-
  teur,
Grand peste & guerre, faim & soif
  fera voir,
Loing ou mourra leur Prince &
  grand recteur.

In Lucca it shall rain blood and
  milk,
A little before the change of the
  magistrate,
A great plague, war, hunger and
  thirst shall be seen,
Along where their Prince and great
  director shall die.

In Italy, there will be alternating periods of depression and prosperity,
then a change of chief magistrate, who will bring a plague, followed by
war and hunger. The leader will die near Lucca.

20

Par les contrees du grand fleuve Be-
  tique
Loing d'Ibere au royanne de Grenade,
Croix respoussees par gens Maho-
  metiques,
Un de Cordobe trahyra la contrade.

Through the countries of the great
  River Betis,
Far off from Iberia, in the kingdom
  of Grenada,
Crosses beaten back by Moham-
  medan people,
One of Cordoba shall at last betray
  the country.

The River Betis (Latin name) is the River Guadalquivir in Spain, on
whose banks is the city of Seville. There Christians shall be betrayed by
a Spaniard of Cordova, who will bring in Moors to slaughter his own
people.

21

Au Crustamin par Mer Adraitique,
Apparoistra vn horrible poisson,
De face humain & de corps aqua-
  tique,
Qui se prendra dehors de l'hame-
  con.

Among the Crustacea, near the
  Adriatic Sea,
A horrid fish shall appear,
Having a man's face and a fish's
  body,
Which shall be taken without a
  hook.

The Manatee, an herbivorous aquatic mammal, inhabiting the African
and Amazonian Coasts, often wanders far from his haunts. It was fre-
quently mistaken for a human being, which its upper half resembles.

22

Six jours l'assaut devant citte
donne,
Livres sera forte & aspre bataille,
Trois la rendront & a eux pardonne,
Le reste a feu & a sang tranche
taille.

Six days shall the assault be in front
of the city,
A great and fierce battle shall be
fought,
Three shall surrender it, and be
pardoned,
The rest shall be put to fire and
sword, cut and slashed.

An episode in the perpetual wars that plague mankind, until the mil-
lennium, which Nostradamus mentions in a later prophecy.

23

Si, France, passe outre me Ligus-
tique,
Tu te verra en isles & mers enclos,
Mahomet contraire plus mer ad-
riatique,
Chevaux & d'asnes tu rongeras les
os.

If France goeth beyond the Li-
gustic Sea,
Thou shalt see thyself enclosed
with islands and seas,
Mahomet, against thee besides the
Adriatic Sea,
Of horses and asses thou shalt
gnaw the bones.

A warning to France not to advance beyond Corsica, or she will be
attacked on all sides, blockaded and will suffer want of food.

24

De l'entreprinse grande confusion,
Perte de gens, tresor innumerables;
Ty ny dois faire encores tension,
France, a mon dire fais que sois
    recordable.

From the undertaking great con-
    fusion,
Loss of people and innumerable
    treasure,
Thou ought not yet to tend that
    way,
France! Endeavor to remember my
    saying.

A continuation of the preceding stanza, and of the same general tenor.

25

Qui au royanne Navarrois par-
    viendra,
Quande le Sicile & Naples seront
    joints,
Bigorre & Landes par Foix lors on
    tiendra,
D'un qui d'espagne sera par trop
    conjoints.

He that shall obtain the kingdom
    of Navarre,
When Sicily and Naples shall be
    joined,
Bigorre and Landes they by Foix
    shall be held,
Of one who shall too much be
    joined to Spain.

At a time when Italy is united, one who is deeply involved with Spain shall also obtain his way in France.

26

Des Roys & princes dresseront si-
    mulachres,
Augures cruez, esclevez aruspices;
Corne victime doree, & d'azur d'-
    nacre,
Interpretez seront les estipices.

Some kings and princes shall set
    up idols,
Divinations and hollow raised di-
    vinators,
Victim with gilded horns, set with
    azure and mother of pearl,
The looking into the entrails shall
    be interpreted.

Some Kings and Princes shall set up idols of Nationalism, supported by a prostituted clergy. Their victims will be glorified and from their remains, seers shall find much to interpret.

27

Prince Lybinique puissant en Occident,	A Libian Prince being powerful in the West,
Francois d'Arabe viendra tant enflammer;	The French shall love so much the Arabian language,
Scavans aux lettres sera condescendent,	That he, being a learned man, shall condescend
La langue Arabe en Francois translater.	To have the Arabian tongue translated into French.

An African potentate, being honored by the French, shall return the honor by translating his orders into the French tongue.

28

De terre foible & pauvre parentelle,	One weak in lands and of poor kindred,
Par bout & paix parviendra dans l'Empire,	By thrusting and peace shall attain to Empire,
Long temps regner une jeune femelle,	Long time, shall reign a young woman,
Qu'onc q'en regne n'en furvint un si pire.	Such as in a reign was never worse.

Madame Du Barry, mistress of Louis XV, is expressly indicated—from a poor milliner, she rose to be the power behind the throne of France.

29

Les deux neveaux en divers lieux nourris,	The two nephews brought up in divers places,
Navale pugne, terre peirres tombees.	A sea fight, fathers fallen to the earth.
Viendront si haut esleve enguerris,	They shall come highly educated and expert in arms,
Venger l'injure ennemys succombez.	To avenge the injury, their enemies shall fall down under them.

Two people of the same blood, from opposite sides of the ocean, shall unite and crush their common enemy.

30

Celuy qu'en luitte & fer au fait
  bellique,
Aura porte plus grand que luy le
  prix,
De nuit au lit six luy feront la
  pique,
Nud sans harnois subit sera surprins.

He who in wrestling and martial
  deeds,
Had carried the prize before his
  better,
By night six shall abuse him in his
  bed,
Being naked and without harness
  he shall suddenly be surprised.

The Earl of Montgomery, who accidentally killed Henry II of France, in a sporting bout, was afterward beheaded for being one of the Protestant Party.

31

Aux champs de Mede, d'Arabe &
  d'armenie
Deux grands copies trois fois s'as-
  sembleront,
Pres du rivage d'Araxes la mesnie,
Du grand Soliman en terre tomberont.

In the fields of Media, Arabia and
  Armenia,
Two great armies shall meet thrice,
Near the shore of Araxes, the peo-
  ple,
Of great Solyman shall fall down.

In the Near East, two great armies will clash, the net result of which will be that the Jews will suffer thereby.

32

Le grand sepulchre du peuple
  Aquitanique,
S'approchera aupres se la Toscane,
Quand Mars sera pres du coing
  Germanique,
Et au terroir de la gent Mantuane.

The great grave of the Aquatanic
  people
Shall approach to Tuscany,
When Mars shall be in the German corner,
And in the territory of the Man-
  tuan people.

When war shall be in Italian territory sponsored by the Germans, then the British shall suffer much loss of life in Tuscany.

33

En la cite ou le loup entrera,
Bien pres de la les ennemis seront;
Copie estrange grand pays gastera,
Aux monts & Alpes les amis pas-
  seront.

In the city wherein the wolf shall
  go,
Near the place the enemies shall
  be,
An army of strangers shall spoil a
  great country,
The friends shall go over the mountains of the Alps.

The city of the Italian Wolf shall be besieged and almost overcome
by a great army of strangers until assistance shall be rendered by those on
the other side of the Alps.

34

Quand le deffaut du soleil lors sera,
Sur le plain jour le monstre sera
  veu;
Tout autrement on l'interpretera,
Cherte n'a garde, nul n'y aura pour-
  veu.

When the eclipse of the sun shall
  be,
At noon day, the monster shall be
  seen,
It shall be interpreted other ways,
Then for a dearth, because nobody
  hath provided for it.

When the eclipse of Liberty shall be at its zenith, a monstrous movement shall arise, disguised as freedom; running its course it will cause
great havoc.

35

Du plus profond de l'Occident d'-
  Europe,
De pauvres gens un jeune enfant
  naistra,
Qui par sa langue seduira grande
  trouppe,
Son bruit au regne d'orient plus
  croistra.

Out of the deepest part of the west
  of Europe,
From poor people a young child
  shall be born,
Who with his tongue shall seduce
  many people,
His fame shall increase in the Eastern Kingdom.

Adolf Hitler, born in Austria of poor parents, with his knowledge
of mob psychology and powers of speech, was successful in seducing many
people, even in the Eastern Empire of Japan

36

Ensevely non mort apoplectique,	One burned, not dead, but apo-
Sera trouve avoir les mains man-	plectical,
gees,	Shall be found to have eaten up
Quand la cite damnera l'heretique	his hands,
Qu'avoit leurs loix ce leur sembloit	When the city shall damn the
changees.	heretical man,
	Who as they thought had changed
	their laws.

The escape of Hitler from embattled Berlin is here foreshadowed.

37

Avant l'assaut l'oraison prononcee,	Before the assault, the prayer shall
Milan prins d'Aigle par embusches	be said,
deceus,	A kite shall be taken by the eagle,
Muraille antique par cannons en-	being deceived by an ambuscade.
foncee.	The ancient wall shall be beaten
Par feu & sang a mercy peu receus.	down with cannons,
	By fire and blood, a few shall have
	quarter.

A play on words, Milan being both the name of an Italian city and a bird.

38

La gent Gaulois & nation estrange,	The French people and another
Outre les monts, prins & profligez;	nation,
Au moys contraire & proche de ve-	Being over the mountains, shall die
dange,	and be taken,
Par les Seigneurs en accord redigez.	In a month contrary to them, and
	near the vintage,
	By the Lords agreed together.

Sometime in the month of September, the French and their Allies, attempting to invade a foreign shore, shall be decisively beaten.

39

Les sept en trois mis en concorde, Pour subjuguer les Alpes Ape- ninnes, Mais le tempeste & ligure courade, Les profligent en subiets ruynes.	The seven shall agree together within three months, To conquer the Apennine Alps, But the tempest and the cowardly Genoese, Shall sink them into sudden ruin.

Seven persons shall take three months to make an agreement to
conquer the Italians, but the invasion shall be held up by bad weather.

40

Le grand theatre se viendra redres- ser, Le dez jette & les rets ia tendus, Trop le premier en glaz viendra lasser, Par arcs prostraits de long temps ia fendus.	The great theatre shall be raised up again, The die being cast and the net spread, The first too much in tolling shall weary, Beaten down by bows, who long before were split.

An ironic commentary on the varying fates of nations, wherein the
vanquished rises to fight and becomes the victor, then in turn is vanquished. And thus there can be no true victory by the sword.

41

Bossu sera esleu par le conseil, Plus hydeux monstre en terre n'- aperceu; Le coup volant prelat crevera l'oeil, Le traistre au Roy pour fidelle re- ceu.	Crook-back shall be chosen by council, A more hideous monster I never saw upon earth, The flying blow shall put out one of his eyes, The traitor to the King shall be admitted as faithful.

A hunchback will be elected to a position of power, but will turn out
to be a traitor to the King.

42

L'enfant naistra a deux dents en la gorge,
Pierre en Tuscie par pluye tomberont;
Peu d'ane apres ne sera bled ne orge,
Pour faouller ceux qui de faim failleront.

A child shall be born with two teeth in his mouth,
It shall rain stones in Tuscany.
A few years after there shall be neither wheat nor barley,
To feed those that shall faint for hunger.

A world famine will occur after the birth of a prodigy and the falling of bombs in Tuscany.

43

Gens d'alentour de Tarn, Loth, & Garonne,
Gardez les monts Apennines passer,
Vostre tombeau pres de Rome & d'Anconne
Le noir poil crespe fera trophee dresser.

People that live about the Tar, Lot and Garonne,
Take heed to go over the Apennine Mountains,
Your grave is near Rome, and Ancona,
The black-haired ones shall set up a trophy.

The people of France, near the Tar, Lot and Garonne Rivers, are warned not to go into Italy, the home of the Black Shirts. The "trophy" refers to the dishonored corpse of the former duce—Mussolini.

44

Quand l'animal a l'homme domestique,
Apres grand peine & saute viendra parler;
Le foudre a vierge sera si malefique,
De terre prinse & suspendue en l'air.

When the beast familiar to mankind,
After great labour, and leaping shall come to speak,
The lightning shall be so hurtful to a virgin,
That she shall be taken from the earth and suspended in the air.

The dogs of war will be unleashed and shall come to "speak." An explosion in a church shall blow a Virgin skyward, and initiate a period of great uncertainty.

45

Les cinq estrangers entrez dedans le temple	The five strangers having come into the church,
Leur sang viendra la terre prophaner;	The blood shall profane the ground,
Aux Thoulouseins sera bien dure exemple	It shall be a hard example to those of Toulouse,
D'un qui viendra les loix exterminer.	Concerning one that came to break their laws.

In Toulouse, five alien officials will be assassinated in a church, profaning the ground according to clerical opinion. The assassins shall be penalized heavily for it.

46

Le Ciel (de Plancus la cite) nous presage	The Heaven foretelleth concerning the city of Plancus,
Par clairs insignes & par estoilles fixes,	By clear signs and fixed stars,
Que de son change subit s'approche l'aage,	That the time of her sudden change is near at hand,
Ne pour son bien ne pour les malefices.	Neither because of her goodness nor wickedness.

The city of Plancus is Lyons, as Plancus was its founder. She is due for a sudden change in fortune.

47

Le vieux monarque dechasse de son regne,	The old monarch being expelled out of his reign,
Aux Orients son secours ira querre,	Shall go into the East to get assistance
Pour peur de croix ployers son enseigne,	For fear of the crosses he shall fold up his colours,
En Mitilens ira par port & par terre.	He shall go into Mitylene by sea and land.

The old King of Norway, Haakon, shall go to Russia for assistance to help expel those of the crooked crosses.

48

Sept cens captifs attachez rudement,	Seven hundred prisoners shall be tied together,
Pour la moitie meurdrir, donne le fort;	To murder half of them, the lot being cast,
La proche espoir si promptement,	The next hope shall come quickly,
Mais non si tost qu 'vne quinziesme mort.	And not so quickly, but fifteen shall be dead before.

An example of Nazi brutality to both civilians and combatants in World War II.

49

Regne Gaulois tu seras bien change,	French Kingdom, thou shalt be much changed,
En lieu estrange l'Empire translate,	The Empire is translated in another place,
En autres loix & moeurs seras range,	Thou shalt be put to other manners and laws,
Rouen & Chartres te fera bien du pire.	Rouen and Chartres shall do the worst they can to thee.

A prediction of the change of form of Government in France from Monarchy to Republic.

50

La Republic de la grande Cite	The Republic of the great City,
A grand rigueur ne voudra consentir;	With great harshness shall not consent,
Roy sortir hors par trompette cite,	That the king should go out being summoned by the city's trumpet,
L'eschelle au mur la cite repentir.	The ladder shall be put to the wall and the city repent.

The government of Paris, with great harshness, summons and arrests the King and the Bastille is stormed.

51

Paris conjure un grand meurtre commettre
Blois le fera sortir en plain effect;
Ceux d'Orleans voudront leur chef remmettre,
Angiers, Troye, Langres leur foront grand forfait.

Paris conspireth to commit a great murder,
Blois shall cause it to come to pass,
Those of Orleans will set up their head again,
Angiers, Troyes, Langres will do them harm.

In Paris the Reign of Terror commences, and spreads to all France. The house of Orleans again will ascend the Throne, in the person of Louis Philippe.

52

En la campagne sera si longue pluye,
Et en l'Apoville si grande siccite,
Coq verra l'Aigle mal acomplie,
Par lyon mise sera en extremite.

In the country shall be so long a rain,
And in Apulia so great a drought,
The cock shall see the eagle with his wing injured,
And by him the lion brought to extremity.

The Gallic Cock shall see the American Eagle and the British Lion in great peril, during a long war.

53

Quand le plus grand emportera le pris,
De Nuremberg, D'usburg, & ceux de Basle,
Par Agripine chef Frankfort repris,
Traverseront par Flamens jusque'en Gale.

When the great one shall carry the prize,
Of Nuremberg, Augsburg and Basle,
By Agrippina the Chief of Frankfort shall be taken,
They shall go through Flanders as far as France.

When the Commander in Chief shall have captured other German cities, after the blasting of Cologne (ancient name, Agrippina), the German Commander shall be captured and imprisoned in France.

54

L'un des plus grands fuyra aux Espagnes,	One of the greatest shall run away into Spain,
Qu'en longue playe apres viendra feigner,	That shall cause a wound to bleed long,
Passant copies par les hautes montainges,	Leading armies over high mountains,
Devastant tout & puis en paix regner.	Destroying all, and afterwards shall reign.

General Franco and his destruction of the Spanish People's Republic are indicated here.

55

En l'an qu'un ceil en France regnera,	In the year that one eye shall reign in France,
La court sera en vn bien fascheux trouble,	The court shall be in the very same trouble,
Le grand de Bloys son amy tuera,	The great one of Blois shall kill his friend,
Le regne mis en mal & doubte double.	The kingdom shall be in an evil way, and double doubt.

A King blind in one eye shall rule a court that is just as shortsighted.

56

Mantauban, Nismes, Avignon, & Besiers.	Montauban, Nismes, Avignon and Besier.
Peste, tonnerre, & gresle a fin de Mars,	Plague, lightning and hail at the end of March,
De Paris pont Lyon mur, Montpellier,	The Bridge of Paris, the Wall of Lyons, and Montpellier shall fall
Depuis six cens et sept vingt, trois parts.	From six hundred and seven score three parts.

Widespread destruction shall befall France in March, in 12,143 parts.

57

Sept fois changer verrez gent Britannique,
Taints en sang en deux cents nonante an;
France, non, point par appuy Germanique,
Aries double son Pole Bastarnan.

Seven times you shall see the English to change,
Dyed in blood, in two hundred and ninety years,
Not France, by the German support,
Aries doubles his Bastarnan Pole.

England will see many changes, and all will occur under bloody circumstances. France, with the support of Germany and under the benevolent influence of Aries, will remain stable.

58

Aupres du Rhin des Montagnes Noriques,
Naistra un grand de gens trop tard venu,
Qui deffendra Saurome & Pannoniques,
Qu'on ne scaura qu'il sera devenu.

Near the Rhine out of the Norick Mountains,
Shall be born a great one, though come too late.
Who shall defend the Poles and Hungarians,
So that it shall not be known what is become of him.

Nostradamus remarks on the above that, "This is plain." It obviously refers to an event and character in his time now lost in the maze of history.

59

Barbare Empire par le iters usurpe,
La plus part de son sang mettre a mort,
Par mort senile, par luy, le quart frappe,
Par peur que sang par la sang en soit mort.

A Barbarian Empire shall be usurped by a third person,
Who shall put to death the greater part of his kindred,
By death of old age, the fourth shall be stricken by him,
For fear that blood should not die by blood.

Henry Pu Yi was installed by Japan in 1934 as Ruler of Manchukuo, usurped from China, and Nostradamus foresees that his dynasty will fail.

60

Par toute Asie grande proscription,
Mesme en Mysie, Lysie, & Pam-
  phylie;
Sang versera par dissolution,
D'un jeunne noir remply de felon-
  nie.

Through all Asia shall be a great
  proscription,
The same as in Mysia, Lydia, and
  Pamphilia,
Blood shall be spilled by the de-
  bauchness
Of a dark young man, full of trea-
  son.

An Asiatic shall force the hordes of Asia into armies of conquest.

61

La grand bande & secte crucigere
Se dressera en Mesopotamie,
Du proche fleuve compagnie legere,
Que telle loy tiendra pour ennemis.

The great band and sect wearing
  a cross,
Shall rise up out of Mesopotamia,
Near the river shall be a light
  company,
Which shall hold that law for the
  enemy.

A great organization, with some kind of cross as its emblem, shall
emerge in a land between two rivers. Near one of those rivers, some traitors
shall give the enemy assistance.

62

Proche del Duero par mer Cyrene
  close,
Viendra percer les grands Monts
  Pyrenees,
La main plus courte & sa percee
  close,
A Carcassonne conduira ses me-
  nees.

Near the Duro, closed by the Cy-
  renian Sea,
Shall come to pierce the Pyrenees
  Mountains,
The shorter hand and his pierced
  criticism,
Shall in Carcassone lead his plot.

Near the Duro River, which rises in Spain near the Pyrenees Mountains, the one with a short hand shall lay a plot that will eventually embroil
the strongest fort of France, Carcassone.

63

Romain pouvoir sera du tout a bas,
Son grand voisin imiter ses vestiges;
Occultes haines civiles & debats
Retarderont aux bouffons leurs fol-
  lies.

The Roman power shall be quite
  put down,
His great neighbor shall follow his
  steps,
Secret and civil hatreds and quarrels,
Shall stop the buffoon's folly.

The collapse of power under Mussolini, the Roman buffoon, was
quickly followed by the downfall of his neighbor, Hitler.

64

Le chef de Perse remplira grands
  Olchades,
Classe trireme contre gent Mahom-
  etique,
De Parthe & Mede, & pilliers les
  Cyclades,
Repos long temps au grand port
  Ionique.

The head of Persia shall fill great
  merchant ships,
A fleet of warships against the
  Mohammedan folk,
From Parthia and Media they shall
  come to plunder the Cyclades,
A long rest shall be on the Ionic
  port.

A great potentate shall send a fleet of warships supported by a well-
supplied group of commercial vessels against a Moslem League, and commerce in the Mediterranean shall be stagnant.

65

Quand le sepulcre du grand Ro-
  main trouve
Le jour apres sera esleu pontife,
Du senat gueres il ne sera prouve
Empoisonne son sang au sacre
  scyphe.

When the sepulcher of the great
  Roman shall be found,
The next day after a Pope shall be
  elected,
Who shall not be much approved
  by the Senate,
Poisoned, his blood in the sacred
  chalice.

On the election of a Pope, great turmoil will arise due to disapproval
by the Senate, and he will be assassinated.

66

Le grand Baillif d'Orleans mis a mort,	The great Bailiff of Orleaas, shall be put to death,
Sera par un de sang vindicatif;	By one of revengeful and vindictive blood,
Demort merite ne mourra ne par fort,	He shall not die of a deserved death nor by chance,
Des pieds & mains mal le faisoit captif.	But the disease of being tied hand and foot. hath made him prisoner.

The grim Rabelaisian humor of the age is well displayed here. A great personage of France will meet an untimely death at the hands of a vindictive enemy.

67

Une nouvelle secte de Philosophes,	A new sect of Philosophers shall rise,
Mesprisant mort, or, honneurs & richesses,	Despising death, gold, honors and riches,
Des monts Germains seront fort limitrophes,	They shall be near the mountains of Germany,
A les ensuyure auront appuy & presses.	They shall have abundance of others to support and follow them.

In Central Germany, near the Alps, a fanatical group shall arise and they will find much support and many followers throughout the world.

68

Peuple sans chef d'Espagne & d'-Italie,	A people of Spain and Italy without a head
Morts profligez dedans la Cherrenosse,	Shall die, being overcome in the Crimea,
Leur duict trahy par legere folie,	Their saying shall be betrayed by their folly,
Le sang nager par tout a la traverse.	The blood shall swim all over at random.

The Blue Division, Fascist Spain's contribution to Hitler's invasion of Russia in World War II, was entirely exterminated on this front.

69

Grand exercite conduit par jou-
venceau,
Se viendra rendra aux mains des
ennemis;
Mais le vieillard nay au demy pour-
ceau.
Fera Chalon & Mascon estre amis.

A great army led by a young man,
Shall yield itself in the hand of
enemies,
But the old man born at the sign
of the Half Hog,
Shall cause Chalon and Mascon to
be friends.

Great French Armies shall be betrayed to the enemy by an inexperi-
enced leader, but the old man shall reunite all.

70

Le grand Bretagne comprinse d'An-
gleterre,
Viendra par eaux si fort a inondre,
La ligue neufue d'Ausonne fera
guerre,
Que contre eux il se viendront
bander.

Great Britain including all of England,
Shall suffer so great an inundation
of waters,
The new league of Italy shall make
wars,
So that they shall stand against
them.

Great Britain will be endangered by floods; and at the same time a
New League, under Italian leadership, will threaten her shores.

71

Ceux dans les Isles de long temps
assiegez,
Prendront vigueur force contre ennemis,
Ceux par behors morts de faim
profligez,
En plus grand faim que jamais
seront mis.

Those in the Islands that have long
been besieged,
Shall take vigour and force against
the enemies,
Those without shall die for hunger,
being overcome,
They shall be put in greater famine
than they were before.

The Dutch, being besieged, shall break the dikes to flood the country,
confronting the enemy with great danger and hunger.

72

Le bon vieillard tout ensevely,
Pres du grand fleuve par faux soup-
    con,
Le nouveau vieux de richesse en-
    nobly,
Prins a chemin tout l'or de la ran-
    con.

The good old man shall be buried
    alive,
Near the great river by a false sus-
    picion,
The new old one made noble by
    his riches,
The gold of his ransom shall be
    taken in the way.

A good ruler, grown old in service to his country, shall be deposed by
a new one, who will gain his ends through bribery.

73

Quand dans le regne parviendra le
    boiteux,
Competiteur aura proche bastard,
Luy & le regne viendront si fort
    rogneux
Qu'ains qu'il guerisse son fait sera
    bien tard.

When the lame man shall attain
    to the kingdom,
He shall have a bastard for his near
    competitor,
He and his kingdom shall be so
    scabby,
That before he be cured it will be
    late.

An event that must have taken place in the days of Nostradamus, and
which has now lost its meaning.

74

Naples, Florence, Fayence, &
    Imole,
Seront en termes·de telles fascherie,
Que pour complaire aux malheu-
    reux de Nole
Plaint d'avoir fait a son chef mo-
    querie.

Naples, Florence, Fayenza and
    Imola,
Shall be put into so much distress,
For being complacent to the un-
    happy one of Nola,
Who was complained of for having
    mocked his superior.

Italian factional disputes shall flourish because of the lack of unity
among the people.

75

Pau, Veronne, Vincence, Sara-
gousse,
De Glaives atteints terriors de sang
humides;
Peste si grande viendra a la grande
gousse,
Proches securs & bien loings les
remedes.

Pau, Verona, Vicenza, Saragossa,
Hit by the Sword, the country shall
be moist with blood,
So great a plague and so vehement
shall come
That though help be near, the
remedy shall be far off.

Italian cities, suffering from plague and famine, shall not be able to
avail themselves of assistance, due to lack of organization.

76

En Germanie naistront diverses
fectes,
S'approchant fort de l'heureux pa-
ganisme,
Le coeur captif, & petites receptes
Feront retour a payer le vray disme.

In Germany shall divers sects arise,
Coming very near to happy paganism,
The heart captivated and small re-
ceivings,
Shall open the gate to pay the true
tithe.

A prophetic description of the rise of the pagan doctrine of National
Socialism.

77

Le tiers climat sous Aries comprins,
L'ans mil sept cens vingt & sept en
Octobre,
Le Roy de Perse par ceux d'Egypte
prins,
Conflit, mort, perte, a la croix
grand opprobre.

The third climate comprehended
under Aries,
In the year 2025, the 27th of October,
The King of Persia shall be taken
by those of Egypt,
Battle, death, loss, a great shame
to the Christians.

In the year 2025, under a special chronology enumerated by Nostradamus, strange events are to take place in the Orient much to the shame
of Christians.

78

Le chef d'Escosse, avec six d'Ale-
  magne,
Par gens de mer Orientaux captifs,
Traverseront le Calpre & Espagne,
Present en Perse au nouveau Roy
  craintif.

The chief of Scotland with the six
  of Germany,
Shall be taken prisoners by the sea-
  men of the east,
They shall go through the Calpre
  and Spain,
And shall be made a present in
  Persia to the new fearful king.

A new King of the East shall arise and conquer many lands, and a
British leader and six Germans shall be brought to him as hostages, by
way of Calpre (the Straits of Gibraltar).

79

Le grand criard sans honte auda-
  cieux,
Sera esle gouverneur de l'armee.
La hardiesse de son contentieux,
Le pont rompu, Cite de peur pa-
  smee.

The great squawker proud without
  shame,
Shall be elected governor of the
  army,
The stoutness of his competitor,
The bridge being broken, the city
  shall faint for fear.

A great demagogue, without shame or conscience, shall obtain control
of the army, much to the citizens' helpless fear.

80

Erins, Antibe villes autour de Nice,
Seront vastees fort, par mer & par
  terre,
Les sauterelles terre & mer vent
  propice,
Prins, morts, trossez, pillez sans loy
  de guerre.

Ervins, Antibes, and the towns
  about Nice,
Shall be destroyed by land and sea,
The grasshoppers shall have the
  land, the sea and wind favorable.
They shall be taken, killed, thrust
  up, plundered, without law of
  war.

The tremendous air fleets used in the invasions of France are clearl··
indicated.

81

L'ordre fatal sempiternel per chaine,
Viendra tourner par ordre consequent;
Du port Phocen sera rompue la chaine,
La cite prinse l'ennemy quant & quant.

The fatal and eternal order by chain,
Shall come to turn by consequent order,
Of Port Phocen the chain shall be broken,
The city taken, and the enemy presently after.

Phocen is the ancient name for Marseilles. Her harbor chain shall be pierced by the enemy and the port captured.

82

Du regne Anglois l'indigne dechasser,
Le conseiller, par ite mis a feu;
Ses adherants iront si bas trasser,
Que le bastard sera demy receu.

From the English Kingdom the unworthy driven away,
The councillor through the anger shall be burnt,
His partners shall creep so low,
That the bastard shall be half received.

Rudolf Hess, as peace messenger to the Cliveden Set, was repudiated both by his master and also by his British partners, after the chief councillor of Britain, Winston Churchill, burnt with anger on the notification of his errand.

83

Les longs cheveux de la Gaule Celtique,
Accompagnez d'estranges nations,
Mettront captif la gent Aquitanique,
Pour succomber a leurs intentions.

The long hairs of the Celtic Gaul,
Joined with foreign nations,
Shall put in prison the Aquatanic agent,
To make him yield to their intentions.

The intellectuals of Northern France, with the support of foreign agents, shall stamp out and imprison their opponents that favor the opposite view.

84

La grand cite sera bien desoles,
Des habitans un seul ny demourra,
Mur, sexe, temple, & vierge violee,
Par fer, feu, peste, canon, peuple
  mourra.

The great city shall be made very
  desolate,
Not one of the inhabitants shall be
  left in it,
Wall, sex, church and virgin ravished,
By sword, fire, plague, cannon,
  people shall die.

This incident occurred many times during the last World War but is especially applicable to Lidice.

85

La Cite prinse par tromperie &
  fraude,
Par le moyen d'un beau jeune at-
  trappe,
L'assaut donne, Raubine pres de
  Laude,
Luy & tours morts pour avoir bien
  trompe.

The City shall be taken by cheat
  and deceit,
By means of a fair young one
  caught in it,
Assault shall be given Raubins near
  Lande,
He and all shall die for having de-
  ceived.

Through the treachery of a light-complexioned person, a City will be pillaged by German robbers (Raubins) but he himself and his fellow conspirators shall not escape.

86

Un chef d'Ausonne aux Espagnes
  ira,
Par mer fera arrest dedans Marseille,
Avant sa mort un long temps lan-
  guira,
Apres sa mort l'on verra grand
  merveille.

A chief man of Ausonne shall go
  into Spain,
By sea, he shall stay at Marseilles,
He shall languish a great while before his death,
After his death great wonders shall
  be seen.

Nostradamus makes constant reference to happenings connected with Ausonne (the city of Bordeaux), and for the most part they are veiled in obscurity.

87

Classe Gauloise n'approches de Corsegne,
Moine de Sardaigne tu t'en repentiras,
Trestous mourrez frustres de l'Aide grogne,
Sang nagera captif ne me Croiras.

French Fleet, do not come near unto Corsica,
Much less to Sardinia, thou shalt repent it.
All of you shall die frustrate of the help of the great ships,
Blood shall swim, being captive thou shalt not believe me.

The French are warned to steer clear of Corsica, the birthplace of Napoleon.

88

De Barcelone par mer si grande armee,
Toute Marseille de frayeur tremblera,
Isles saisies, de mer aide fermes,
Ton traditeur en terre nagera.

From Barcelona, shall come by sea, so great an army,
That Marseilles shall quake for fear,
The Islands shall be seized, help by sea shut up
Thy traitor shall swim to land.

The victory of a force coming from Barcelona is predicted.

89

En ce temps la sera frustre Cypres,
De son secours de ceux de Mer Aegee,
Vieux trucidez, mais par Mesles & Lipre,
Seduict leur Roy, Royne plus outragee.

At the time Cyprus shall be frustrated,
Of its help, those of the Aegean Sea,
Old ones shall be killed, but by Mesles and Lipre,
Their King shall be seduced, and the Queen more wronged.

The Island of Cyprus will be besieged, the Greeks will not be able to come to their assistance; at the same time the King and Queen will be in exile.

90

Le grand Satyre & Tygre d'Hycarnie,	The great Satyr and Tiger of Hircania,
Don presente a ceux de l'Ocean,	Shall be a gift presented to those of the Ocean,
Un chef de classe iastra de Carmanie,	An admiral of a fleet shall come out of Carmania,
Que prendra terre au Tyrran Phocean.	Who shall land in the Thyrren Phocean.

Hercynia, in ancient geography, is the mountain region of Germany. The Tiger will be taken prisoner and turned over to a maritime people. Carmania (now called Kerman) is in Persia, and the Thyrren Phocean is Marseilles.

91

L'arbre qu'estoit nar si long temps seche,	The tree that has been long dead and withered,
Dans une nuict viendra a reverdir;	In one night shall grow green again,
Son Roy malade, prince pied estache,	His king shall be sick, the prince shall have his foot tied,
Craint d'ennemis fera voiles bondir.	Being feared by his enemies, he shall make his sail rebound.

A metaphorical description of a renaissance of human understanding to take place in the future.

92

Le monde proche du dernier periode,	The world being near its last period,
Saturne encor tard sera de retour;	Saturn shall come yet late to his return,
Translat empier devers nation Brodde,	The empire shall be changed into black nations,
L'oeil arrache a Narbon par autour.	Narbonne shall have her eye picked out by a hawk.

Along toward the end of the world, the dark nations shall reign supreme.

93

Dans Avignon tout le chef de l'Empire,
Fera appreste, pour paris desole;
Tricast tiendra l'Annibalique ire,
Lion par change sera mal console.

In Avignon all the chief of the Empire
Shall stay, by reason of Paris being desolate,
Tricast shall stop the Hanniballic anger,
The Lion by change shall be ill-comforted.

Avignon, once the seat of the Papal government (1307-76), shall again have power, after Paris is desolate by reason of an African (Hanniballic) anger, and much to the disappointment of the British Lion.

94

De cinq cens ans plus compte l'on tiendra,
Celuy qu'estoit l'ornament de son temps,
Puis a un coup grande clarte donra,
Que par es siecle les rendra tres contens.

For five hundred years no account shall be made
Of him who was the ornament of his time.
Then of a sudden he shall give so great a light,
That for that age he shall make them to be most contented.

Sir Francis Bacon (1561-1620), scientist, philosopher, statesman, and alleged author of the Shakespearean plays, shall be disclosed in a new light.

95

La Loy Moricque on verra deffaillir,
Apres une autre beaucoup plus seductive,
Boristhenes premier viendra faillir.
Par dons & langues une plus attractive.

We shall see the Moorish Law to decline,
After which another more seducing shall arise,
Boris Thenes shall be the first that shall fall,
By gifts and tongue that law shall be most seducing.

After religious intolerance falls, a new ideology shall seduce mankind; the first ones to be attracted to this revolutionary concept shall be the Russians.

96

Chef de Fossan aura gorge couppes,
Par le ducteur du Limier & L'-
  curier,
Le fait patre par ceux du mont
  Tarpee,
Saturns en Leo treziesme Fevrier.

The chief of Fossan shall have his
  throat cut.
By the leader of Hunt and Grey-
  hound,
The act committed by those of the
  Tarpian Rock,
Saturn being in Leo, the Thir-
  teenth of February.

The chief man of Northern Italy shall be hunted down by those of
Rome and shall die an infamous death.

97

Nouvelle loy terre neuve occuper,
Vers la Syrie, Judee & Palestine,
Le grand Empire Barbare corruer,
Avant que Phebe son siecle deter-
  mine.

A new law shall occupy a new
  country,
Towards Syria, Judea and Palestine,
The great Barbarian Empire shall
  fall down,
Before Phoebe makes an end of
  her course.

BALFOUR ACT.

The Arab Confederacy shall fall of its own weight and a new Judea
and Palestine shall occupy the place of Syria.

98

Deux Royals Freres si fort guer-
  royeront,
Qu'entre 'eux sera la guerre si mortelle,
Qu'un chacun places fortes occuperont,
De regne & vie sera leur grand que-
  relle.

Two Royal Brothers shall war so
  much one against the other,
That the war between them shall
  be mortal,
Each of them shall seize upon
  strong places,
Their quarrel shall be concerning
  kingdom and life.

An incident to occur before the World Organization of Nations out-
laws wars for personal aggrandizement.

99

Aux champs herbeux d'Alein & du
   Varneigne,
Du Mont Lebron proche de la Du-
   rance,
Camp des deux parts conflit sera
   si aigre.
Mesopotamie deffaillira en la
   France.

In the meadow fields of Alein and
   Varneigre,
Of the brown mountains near the
   Durance,
Armies on both sides, the fight
   shall be so sharp,
That Mesopotamia shall be want-
   ing in France.

France is to be the battleground for contending armies in a decisive
engagement involving heavy losses.

100

Entre Gaulois le dernier honore,
D'homme ennemy sera victorieux,
Force & terrior en moment explore,
D'un coup de trait quand mourra
   l'envieux.

He that least honored among the
   French,
Shall be conqueror of the man that
   was his enemy,
Strength and terror shall in a mo-
   ment be tried,
When the envious shall be killed
   with an arrow.

The underprivileged classes of France shall emerge victors after overthrowing a conspirator who will continue to be their greatest enemy.

CENTURY IV

1

Cela du reste de sang non espande,
Venise quiert secours esntre donne,
Apres avoir bien long temps at-
    tendu,
Cite livree au premier cornet
    sonne,

There shall be a remnant of blood
    unspilt,
Venice shall seek for succour,
After having long waited for it,
The city delivered at the first sound
    of the trumpet.

This concerns the Siege of Candia which lasted for twenty years. The Venetians fought a losing battle with the Turks, expecting, but never receiving, help from the Christian Princes, until eventually the city was compelled to surrender.

2

Par mort la France prendra voyage
    a faire,
Classe par mer, marcher monts
    Pyrenees.
Espagne en trouble, marcher gent
    militaire,
Des plus grand; dames en France
    emmences.

By reason of a death, France shall
    undertake a journey,
They shall have a fleet at sea, and
    march towards the Pyrenees,
Spain shall be in trouble by an
    army,
Some of the greatest ladies in
    France carried away.

Conditions in France and Spain during a revolutionary period are forecast in this verse.

3

D'Arras & Bourges de Brodes grands enseignes.
Unplus grand nombre de Gascons battre a pied,
Ceus long du Rhosne saigneront les Espagnes,
Proche du mont ou Sagonte s'assied.

From Arras and Bourges many colours of Dark men shall come.
A great number of Gascons shall go on foot,
Those along the Rhone shall let Spain blood,
Near the mountain where Saguntus is seated.

Saguntus, a city in Spain destroyed by the Romans, is here used symbolically. Men of the dark Mediterranean races shall roam widespread over Spain, to her detriment.

4

L'impotent prince fasche, plainte & querelles,
De raps & pilles par coqs & par Lybiques,
Grand est par terre, par mer infinies voilles,
Seule Italie sera chassant Celtiques.

The impotent prince angry complains and quarrels,
Concerning rapes and plunderings done by the cocks and Libiques.
Great trouble by land, by sea infinite sails.
Italy alone shall drive away the French.

French and African forces joined together shall sack and pillage a helpless country, while Italy alone will be able to defend her shores.

5

Croix paix soubs un, accomply divin verbe,
Espaigne & Gaule seront unis ensemble,
Grand clad proche, & combat tresacerbe,
Coeur si hardy ne sera qui ne tremble.

The cross shall have peace, under an accomplished divine word,
Spain and France shall be united together,
A great battle near hand and a most sharp fight,
No heart so stout but shall tremble.

After a terrific struggle Spain and France shall be united in a form of government satisfactory to Christians.

6

D'habits nouveaux apres fait la
treuve,
Malice tramme & machination;
Premier mourra qui en sera la
preuve,
Couleur Venise insidiation.

After the new clothes shall be
found out,
There shall be malice, plotting and
machination,
He shall die the first, that shall
make trial of it.
Under cover of Venice, shall be a
conspiracy.

A new form of government, by conspirators cast out by the Italians,
shall destroy the innovators.

7

Le mineur fils du grand & hay
prince,
De lepre aura a vingt ans grande
tache;
De dueil sa mere mourra bien trist
& mince,
Et it mourra la ou tombe chef
lasche.

The younger of the great and hated
prince,
Being twenty years old shall have
a great touch of leprosy,
His mother shall die of grief, very
sad and lean,
And he shall die of the disease
loose flesh.

The King of Rome, Napoleon II, son of Napoleon and the ill-fated
Marie Louise, died in 1832 after a wasting sickness lasting a year, at the age
of twenty.

8

La grand cite d'assaut pront & re-
pentin,
Surprins de nuict, gardes inter-
rompus,
Les excubies & veilles saint Quintin,
Trucidez gardes & les portails
rompus.

The great city shall be taken by a
sudden assault,
Being surprised by night, the watch
being beaten,
The court of guard and watch of
St. Quentin,
Shall be killed, and the gate
broken.

The battle of St. Quentin was one of the decisive fights in World
War I. The Germans almost broke the Allied lines at this point in a surprise attack.

9

Le chef du camp au milieu de la presse,
D'un coup de flesche blesse aux cuisses.
Lors que Geneve en larmes & en detresse
Sera trahy par Lozan & Souysses.

The chief of the camp in the middle of the crowd,
Shall be wounded with an arrow through both his thighs,
When Geneva being in tears and distress,
Shall be betrayed by Lausanne and the Swiss.

The Treaty of Lausanne completely sabotaged the work of the League of Nations.

10

Le jeune Prince accuse feucement,
Mettra en trouble le camp & en querelles;
Meurtry le chef pour le sous Levement,
Scepter appraiser, puis guerur escrouelles.

The young prince being falsely accused,
Shall put the camp in trouble and in quarrels.
The chief shall be murdered by the tumult,
The scepter shall be appeased and later cure the king's evil.

A young prince shall be falsely accused of treason. After being found innocent, he shall take his rightful place as the head of the State, and his accuser shall be slain by the people.

11

Celuy qu'aura couvert de la grand cappe,
Sera induit a quelque cas patrer;
Le douze rouges viendront souiller la nape,
Soubs meurtre, meurtre se viendra perpetrer.

He that shall be covered with a great cloak
Shall be induced to commit some great act,
The twelve red ones shall soil the table cloth,
Under murder, murder shall be committed.

Evidently a phase of the activities of the Roman Catholic Church—the Twelve Red Ones, being Cardinals, and the Great Cloak, the Pope.

12

Le camp plus grand de route mis en suit,	The greatest camp being in disorder shall be routed,
Geures plus outre ne sera pourchasse;	And shall be pursued not much after,
Ost recampe & region reduicte	The army shall encamp again, and the troops set in order,
Puis hors de Gaule du tout sera chasse.	Then afterwards, they shall be wholly driven out of France.

The invasions of France by the Germans are here predicted. Nostradamus forecasts the eventual, and complete, victory of France.

13

De plus grand perte nouvelles rapportees,	News being brought of a great loss,
Le rapport fait le camp s'eslongnera,	The report divulged, the camp shall be astonished,
Bendes unies encontre revoltes,	Troops being united and revolted,
Double phalange, grand abandonnera.	The falange shall forsake the great one.

The revolt of the Spanish Army and Falangists against Franco's dictatorial power is predicted.

14

La mort subiette du premier personnage,	The sudden death of the chief man,
Aura change & mis un autre au regne,	Shall cause a change, and put another in the reign soon,
Tost, tard venu a si haut & bas age,	Late come to so high a degree in a low age,
Que terre & mer faudra qu'on le craingne.	So that by land and sea he must be feared.

A regency shall be proclaimed when a young person is raised to the throne, and the clique in control shall misrule for a considerable period.

15

D'ou pensera faire venir famine,
De la viendra le rassassiement;
L'oeil de la mer par avare canine,
Pour de l'un l'autre donra huille
  froment.

Whence one thought to make
  famine to come,
Thence shall come the fullness,
The eye of the sea through a dog-
  gish covetousness,
Shall give to both, oil and wheat.

The low lands of Holland and the Zuider Zee were flooded by the Germans, but Nostradamus assures us that they will again be fertile.

16

La cite franche de liberte fait serue,
Des profligez & resueurs fait azyle;
Le Roy change a eux non si pro-
  terue,
De cent seront devenus plus de
  mille.

The free city from a free one shall
  become slave,
And of the banished and dreamers
  shall be a retreat,
The King changed in mind shall
  not be so unfavorable to them,
Of one hundred, they shall become
  more than a thousand.

The Free City of Danzig, enslaved by the Nazis, was nevertheless highly favored by them, even to the point of expansion.

17

Changer a Beaune, Nuis, Chalons,
  Dijon,
Le Duc voulant amender la barree,
Marchant pres fleuve, poisson bec
  de Plongeon,
Verra la queue port sera serree.

There shall be a change at Beaune,
  Nuis, Chalons, Dijon,
The Duke going about to raise
  taxes,
The Merchant near the river shall
  see the tail
Of a fish, having the bill of a loon,
  the door shall be shut.

A submarine shall be seen by a merchant, in a river near the above-mentioned French towns.

18

Des plus lettrez dessus les faits celestes,	The most learned in the celestial sciences,
Seron par princes ignorans reprouvez,	Shall be found fault with by ignorant princes,
Punis d'edit, chassez comme celestes,	Punished by a proclamation, chased away as wicked,
Et mis a mort la ou seront trouvez.	And put to death where they shall be found.

The warnings of learned scientists shall be scoffed at by ignorant persons in power, even to the point of persecution.

Nostradamus explicitly charges mankind to heed the warnings of science and take atomic power under international control.

19

Devant Rouan d'insubres mis le siege,	Before Rouen, a siege shall be laid by the Italians,
Par terre & mer enfermez les passages,	By sea and land the passages shall be shut up.
D'Haynaut, & Flandres de Gand & ceux de liege,	Those of Hianaut, Flanders, Ghent and Liege,
Par dons levees raviront les rivages.	With them troops shall plunder the sea shore.

An incident in the many wars among the European nations is here forecast.

20

Paix ubertre long temps Dieu louera,	Peace and plenty shall be not long praised,
Par tout son regne desert la fleur de lis	All the time of his reign the Fleur de Lys shall be deserted,
Corps morts d'eau, terre la l'on apportera,	Bodies shall die by water, earth shall be bought,
Aperant vain heur d'estre la ensevelis.	Hoping vainly to be there buried.

This predicts a great famine and flood in France, here signified by the Fleur de Lys.

21

Le changement sera fort difficile,
Cite province au change gain sera,
Coeur haut, prudent mis, chasse
  luy habile,
Mer, terre, peuple, son estat chang-
  era.

The change shall be very hard,
The city and country shall gain by
  the change,
A high prudent heart shall be put
  in, the unworthy expelled,
Sea, land, people, its state shall
  change.

This is the forecast of a revolution that will bring great and good changes to all.

22

La grand copie que sera dechassee,
Dans un moment fera besoin au
  Roy,
La foy promise de loing sera faus-
  see,
Nud se verra en piteux desarroy.

The great army that shall be rejected,
In a moment shall be wanted by
  the King,
The faith promised afar off shall
  be broken,
So that he shall be left naked in a
  pitiful case.

A continuation of the preceding stanza, this tells of the disintegration of the royal army and their desertion from the King to the cause of revolution.

23

La Legion dans la Marine classe,
Calcine, Magne, souphre & poix
  bruslera,
Le long repos de l'asseuree place,
Port Selyn chercher feu les con-
  sumera.

The Legion in the Maritime Fleet,
Calcining greatly, shall burn brim-
  stone and pitch,
After a long rest in the secure
  place,
They shall seek Port Selyn, but
  fire shall consume them.

A terrific assault by a great fleet equipped with weapons employing potent chemical agents, shall attack a country which has long enjoyed peace and security. They shall attack the great Port of LES N. Y. but will be repulsed by weapons even more terrible.

24

Ouy sous terre saincts d'ame voix
    fainte,
Humains flamme pour divin voir
    luire,
Fera des seuls de leur sang terre
    tainte,
Et les saints temples pour les im-
    pure destruire.

Underground, shall be heard the
    feigned voice of a holy dame,
A human flame to see a divine one
Shall cause the ground to be dyed
    with their own blood,
And the holy temples to be de-
    stroyed by the wicked.

Under the guise of a so-called reform movement, humanity shall suffer
much and the holy temples shall be destroyed.

25

Corps sublimes sans fin a l'oeil visi-
    bles,
Obnubiler viendra par ses raisons,
Corps, front comprins, sense, chef
    & invisibles,
Dimineant les sacrees oraisons.

The celestial bodies that are always
    visible to the eye,
Shall be darkened for these reasons,
The body with the forehead, sense
    and head invisible,
Diminishing the sacred prayers.

The occult knowledge of "prophets" shall flourish during this period,
keeping alive the hope of the world.

26

Lou grand cyssame le levera d'al-
    belhos,
Que non sauran don, te signen ven
    guddos,
Denech l'embousq, sou gach sous
    las treilhos,
Cuitad trahido per cinq lengos non
    nudos.

The great swarm of bees shall rise,
And it shall not be known whence
    they come,
Towards the ambush, the jay shall
    be under a trellis,
A city shall be betrayed by five
    tongues not naked.

When a swarm of bees alight from an unknown source, then shall be
seen a Jay under the trellis and the city shall be betrayed by five different
nations.

27

Salon, Mansol, Tarascon de Sex l'arc,
Ou est debout encor la pyramide;
Viendront livrer le prince d'Denemark,
Rachapt honny au temple d'Artemide.

Salon, Mansol, Tarascon of six arches
Where is still standing the pyramids,
Shall come to deliver the Prince of Denmark,
A shameful ransom shall be paid into the temple of Artemis.

Provincial towns are named here and the arches mentioned are the ruins of ancient triumphal monuments erected by the Romans. Artemis is another name for Diana.

28

Lors que Venus du Sol sera couvert;
Soubs l'esplendeur sera forme occulte;
Mercure au feu les aura descouvert,
Par bruit bellique sera mis a l'insulte,

When Venus shall be covered by the Sun,
Under the splendor it shall be an occult form,
Mercury in the fire shall discover them,
And by a warlike rumor shall be provoked.

An allegorical stanza, wherein is expressed a hidden formula, having to do with the preparation of the elixir to make the hermetic Philosophers' Stone. The same occult directions are given also in the three stanzas following.

29

Le Sol cache eclipse par Mercure,
Ne sera mis que pour le ciel second;
De Vulcan Hermes sera faite pasture,
Sol sera veu pur rutilant & blond.

The Sun shall be hid and eclipsed by Mercury,
And shall not be set but for the second heaven,
Hermes shall be made a prey to Vulcan,
And after that the Sun shall be seen pure, shining and yellow.

The Sun refers to gold, the second heaven means a furnace. "Hermes a prey to Vulcan" indicates the elixir to be put upon the fire in a furnace.

30

Plus unze fois Lune Sol ne voudre,
Tous augmentez & baissez de de-
gree;
Et si bas mis que peu d'or le secret,
Qu'apres faim, peste, decouvert le
secret.

The Moon will not have the Sun
above eleven times.
Then both shall be increased and
lessened in degree,
And put so low, that a little gold
shall be sewed up,
So that hunger and plague, the
secret shall be discovered.

Alchemical formulae and processes are clearly expressed for the adept,
but are most confusing for the uninitiated.

31

Le lune au plain de nuict sur le
haut mont
Le nouveau sophe d'vn seul cerveau
l'a veu,
Par ses disciples estre immortel se-
mond,
Yeux au midy, en sens mains corps
au feu.

The moon at full by night upon
the high mount,
The new Sophe with only one
brain has seen it,
Invited by his disciples to become
immortal,
His eyes to the south, his hands
and body to the fire.

The Sophe, or wise man, has mastered the secret. Invited to reveal
the secret to the world, by his disciples, he refuses, and does not become
immortal.

32

Es lieux & temps chair au poisson
dorna lieu.
La loy commune sera faite au contraire,
Vieux tiendra fort, puis este du
milieu,
Le Panta, Choina Philon, mis fort
arriere.

In places and times, flesh shall give
way to flesh,
The common law shall be made
against it;
The old man shall stand fast, then
being taken away,
Then all things common among
friends, shall be set aside.

Panta, Choina Philon are Greek words expressed best in English as
"All things are common among friends."

33

Jupiter joint plus Venus qu'a la
Lune,
Apparoissant de plentitude
blanche;
Venus cachee sous la blancheur
Neptune,
De Mars frappee par la grande
branche.

Jupiter being more joined to Venus
than to the Moon,
Appearing in a full whiteness,
Venus being hid under the whiteness of Neptune,
Stricken by Mars through the en-
graved branch.

Those in power shall give more time to the pleasures of Venus than to
other activities, until the sudden onslaught of a war.

34

Le grand mene captif d'estrange
terre,
D'or enchaine au Roy Chyren of-
fert;
Qui dans Ausonne, Milan perdra la
guerre,
Et tout son ost mis a feu & a fer.

The great one brought prisoner
from a far country,
And chained with gold, shall be
presented to Henry, the ruler,
Being then at Ausonne, Milan shall
lose the war,
And all its host put to fire and
sword.

Nostradamus interprets this literally, thus: When a great one from a
far country shall be brought prisoner chained with gold, and presented to a
King called Henry (for Chyren by transposition of letters is Henryc) who
then shall be at Bordeaux (Ausonne), Milan shall lose a great army.

35

Le feu estaint les vierges trahyront,
La plus grand part de la bande vou-
velle;
Poudre a fer, lance les seule Roy
garderont,
Etrusque & Corse de nuict gorge
allumelle.

The fire being put out, the virgins
shall betray,
The greatest part of the new troup,
Gunpowder, lance, shall keep only
the King,
In Etruria and Corsica by night,
throats shall be cut.

An insurrection in Italy (Etruria) is predicted, which shall take place at
night and be betrayed by Virgins.

36

Les jeux nouveaux en Gaule redressez,	The new plays shall be set up again in France,
Apres victoire de l'Insubre campagne,	After the victory obtained in Piedmont,
Monts d'Esperie, les grands liez troussez,	Mountains of Spain, the great ones tied and carried away,
De peur trembler la Romaine & Espagne.	Romania and Spain shall quake for fear.

France again will be triumphant after a victory over the Italians. Over the mountains of Spain the great ones will be carried away, and Romania and Spain shall be in terror.

37

Gaulois par sauts, monts viendra penetrer.	The French by leaping shall go over the mountains,
Occupera le grand lieu de l'Insubre;	And shall seize the great mount of the Savoyard,
Au plus profond son ost fera entrer,	He shall cause his army to go to the furthermost,
Gennes, Monech pousseront classe rubre.	Genoa, and Monaco shall set out their red fleet.

This prophecy concerns Henry IV, King of France, who went over the Alps and conquered the dukedom of Savoy.

38

Pendant que Duc, Roy, Roynes occupera,	While the Duke shall keep the King and Queen busy,
Chef Bizantin captif en Samothrace;	A great man of Constantinople shall be prisoner in Greece;
Avant l'assaut l'vn l'autre mangera,	Before the assault one shall eat up the other,
Rebours ferre suyura de sang la trace.	Rebours armored shall trace one by the blood.

A great tumult and riot will occur before the city is captured by the heavily armored enemy.

39

Les Rodiens demanderont secours,	The Rhodians shall ask for aid,
Par le neglet de ses hoirs delaisses,	Being forsaken by the neglect of her heirs,
L'empire Arabe revalera son cours,	The Arabian Empire shall slack his course,
Par Hesperies la cause radressee.	By means of Spain the care shall be mended.

Nostradamus looks into time, and see the Turks assuming a minor role in history. In 1555, when the Centuries were first issued, Turkey was in a position to challenge the Christian nations for a position of world supremacy.

40

Les forteresses des assiegez ferrez,	The strong places of the besieged shall be pressed.
Par poudre a feu profondes en abysme;	By gunpowder they shall be plunged into a pit,
Les proditeurs seront tous vifs serrez,	The traitors shall be shut up alive,
Onc aux Sacristes n'advint si piteux scisme.	Never did happen so pitiful a schism to the Sacristes.

By Sacristes, the author means that part of the Roman Catholic Church that is in charge of the books and property. There seems to be a warning implicit in this quatrain—probably slanted against those whom Nostradamus considered heretics.

41

Gynique sexe captive hostage,	Gynical sexe being captive by hostage,
Viendra de nuict custodes decevoir;	Shall come by night to deceive her keepers,
Le chef du camp deceu par son lignage,	The chief of the camp being deceived by her language,
Liarra le genre, fera piteux avoir.	Shall keep her folks, a thing pitiful to behold.

Gynical sexe is taken from a Greek word meaning woman. A woman shall captivate the chief of her captors, and cause him to betray his trust.

42

Geneve & Langres par ceux de
  Chartre & Dole
Et par Grenoble captif au Montli-
  mar,
Seysset, Losanne par fraudulente
  dole,
Les trahyront par or soixante marc.

Geneva and Langres by those of
  Chartres and Dole,
And by one of Grenoble captive at
  Montlimar,
Seisset, Lausanne by a fraudulent
  deceit,
Shall betray them for thirty pounds
  weight of gold.

The sense is plain, and this apparently refers to struggles among various towns in France.

43

Seront ouys au ceil les armes battre,
Celuy an mesme les divins ennemis,
Voudront Loix Sainctes injuste-
  ment debatre,
Par foudre & guerre bien croyants
  a mort mis.

There shall be heard in the air the
  noise of weapons,
And in that same year, the divines
  shall be enemies,
They shall unjustly put down the
  Holy Laws,
And by thunder and the war, true
  believers shall die.

A religious war shall break out, during which many true believers will suffer greatly.

44

Deux gros de Mende de Rhodes &
  Millaud,
Cahors, Limoges, Castre malo sep-
  mano,
De nuech l'intrado, de Bordeaux
  an cailhau,
Par Perigort au toc de la Campano.

Two great ones of Mendes, of
  Rhodes and Millaud,
Cahors, Limoges, Castres, an evil
  week,
By might the entry shall be from
  Bordeaux one cailhau,
Through Perigort at the ringing of
  the bell.

Towns near the home of Nostradamus are spoken of here, and a rising against tax collectors is indicated.

45

Par conflit Roy Regne abandon-
nera,
Le plus grand chef faillira au beso-
ing,
Morts profligez, peu en rechappera,
Tous destranchez, un en sera tes-
moin.

By a battle the King shall forsake
his kingdom,
The great commander shall fail in
time of need,
They shall be killed and routed,
few shall escape,
They shall be cut off, one only shall
be left for a witness.

The Battle of Waterloo is prognosticated. His defeat in this battle, due
to the failure of Marshal De Grouchy, caused Napoleon to lose his Empire.

46

Bien deffendu le fait par excellence,
Garde toy Tours de ta proche
ruyne;
Londres & Nantes par Rheims fera
deffence
Ne passez outre au temps de la
bruyne.

The fact shall be defended excel-
lently well,
Tours beware of thy approaching
ruin,
London and Nantes by Rheims
shall stand upon their defence,
Do not go further in foggy weather.

Tours, a city in France, is warned of a fog, and told to beware of her
approaching ruin.

47

Le noir farouche quand aura essaye,
Sa main sanguine par feu, fer arcs,
tendus,
Trestout le peuple sera tant effraye,
Voir les plus grands par col & pieds
pendus.

The wild black one, after he shall
have tried,
His bloody hand by fire, sword,
bended bows,
All the people shall be so frightened,
To see the greatest hanged by neck
and feet.

Astonishingly accurate prophecy of the fate of Mussolini, Leader
of the Black Shirts. After his death, he was hung by his feet for the mob to
spit upon.

48

Plannure, Ausonne fertille, spa-
cieuse,
Produira tahons si tant de sauterelles,
Clarte solaire viendra nubileuse,
Ronger le tout, grand peste venir
d'elles.

The plain about Bordeaux fruitful
and spacious,
Shall produce so many hornets and
so many grasshoppers,
That the light of the sun shall be
darkened,
They shall fly so low, a great plague
shall come from them.

The prediction here is of the D-Day invasion of France by the Allies
in World War II; at that time the sky was darkened by the tremendous
concentration of Air Power.

49

Devant le peuple sang sera respandu,
Que du haut ciel ne viendra eslong-
ner;
Mais d'un long temps ne sera en-
tendu,
L'esprit d'un seul le viendra tes-
moigner.

Before the people, blood shall be
spilt,
Who shall not come far from high
heaven,
But it shall not be heard of for a
great while,
The spirit of one shall come to
witness it.

A worthy person shall be murdered openly. His blood shall cry to
heaven, but shall not be heard for a time, but at last it shall be discovered.

50

Libra verra regner les Hesperies,
De Ciel & Terra tenir la mon-
archie,
D'Asie forces nul ne verra peries,
Que sept ne tiennent par rang la
Hierarchie.

Libra shall see Spain to reign,
And have the monarchy of Heaven
and Earth,
Nobody shall see the forces of Asia
to perish,
Till seven have kept the Hierarchy
successively.

A Spaniard shall attain to the office of Pope, Monarch of Heaven and
Earth, and after seven of the Spanish faction have reigned successively
then the Asiatic forces will be overcome.

51

Un Duc cupide son ennemy en-
suyvre,
Dans entrera empeschant la pha-
lange,
Hastez a pied si pres viendront
poursuyvre,
Que la journee conflit pres de
Gange.

A Duke being earnest in the pursuit of his enemy,
Shall come in, hindering the falange,
Hastened on foot shall follow them
so close,
That the day of the battle shall be
near Ganges.

In India, near the Ganges, there will be a battle, involving a falange (squadron of soldiers) and a Duke.

52

En cite obsessee aux murs hommes
& femmes,
Ennemys hors le chef prest a soy
rendre,
Vent sera fort encontre les gens-d'-
armes,
Chassez seront par chaux, poussiere
& cendre.

In a besieged city, men and women
being upon the walls,
The enemy without, the governor
ready to surrender,
The wind shall be strong against
the soldiers
They shall be driven away by lime,
dust and cinders.

A besieged city shall be saved from captivity by means of a powerful chemical apparently borne by a strong wind, which will drive away the besiegers.

53

Les fugitifs & bannis revoquez,
Peres & fils grand garnissant les
haut poits;
Le cruel pere & les siens suffoquez,
Son fils plus pire submerge dans le
puis.

The fugitive and banished men being rescued,
Fathers and sons garnishing the
high walls,
The cruel father and his retinue
shall be suffocated,
His son, being worse, shall be
drowned in the well.

The reappearance of evil men, banished because of their part in the making of war, once again shall usher in a period of destruction.

54

Du nom qui onc ne fut au Roy Gaulois,	Of a name that a French King never was,
Jamais ne fut un foudre si crain-tif,	There was never a lightning so much feared,
Tremblant l'Italie l'Espagne & les Anglois,	Italy shall tremble, Spain and the English
De femme estrangers grandement attentif.	He shall be much taken with women strangers.

This concerns Napoleon Bonaparte, even to his many amours.

55

Quand la Corneille sur tour de brique jointe,	When the Crow on a tower made of brick
Durant sept heures ne fera que crier,	For seven hours shall do nothing but cry,
Mort presagee de sang statue tainte,	Death shall be foretold and the statue dyed with blood,
Tyran meurtry, aux Dieux peuple prier.	Tyrant shall be murdered and the people pray to the Gods.

The extraordinary spectacle of a continuous alarm, by a crow, for seven hours from a brick tower will be a sign that some infamous tyrant will meet his end, and the populace shall show fear.

56

Apres victoire de raibeuse langue,	After victory over a raging tongue,
L'esprit tempte en tranquil & re-pos;	The mind that was tempted shall be in tranquility and rest,
Victeur sanguin par conflit fait harangue,	The bloody emperor by battle shall make a speech,
Rostir la langue, & la chair & les os.	And roast the tongue, the flesh and the bones.

Vengeance shall be taken by a conqueror over his critics who had spoken against him.

57

Ignare envie du grand Roy sup-
portee,
Tiendra propos deffendre les escrits;
Sa femme non femme par un autre
tentee,
Plus double deux ne feront ne cris.

Ignorant envy being supported by
the great King
Shall talk of prohibiting the writings,
His wife no wife, being tempted
by another,
Shall no more than they two prevail by crying.

Envious persons, in favor with the King, shall attempt to suppress
learning. But the King's mistress shall persuade him to the contrary, and
shall prevail.

58

Soleil ardant dans le gosier coller,
De sang humain arroser terre
Etrusque;
Chef seille d'eau mener son fils
filer,
Captive dame conduite en terre
Turque.

Burning sun shall pour into the
throat,
This human blood shall wet the
Etruscan ground,
The chief pail of water shall lead
his son to spin,
A captive lady shall be carried into
the Turkish country.

Molten gold shall be poured into a throat and human blood shall
flow. Because of this, a great water carrier shall make his son effem-
inate, and a captive lady shall be exiled.

59

Deux assiegez en ardante fureur,
De soif estaints pour deux plaines
tasses,
Le fort limen & vn viellard resueur,
Aux Genois de Nizza monstrera
trasse.

Two besieged, being in a burning
heat,
Shall die for thirst, want of two
cups full,
The fort being filed, an old doting
man,
Shall show to the Genoese the way
to Nice.

Nice shall be taken by the Italians through the help of an old dotard.

60

Les sept enfans en hostage laissez,	The seven children being left in hostage,
Le tiers viendra son enfant trucider;	The third shall come to kill his child,
Deux par son fils seront d'estoc percez,	Two by their sons shall be run through,
Gennes, Florence, lors viendra enconder.	Genoa and Florence shall second them.

Evidently this indicates an event which occurred during the time of Nostradamus, and according to him should be understood by all.

61

Le vieux mocque, & prive de sa place,	The old man shall be baffled and deprived of his place,
Par l'estranger qui le subornera;	By the stranger that shall have instigated him,
Mains de son fils mangees devant sa face	But his sons shall be eaten before his face,
Les freres a Chartres, Orleans, Rouen trahyra.	The brother at Chartres, Orleans shall betray Rouen.

General Henri Petain, dictator of Vichy France, under Nazi supervision, was deposed by General De Gaulle. During the time Petain was in power the captured French were used by the Germans as slave laborers.

62

Un coronel machine ambition,	A colonel intrigues a plot by his ambition,
Se saisira de la plus grande armee;	He shall seize upon the best part of the army,
Contree son prince fainte invention,	Against the prince he shall have a feigned invention.
Et descouvert sera sous sa ramee.	And shall be discovered under the harbour of the vine.

An accurate picture of the rise of Oliver Cromwell to the height of power in England.

63

L'armee Celtique contre les Mon-
tagnars,
Qui seront sceus & prins a la pipee;
Paysans irez pouseront tost faug-
nars,
Precipitez tous au fil de l'espee.

The Celtic army shall go against
the Highlanders,
Who shall stand upon their guard,
and being taken with trickery,
The peasant being angry, shall roll
down the stones,
They shall be all put to the edge
of the sword.

The heroic peasant rebellion of the Austrian Tyrol, under Andreas Hofer, against the French Republican Army, is here prophesied by our author.

64

Le deffaillant en habit de bou-
geois,
Viendra le Roy tempter de son of-
fense,
Quinze soldats la plus part osta-
gois,
Vie derniere & chef de sa chevance.

The guilty, in a citizen's habit,
Shall come to tempt the King concerning his offense,
Fifteen soldiers the most part hostages,
Last shall be his life and the best
part of his estate.

The King shall be taunted by the citizens, and a guard of fifteen soldiers shall be put over him.

65

Au deserteur de la grand forteresse,
Apres qu'aura son lieu abandonne;
Son adversaire fera si grand pro-
vesse,
L'Empereur tost mort sera con-
damne.

To the deserter of the great for-
tress,
After having forsaken his place,
His adversary shall do great feats,
That the Emperor shall soon be
condemned to death.

Treachery shall play a prominent part in the destruction of a future emperor who will be condemned to a living death.

66

Soubs couleur fainte de sept'testes rasees,	Under the feigned colour of seven shaven heads,
Seront semez divers explorateurs;	Shall divers spies be framed,
Puys & fontaines de poison arrousees,	Wells and fountains shall be sprinkled with poison,
Au fort de Gennes humaine devorateurs.	In the fort of Genoa shall be human devourers.

Seven priests or monks shall poison the well of public opinion, and in Genoa shall be those that live on human flesh.

67

L'an que Saturne & Mars eagaux combust,	In the year that Saturn and Mars shall be fiery,
L'air fort seiche, longue trajection;	The air shall be very dry, in many countries,
Par feux secrets, d'ardeur grand lieu adust	By secret fires, many places shall be burnt with heat,
Peu pluye, vent, chaud, guerres, incursions.	There shall be scarcity of rain, hot winds, wars, wounds.

A prognostication that Saturn (Commerce) and Mars (War) shall have a Roman Holiday.

68

En l'an bien proche eslongue de Venus,	In the year that is to come soon, and not far from Venus,
Les deux plus grands de L'Asie & d'Affrique;	The two greatest ones of Asia and Africa,
De Rhin, & Hyster, qu'on dira sont venus.	Shall be said to come from the Rhine and Ister,
Cris, pleurs a Malte & coste a Lycustique.	Crying and tears shall be at Malta and on the Italian Shore.

From the shores of the Rhine and Danube shall come those who will bring woe on Malta and also to the Italian shores.

69

La cite grande les exilez tiendront,
Les citadins morts meurtris & chas-
    sez;
Ceux d'Aquilee a Parmee promet-
    tront,
Monstrer l'entree par les lieux non
    trassez.

The banished shall keep the great
    city,
The citizens being dead, murdered
    and expelled,
Those of Aquelia shall promise to
    Parma,
To show the entrance by unknown
    paths.

Aquelia and Parma are Italian cities and, according to Nostradamus,
they will be involved in inter-city warfare.

70

Bien contigue des grands monts
    Pyrenees,
Un contre l'Aigle grand copie ad-
    dresser;
Ouvertes vaines, forces extermi-
    nees,
Que jusque a Pau, le chef viendra
    chasser.

Near the great Pyrenees Moun-
    tains,
One shall raise a great army against
    the Eagle,
Veins shall be opened, forces
    driven out,
So that the chief shall be driven
    as far as the Po.

Near the Spanish border one shall raise an army against an Emperor,
whose emblem is the Eagle, but to no avail, as the chief of the army will
flee and his forces will be scattered.

71

En lieu d'espouse les filles truci-
    dees,
Meurtre a grand faute ne sera su-
    perstile;
Dedans le puys vestuies inondees,
L'espouse estaint par hauste d'-
    Aconite.

Instead of the bride, the maid shall
    be killed,
The murder shall be a great fault,
    none shall be surviving,
In the well they shall be drowned
    with their clothes,
The bride shall be disposed of by
    high Aconite.

This tells of the tragic aftermath of a marriage, in which the bridesmaids
shall be drowned in their wedding finery and the bride poisoned by Aconite.

72

Les Artomiques par Agen & Lectoure,
A saint Felix feront leur parlement,
Ceux de Basas viendront a la mal-
heure,
Saisir Condon & Marsan promptement.

The Artomiques, through Agen
and Lectoure,
Shall keep their parliament at Saint
Felix,
These of Bazan shall come in an
unhappy hour,
To seize Condon and Marsan
speedily.

By Artomiques, our author means the Protestants, who take the Com-
munion with leavened bread, called in Greek, Artos. The towns mentioned
are all in Gascony.

73

Le nepveu grand par forces prou-
vera,
Le peche fait du coeur pusillanime;
Ferrare & Ast le Duc esprouvera,
Par lors qu'au soir fera la panto-
mime.

The great nephew by force shall
provoke,
The sin committed by a pusillan-
imous heart,
Ferrari and Asti shall make a trial
of the Duke,
When the pantomime shall be in
the evening.

While the performance of a comedy is being enacted, a cowardly person,
provoked by his nephew, shall go on a rampage.

74

Du lac Leman & ceux de Bran-
nonices,
Tous assemblez contre ceux d'Aquitaine,
Germains beaucoup encor plus
souisses,
Seront defaicts avec ceux d'Humaine.

From Lake Geneva and to Verona,
They shall be gathered against
those of England,
Great many Germans and many
more mercenaries,
Shall be routed together with
many people.

The Germans and their allies shall be decisively beaten by the English-
speaking allies during a great campaign in Italy.

75

Prest a combattre fera defection,	One being ready to fight shall faint,
Chef adversaire obtiendra la victoire,	The chief of the adverse party shall obtain the victory,
L'arriere garde fera defension,	The rear guard shall fight it out,
Les deffaillans mort au blanc territoire.	Those that fall away shall die in the white country.

1945

In a time of stress, the leader of one side, profiting by his opponent's weakness, shall grasp power, and the northern nations shall be worsted in the struggle.

76

Les Nictobriges par ceux de Perigort,	The Nictobriges by those of Perigort,
Seront vexez tenant jusques au Rhosne,	Shall be vexed as far as the Rhone,
L'associe de Gascons & Bigorre,	The associate of the Gascons and Bigorre,
Trahir le temple, le prestre estant au prosne,	Shall betray the church while the priest is in his pulpit.

Nictobriges, in Greek, signifies a people of a dark and moist country. —Perigort and Bigorre are towns in France.

77

Selyn monarque, L'Italie pacifique,	Selyn being monarch, Italy shall be in peace,
Regnes unis Roy Chrestien du monde;	Kingdoms shall be united, a Christian King of the world,
Mourant voudra coucher en terre belsique,	Dying, shall desire to be buried in Europe.
Apres pyrates avoir chasse de l'onde.	After he shall have driven the pirates from the sea.

During a time of peace, all the world will be united under a great and noble king who will be a Christian.

78

La grand armee de la pugnee civille,
Pour de nuict Parme a l'estrange
trouvee
Septante neuf meurtris dedans la
ville,
Les estrangers passez tous a l'espee.

The great army belonging to the
civil war,
Having found by night Parma possessed by strangers,
Shall kill seventy-nine in the town
And put all the strangers to the
sword.

Great civil wars are promised for Parma and other Italian cities.

79

Sang Royal fuis, Monheurt, Mas
Aiguillon,
Remplis seront de Bourdelois les
Landes,
Navarre, Bigorre, pointes & eguil-
lons,
Profonds de faim, vorer de liege,
glandes.

Royal Blood run away from Monheurt, Marsan, Aiguillon,
The Landes shall be full of Bourdelois,
Navarre, Bigorre, shall have points
and pricks,
Being deep in hunger, they shall
devour the cork and acorns.

Bourdelois refers to the people of Bordeaux. Landes is a desert region in France near the towns of Navarre and Bigorre. As in quatrain 76, there seems to be no deeper significance beyond Nostradamus' concern with these French towns and their current troubles.

80

Pres du grand fleuve grand fosse
terre egeste
En quinze part sera l'eau divisee,
La cite prinse, feu, sang cris, conflit mestre,
Et la plus part concerne au colli-
see.

Near the great river, a great pit,
earth dug out,
In fifteen parts, the water shall be
divided,
The city taken, fire, sword, blood,
cries, fighting,
The greatest part concerns the Col-
osseum.

In Rome there shall be a great tumult and fighting, concerning in most part a revival of ancient ideas.

81

Pont on fera promptement de na-
celles,
Passer l'armee du grand prince Bel-
gique;
Dans profondrees & non loing de
Bruxelles,
Outre passez, destrenchex sept a
picque.

A bridge of boats shall suddenly
be made,
To pass over the army of the great
Belgian Prince.
In deep places, and not far from
Brussels,
Being gone over, there shall be
seven cut with a pike.

A prophecy of the Siege of Antwerp by the Spanish under the Prince
of Parma, who eventually erected a pontoon bridge over the River Schelde
and captured the city.

82

Amas s'approche venant d'Escla-
vonie,
L'Olestant vieux cite ruynera;
Fort desclee vera sa Romaine,
Puis la grand flamme estaindre ne
scaura.

A great troop gathered shall come
from Russia,
The old Olestant shall ruin a city,
He shall see his Romania very
desolate,
And after that, shall not be able
to quench that great flame.

A Russian advance to the West shall be slowed up by an attack by an
Olestant (Duke). But he will thus meet his ruin and his country will be
made desolate.

83

Combat nocturne le vaillant capitaine,
Vaincu fuyra, peu de gens profli-
gee;
Son peuple esmeu, sedition non
vaine,
Son propre fils le tiendra assiege.

In a fight by night, the valiant captain
Being vanquished shall run away,
overcome by few.
His people being moved, shall
make no small mutiny,
His own son shall besiege him.

An event in Nostradamus' time which he felt needed no explanation.

84

Un grand d'Auxerre mourra bien miserable,	A great man of Auxerre shall die very miserably,
Chasse de ceux qui soubs luy ont este,	Being expelled by those who have been under him,
Serre de chaisnes, apres d'un rude cable,	Bound with chains, and after that, with a strong cable,
En l'an que Mars, Venus, Sol mis en este.	In the year that Mars, Venus, and Sol shall be in conjunction.

Auxerre is a city in France about fifty miles from Paris. And this stanza merely concerns the unhappy fate of one of its chief men—many, many years ago.

85

Le charbon blanc du noir sera chasse,	The white coal shall be expelled by the black one,
Prisonnier fait mene au tumbereau,	He shall be made prisoner carried in a dung cart,
More chameau sus pied estrelassez,	His feet twisted on a black camel,
Lors le puisne fillera l'aubereau.	Then the youngest, shall suffer the Falcon to have more freedom.

A white prince shall be overcome by a black one, and carried to his execution in a dung cart. According to Nostradamus, this is both "allegorical and metaphorical, and the judgment must be left to the reader."

86

L'an que Saturne en eau sera conjoinct,	In the year that Saturn in Aquarius shall be in conjunction
Avec Sol, le Roy fort & puissant,	With Sol, the King being strong and powerful,
A Rheims & Aix sera receu & oingt,	Shall be received and anointed at Rheims and Aix,
Apres conquestes meurtrura innocens.	After conquest he shall murder innocent persons.

Rheims, a city in France, and Aix, a city in Germany, shall both be the scene of the coronation of a common ruler. Afterwards his actions shall be ominous.

87

Un fils du Roy tent de langues
  aprins,
A son sisne au regne different,
Son pere beau au plus beau fisz
  comprins,
Fera perir principe adherent.

A son of a King having learned
  divers languages
Shall fall out with his elder brother
  for the kingdom,
His father-in-law being more concerned with his elder son,
Shall cause the principal adherent
  to perish.

A King having two sons, the elder shall succeed him. The younger,
being well educated, shall rebel against the King, his father, but shall be
slain by his own father-in-law.

88

Le grand Anthoine du moindre
  fait sordide,
De Phytriase a son dernier ronge,
Un qui de plomb voudra estre cu-
  pide,
Passant le Port d'Esleu sera plonge.

The great Anthony by name, but,
  in effect sordid,
By lice, shall at last be eaten up,
One that shall be covetous of lead,
Passing the Port Esleu shall fall
  into the water.

One who pretends to greatness shall at last realize his failure. He
shall commit suicide by drowning himself.

89

Trente de Londres secret conjur-
  eront,
Contre leur Roy, sur le pont l'en-
  treprinse,
Les satalites la mort degousteront,
Un Roy esleu blonde, natif de
  Frize.

Thirty of London shall secretly
  conspire,
Against the King, upon the bridge
  the plot shall be made,
These satellites shall taste of
  death,
A King shall be elected, fair, and
  born in the low countries.

The Guy Fawkes gunpowder plot against the British Throne is clearly
outlined here.

90

Les deux copie aux murs ne pour-
ront joindre,
Dans cest instant trembler Milan
Ticin,
Faim, soif, doutance si fort les
viendra poindre,
Chair, pain, ne vivres, n'auront un
seul bouncin.

The two armies shall not be able
to join by the walls,
At the instant Milan and Ticin
shall tremble
Hunger, thirst, and fear shall so
seize upon them
They shall not have a bit of meat,
bread nor victuals.

A description of conditions in Italy during a war is here given, referring specifically to the city of Milan.

91

Au Duc Gaulois constranet battre
au duelle,
La nef Mole Monech n'appro-
chera,
Tort accuse prison perpetuelle,
Son fils regner auant mort taschera.

A French Duke compelled to fight
a duel,
The ship of Mole shall not approach Monaco,
Wrongfully accused, shall be perpetually imprisoned,
His son shall endeavor to reign before his death.

"The Man in the Iron Mask," whose name was never known, was a French prisoner who died on November 19, 1703. His identity has been the source of much romantic speculation. Here Nostradamus gives us a clue.

92

Teste trenchee du vaillant Capitaine,
Sera jette devant son adversaire,
Son corps pendu de sa classe a l'an-
tenne,
Confus furia par rames a vent contraire.

The head cut off of the valiant
Captain,
Shall be thrown down before his
adversary,
His body hanged from the ship's
antenna,
Confused, they shall fly with oars
against the wind.

This quatrain caused confusion in the mind of Nostradamus. To us, there is an obvious reference to radio in it—but the event itself remains obscure.

93

Un serpent veu proche du lit Royal,
Sera par dame, nuict chiens n'ab-
bayeront;
Lors naistre en France un Prince
tant Royal
Du ciel venu tous les Princes ver-
ront.

A serpent shall be seen near the
Royal bed,
By a lady of the night, the dogs
shall not bark,
Then shall be born in France a
Prince so much royal,
Come from heaven all the Princes
shall see it.

All the princes of the world will acknowledge a French Prince as the
greatest of them all. The serpent is an allusion to his greatness, as when
Alexander was born, a serpent was seen near his mother's bed.

94

Deux grands freres seront chassez
d'Espaigne,
Laisne vaineu soubs les monts Py-
renees;
Rougir mer, Rosne sang Leman d'-
Alemagne,
Narbon, Blyterres, d'Agath, con-
taminees.

Two great brothers shall be driven
from Spain,
The elder of them shall be overcome under the Pyrenean Mountains,
Bloody sea, Rhone, bloody Geneva
of Germany,
Narbonne, the Land of Agath con-
taminated.

The two great brothers in crime, Nazism and Fascism, will be driven
from Spain, but not before a great struggle takes place near the border
of France.

95

Le regne a deux laisse bien peu
tiendront,
Trois ans sept mois passez feront
la guerre;
Les deux vestales contre rebeller-
ont,
Victor puis nay en Armorique
terre.

The reign left to two they shall
not keep it long,
Three years and seven months be
ing past,
The vestals shall rebel against
them,
The youngest shall be the conqueror of the Armorick country.

This signifies a Kingdom that shall be left to two, who shall keep it
but a short while. Their title will be challenged by two Nuns.

96

La soeur aisnee de l'Isle Britannique,
Quinze ans devant le frere aura
naissance,
Par son promis moyennant verri-
fique,
Succedera au regne de Balance.

The eldest sister of the Britannic
Island
Shall be born fifteen years before
her brother,
By what is promised her and by
help of truth,
She shall succeed in the Kingdom
of Libra.

The eldest sister of Britain, the U. S. A., was born in 1776. Fifteen
years later, 1791, the Republic of France (brother) came into being.

97

L'an que Mercure, Mars, Venus
retrograde,
Du grand Monarque la ligne ne
faillir,
Esleu du peuple lusitant pres de
Pactole,
Que'n paix & regne viendra fort
envillir.

When Mercury, Mars and Venus
shall retrograde,
The line of the great Monarch shall
be wanting,
He shall be elected by the Portu-
guese near Pactole,
And shall reign in peace a good
while.

This signifies the change of state in Portugal, when they threw off
the yoke of Spain, and chose their own King.

98

Les Albanois passeront dedans
Rome,
Moyennant Langres dimiples affu-
blez,
Marquis & Duc ne pardonner a
homme,
Feu, sang morbile, point d'eau,
faillir les bleds.

The Albanians shall pass through
Rome,
By means of Langres covered with
half helmets,
Marquis and Duke shall spare no
man,
Fire, blood, smallpox, water shall
fail us, also corn.

The Albanians shall conquer a large territory and take Rome, and
desolation shall follow in their wake.

99

L'aisne vailland de la fille du Roy,
Repoussera si avant les Celtique,
Qu'il mettra foudres, combien en
   tell arroy,
Peu, & loing puis profondes Hes-
   perique.
	The valiant eldest son of the
	   daughter of the King,
	Shall beat back so far, those of
	   Flanders,
	That he shall employ lightnings,
	   how many in such order,
	Little and far, after shall go deep
	   in Spain.

An able leader of noble birth shall show great skill in employing the forces of nature in conquering Flanders and Spain.

100

De feu celeste au Royal edifice,
Quand la lumiere du Mars deffail-
   lira,
Sept mois grand' Guerre, mort
   gent de malefice,
Rouen Eureux, au Roy ne faillira.
	Fire shall fall from the skies on
	   the King's palace
	When Mar's light shall be eclipsed,
	Great war shall be for seven
	   months, people shall die by
	   witchcraft,
	Rouen and Eureux shall not fail
	   the King.

A seven months' war, of tremendous destructive force such as the world has never seen before, shall terrify mankind.

CENTURY V

1

Avant venus du ruyne Celtique,
Dedans le temple deux parlemente-
ront,
Poignart coeur, d'un monte au
coursier & pique,
Sans faire bruit le grand enterre-
ront.

Before the coming of the ruin of
the Celts,
Two shall discourse together in the
church,
Dagger in the heart of one, on
horseback and spurring,
Without noise they shall bury the
great one.

The Irish, or Celts, shall be eventually ruined but, before this happens,
two shall talk together in a church; one of these will be stabbed and the
other will flee.

2

Sept conjurez au banquet feront
luyre,
Contre les trois le fer hors de na-
vire,
L'un les deux classes au grand fera
conduire,
Quand par le mail denier au front
luy tire.

Seven conspirators at a banquet
shall make their iron glisten
Against three, out of a ship,
One shall carry the two fleets to
the great one,
When in the promenade, the last
one shall shoot him in the forehead.

At a banquet a conspiracy of seven shall succeed against three. A
naval officer shall deliver two fleets to a great one, and for his treachery
shall be shot in the forehead.

3

Le successeur de la Duche viendra,
Beaucoup plus outre que la mer de
    Toscanne,
Gauloise branche la Florence
    tiendra,
Dans son giron d'accord nautique
    Rane.

The successor to the Dukedom
    shall come
Far beyond the Tuscan sea,
A French branch shall hold Flor-
    ence,
In its lap, to which the Sea Frog
    shall agree.

Il Duce, after his fall, shall be succeeded by a non-Italian. Florence will be under French influence.

4

Le gros mastin de cite dechasse,
Sera fasche de l'estrange alliance,
Apres aux champs avoir le chef
    chasse,
Le loup & l'ours se donneront de-
    fiance.

The great mastiff being driven from
    the city,
Shall be angry at the strange alli-
    ance,
After he shall have hunted the hart
    in the fields,
The wolf and the bear shall defy
    one another.

England shall be angry at a strange alliance, whereby the helpless are hunted down. The Italian Wolf and the Russian Bear shall defy one another.

5

Sous ombre saincte d'oster de servi-
    tude,
Peuple & cite l'usurpera luy-mes-
    mes,
Pire fera par faux de jeune pute,
Libre au champ lisant le faux pro-
    esme.

Under the feigned shadow of free-
    ing people from slavery,
He shall usurp the people and city
    for himself,
He shall do worse by the deceit of
    a young whore,
For he shall be betrayed in the field
    reading a false proem.

This prognosticates the "final" days and actions of Hitler, his false marriage to the actress Eva Braun, and his spurious will at his supposed death.

6

Au Roy l'augure sur le chef la main mettre,	The augur shall come to put his hand on the King's head,
Viendra prier pour la paix Italique,	And pray for the peace of Italy,
A la main gauche viendra changer le sceptre,	In the left hand he shall change the scepter,
De Roy viendra Empereur pacifique.	From a King he shall become a pacific Emperor.

The Latin word augur may mean one who foretells events, or may also be taken for a clergyman. Here the significance is, that a priest shall put his hand upon a King's head (Napoleon) and, praying for the peace of Italy, shall place a scepter in his hand, and install him as Emperor.

7

Du triumvir seront trouvez les os,	The bones of the triumvirate shall be found out,
Cerchant profond tresor enigmatique,	When they shall seek for a deep and enigmatical treasure,
Ceux d'alentour ne seront en repos,	Those there about shall not be in rest,
De concaver marbre & plomb metalique.	This concavity shall be of marble and metallic lead.

This delves into Roman history, and tells of the plot of Octavius Caesar, Marcus Antonius and Lepidus to make themselves masters of the Roman Empire and to divide the spoils among the three of them.

8

Sera laisse le feu mort vif cache,	The fire shall be left burning, the dead shall be hid,
Dedans les globes horribles espouventable	Within the globes terrible and fearful,
De nuict a classe cite en poudre lache,	By night the fleet shall shoot against the city,
La cite a feu, l'ennemy favorable.	The city shall be on fire, the enemy shall be favorable to it.

Terrible new weapons launched from ships shall create fearful destruction and cause unquenchable fires; and so complete will be the havoc, it will be impossible to count the dead.

9

Jusques au fond la grand arq de
malve
Par chef captif l'amy anticipe,
Naistra de dame front face cheve-
lue,
Lors par astuce Duc a mort at-
trapppe.

At the bottom of the great evil
arch,
By a chief that is a captive, the
friend shall be anticipated,
One shall be born of a lady with
hairy face and forehead,
Then by craft shall a duke be put
to death.

These words are too veiled in obscurity for either Nostradamus or
myself to render a clear interpretation.

10

Un chef Celtique dans le conflit
blesse,
Aupres de cave vouant siens mort
abbatre,
De sang & playes & d'ennemis
presse,
Et securs par incogneuz de quatre.

A Celtic leader wounded in battle,
Near a cellar, seeing death about
to overthrow his people,
Being much oppressed with blood,
wounds and enemies,
Is succoured by four unknown.

An event that needs no interpretation as it is self-explanatory.

11

Mer par solaires seure ne passera,
Ceux de Venus tiendront toute
l'Affrique;
Leur regne plus Sol, Saturne n'oc-
cupera,
Et changera la mort Asiatique.

Sea by solars, she shall pass safely,
Those of Venus shall hold all Af-
rica,
Saturn shall hold their kingdom
no longer,
And shall change the Asiatic port.

Those of Venus, born to the sea, are the English; as a maritime nation
they shall hold great colonial possessions.

12

Aupres de Lac Leman sera conduite,
Par garse estrange cite voulant
trahir,
Avant sen meurtre a Aspurg la
grand suitte,
Et ceux du Rhin la viendront envahir.

Near Lake Geneva shall be a plot,
By a strange whore to betray a city,
Before she be killed, her great reti-
nue will come to Augsburg,
And those of the Rhine shall come
to invade her.

The corrupting influence of Fascism had its inception in northern Italy, close to Lake Geneva. Before it ran its mad course it also ruined the Germans.

13

Par grand fureur le Roy Roman
Belgique,
Vexer voudra par phalange barbare,
Fureur grincent chassera gent Ly-
bique,
Depuis Pannons jusques Hercules
la Bare.

By great fury, the Roman-Belgic
Kingdom,
Shall come to vex, by their bar-
barian falange,
Gnashing fury shall pursue the
Savage people,
From Hungary as far as the Straits
of Gibraltar.

A coalition of nations shall vex Europe sorely with its barbarian tactics; the climax of its misdeeds is clearly indicated.

CENTURY I
9   PAGE 12

14

Saturne & Mars en Leo Espagne
captive,
Par chef Libique au conflit attrape;
Proche de Malte, heredde Prinse
vive,
Et Romain sceptre sera par coq
frappe.

Saturn and Mars being in Leo,
Spain shall be captive,
By an African general taken in
battle,
Near Malta, a hereditary Prince
shall be taken alive,
And the Roman sceptre shall be
struck by the cock.

Under the joint influence of Saturn (commerce) and Mars (war) Spain shall suffer great defeat. France (the cock) shall contribute to her downfall.

15

En navigant captif prins grand pontife;
Grands apprestez saillir les clercs tumultuez,
Second esleu absent son bien debise,
Son favory bastard a mort tue.

In sailing a pope shall be taken captive,
After which, shall be a great uproar amongst the clergy,
A second absent elected, consumed his goods,
His favorite bastard shall be killed.

A controversy shall arise in the Catholic Church, caused by the election of a Pope who is in disfavor with the clergy.

16

A son haut prix la lerme Sabee,
D'humains chair pour mort en cendre mettre,
A l'isle Pharos par croisars perturbee,
Alors qu'a Rhodes paroistra dure espectre.

The Sabean tear shall be no more at its high price,
To turn human flesh by death into ashes,
The island Pharos shall be troubled by croisars,
When at Rhodes shall a hard phantom appear.

Sabean tear, a term used to describe frankincense, was a vegetable product extensively used in embalming. Pharos, an island opposite Alexandria, shall be troubled by Christians (croisars) when a vision appears in Rhodes.

17

De nuict passant le Roy pres d'une Andronne
Celuy de Cypres & principal guerre,
Le Roy failly la main fuit long du Rhosne,
Les conjurez l'iront a mort mettre.

The King going by night near an Andronne,
He of Cyprus and chief of war,
The King having missed the hand, along by the Rhone,
The conspirators shall put him to death there.

A noted military figure shall conspire against France, but in southern France he shall meet his just fate.

18

De dueil mourra l'infelix proflige,
Celebrera son vitrix l'heccatombe;
Pristine loy, franc edit redige,
Le mur & Prince au septieme jour
    tombe.

The unhappy one, being overcome,
    shall die of grief,
His victrix shall celebrate the heca-
    tomb,
The former law and free edict shall
    be brought again,
The wall and seventh Prince shall
    go to the grave.

Victrix is a Latin word, the feminine gender of the word victor; Hecatomb was a Grecian sacrifice whereby 100 oxen were killed.

19

Le grand Royal d'or, d'airain aug-
    mente,
Rompu la pache, par ieune ouverte
    guerre,
Peuple afflige par unchef lamente,
De sang barbare sera couvert de
    terre.

The great golden Royal, being in-
    creased with copper,
The agreement being broken by a
    young man, there shall be open
    war,
People afflicted by the loss of a
    chief lamented,
The ground shall be covered with
    barbarous blood.

An alliance between a rich nation with one of little wealth shall result
in an open warfare, in which the chief will lose his life.

20

De la les Alpes grande armee pas-
    sera,
Un peu devant naistra monstre va-
    pin;
Prodigieux & subit tournera,
Le grand Toscan a son lie plus pro-
    pin.

Beyond the Alps shall a great army
    go,
And a little while before shall be
    born a vapin monster,
Prodigious and suddenly the great
    Tuscan,
Shall return to his own nearest
    place.

Napoleon shall cross the Alps with a great army.

21

Par les trespas du Monarque Latin, Ceux qu'il aura par regne secourus; Le feu livra divuse le butin, La mort publique au hardis incorus.	By the death of the Latin Monarch, Those that he shall have succoured in his reign, The fire shall shine, the booty shall be divided, The bold comers in, shall be put to public death.

A people shall be pillaged after the death of a monarch of Latin origin. However, the persecutors will eventually be publicly executed.

22

Avant qu'a Rome grand aye rendu l'ame, Effrayeur grand a l'armee estrangere; Par escadrons l'embusche pres de Parme, Puis des deux rouges ensemble feront chere.	Before a great man renders up his soul at Rome, The army of strangers shall put into a great fright, By squadrons the ambush shall be near Parma, After that, the two red ones shall make good cheer together.

The invaders of Italy shall be put into a great fright and driven out of the country; after that, two red ones (cardinals) will be highly satisfied.

23

Les deux contents seront unis ensemble, Quand la pluspart a Mars sera conjonct, Le grand d'affrique en effrayeur & tremble, Duumvirat par la classe des joints.	The two contested shall be united together, When the most part shall be joined to Mars, The great one of Africa shall be in fear and terror, Duumvirat shall by the pursuit be disjointed.

Two nations, previously at war with each other, shall ally themselves against a great one, of Africa. But this alliance (duumvirat) shall not last long.

24

Le Kegne & Roy soubs Venus
  esleve,
Saturne aura sur jupiter empire,
Be loy & regne par le Soleil leve,
Par Saturnius endurera le pire.

The Kingdom and King being
  joined under Venus,
Saturn shall have power over Jupi-
  ter,
The law and reign raised by the
  Sun,
Shall be put to the worse by the
  Saturnians.

The frivolous court of Louis XV, led by Madame Du Barry, made a
farce of law and order, by their Saturnine revels.

25

Le prince Arabs, Mars, Sol, Venus,
  Lyon,
Regne d'Eglise par mer succom-
  bera,
Devers la Perse bien pres d'un mil-
  lion,
Bisance, Egypte, Ver. Serp. in-
  vadera.

The Arab Prince, Mars, Sol, Venus,
  Leo,
The Kingdoms of the Church
  shall be overcome by the sea,
Towards Persia very near a million,
Turkey, Egypt, Ver. Serp. shall
  invade.

Christian ideals will be overcome by Oriental ideology (Ver. Serp.
meaning true serpents).

26

La gent esclave par un heur martiel,
Viendra en haut degre tant esleve,
Changeront prince, naistra un pro-
  vincial,
Passer la mer, copie aux monte leve.

The Slavic Nation shall by martial
  luck,
Be raised to so high a degree,
That they shall change their Prince
  and elect one among themselves,
They shall cross the sea with an
  army raised in the mountains.

Russians, by a military revolution, shall change their form of government and they will grow to be a great power and invade many countries.

27

Par feu & armes non loing de la
  Mer Negro,
Viendra de Perse occuper Trebi-
  sonde;
Trembler Pharos Methelin, Sol ale-
  gro,
De sang Arabe d'Adrie covert
  l'onde.

By fire and sword not far from the
  Black Sea,
They shall come from Persia to
  seize upon Trebisonde,
Pharos and Methelin shall quake,
  Sun be merry,
The sea of Adria shall be covered
  with Oriental blood.

A Russian invasion, coming through Iran, shall seize Mediterranean ports. In the Adriatic Sea they shall be driven back with great losses.

28

Le bras pendu & la jambe liee,
Visage pasle, au sein poignard
  cache;
Trois qui seront jurez de la meslee,
Au grand de Gennes sera le Fer
  lasche.

The arm hanging and the leg
  bound,
With a pale face, a dagger in the
  bosom,
Three shall be sworn to the fray,
To the great one of Genoa the Iron
  shall be darted.

Three wounded men shall conspire to stab the great one of Genoa.

29

La liberte ne sera recouvres,
L'occupera noir, fier, vilain inique;
Quand la matiere du pont sera
  ouvree,
D'Hister, Venise faschee la repub-
  lique.

Liberty shall not be recovered,
It shall be occupied by a black,
  fierce and wicked villain,
When the work of the Danube
  bridge shall be ended,
The Italian commonwealth shall
  be angry.

The black-shirted villain shall destroy Italian liberty. When the wreck of the German alliance is complete, then Italy will really show her anger.

30

Tout a l'entour de la grande cite,	Round about the great city,
Seront soldats logez par champs & villes,	Soldiers shall be in fields and towns,
Donner l'assaut Paris, Rome incite,	Paris shall give the assault, Rome shall be incited,
Sur le pont lors sera faite grand pille.	Then upon the bridge shall be great plunderings.

The capture and sacking of Rome by the French Duke of Bourbon is here described.

CENTURY V
96 : /77

31

Par terre Attique chef de la sapience,	In the country of Attica which is the head of wisdom
Qui de present est la Rose du Monde;	And now is the Rose of the World,
Pont ruyne & sa grand preeminence,	A bridge shall be in ruins with its great preeminence,
Sera subdite & naufrage de undes.	It shall be subdued and made a wreck by the waves.

The country of Attica, or Greece, famed for its wisdom, shall be corrupted by the usages of mankind.

32

Ou tout bon est, tout bien Soleil & Lune,	Where all well is, are good Sun and Moon,
Est abondent, sa ruyne s'approche,	Is existent, its ruin approaches near,
Du ciel s'advance vaner ta fortune,	The heaven is making haste to change thy fortune,
En mesme estat que la septiesme roch.	Into the same state as the seventh rock.

This dark stanza seems to predict the bad times that shall exist during a civil war between the Catholics and Protestants.

33

Des principaux de cite rebellee,
Qui tiendront fort pour liberte
    r'avoir,
Detrencher masses infelice meslee,
Cris hurlemens a Nante; piteux
    voir.

Of the principal men in a rebelled
    city,
Who shall stand out to recover
    their liberty,
The males shall be cut in pieces, O
    unhappy quarrels!
Cries and howlings, it shall be pity
    to see at Nantes.

Nantes in France, shall be the seat of a rebellion against the rest of
France. Tremendous massacres of the natives shall follow.

34

Du plus profond de l'occident An-
    glois,
Ou est le chef de l'isle Britannique;
Entrera classe dans Garonne par
    Blois,
Par vin & sel, feux cachez aux bar-
    riques.

From the most westerly part of
    England,
Where the chief of the British Is-
    land is,
A fleet shall come into the Ga-
    ronne by Blois,
By wine and salt, fire shall be hid-
    den in barrels.

A British Fleet shall plant mines (barrels) in French waters.

35

Par cite franche de la grand Mer
    Seline,
Qui porte encore a l'estomach la
    pierre;
Angloise classe viendra sous la bru-
    ine,
Un rameau prendre du grand ou-
    verte guerre.

By a free city of the Mediterranean
    Sea,
Which carries yet the stone in the
    stomach,
An English Fleet shall come under
    a fog,
To take a branch of great open
    war.

The Free City of Venice in the Mediterranean, shall be invaded by an
English Fleet under cover of a fog.

36

De soeur le frere par simulte fain-
  tise,
Viendra mesler rosee en mineral;
Sur la placente donne a vieille tar-
  dive,
Meurt le goustant sera simple &
  rural.

The brother of the sister, by
  feigned simulation,
Shall mix dew with mineral;
The aftermath being given to a
  slow old woman,
She died tasting, the deed shall
  be simple, and rural.

A brother shall poison his sister during childbirth.

37

Trois sens seront d'un vouloir &
  accord,
Qui pour venir au bout de leur
  attainte,
Vingt mois apres tous & records,
Leur Roy trahir simulant haine,
  fainte.

Three hundred shall be of one
  mind and agreement,
That they may attain their ends.
Twenty months after by all of
  them and their partners,
Their King shall be betrayed by
  simulating a feigned hatred.

The Legislative Assembly after a period of deliberation finally ordered
King Louis XVI to stand trial for treason.

38

Ce grand monarque qu'an mort
  succedera,
Donnera vie illicite & lubrique;
Par nonchalance a tous concedera,
Qu'a la parfin faudra la loy Salique.

The great monarch that shall succeed to the great one,
Shall lead a life unlawful and
  lecherous,
By carelessness he shall give to all,
So that in conclusion, the Salic
  law shall fail.

The Salic law, most famous for its chapter on succession to private
property, which declares that daughters cannot inherit land, is here referred
to in an incident which seems to indicate the degeneracy of the males of
a royal line, which eventually led to the enthroning of a woman.

39

Du vray rameau des fleurs de lys
  issu,
Mis & loge heritier d'Hetrurie;
Son sang antique de longue main
  tissu,
Fera Florence florir en l'Armoirie.

Issued out of the true branch of
  the city,
He shall be set for heir of Etruria;
His ancient blood weaned by a long
  while,
Shall cause Florence to flourish in
  the coats of arms.

A reference to the Medici family and their alliance with the Crown of France—Catherine de Medici, wife of Henry II, was Queen of France when Nostradamus lived.

40

Le sang Royal sera si tresmesle,
Contrainct seront Gaulois de l'-
  Hesperie;
On attendra que terme soit coule,
Et que memoire de la voix soit
  perie.

The Royal blood shall be so much
  mixed,
The French shall be constrained
  by the Spaniards,
They shall stay till the term is past,
And the remembrance of the voice
  is over.

This merely signifies the alliance between France and Spain by reason of royal intermarriages.

41

Nay sous les umbres & journee
  nocturne,
Sera en regne & bonte souveraine,
Fera renaistre son sang de l'antique
  urne,
Renouvellant siecle d'or pour l'airain.

Being born in the shadows and
  nocturnal time,
He shall be a sovereign in kingdom and bounty,
He shall cause his blood to be born
  again from the antique urn,
Renewing a golden age instead of
  a brass one.

A great king, born in a time of darkness, shall reign with a bountiful sceptre and lead the land to a golden age.

42

Mars esleve en son plus haut beffroy,
Fera retraire les Allobrox de France,
La gent Lombarde fera si grand effroy,
A ceux de l'aigle compris sous la Balance.

Mars being raised in its highest watch tower,
Shall cause the Allobrox to retreat from France,
The people of Lombardy shall be in so great fear
Of those of the eagle, comprehended under Libra.

The Allobrox are those of Savoy, or Italians; retreating from France, they shall cause great havoc.

43

La grand ruyne des sacrees ne s'eslongne,
Provence, Naples, Sicile, Seez & Ponce,
En Germanie, au Rhin & la Cologne,
Vexez a mort par tous ceux de Mogonce.

The great ruin of the sacred things is not far off.
Provence, Naples, Sicily, Sez and Ponce,
In Germany towards the Rhine and Cologne,
They shall be vexed to death by those of Moguntia.

Great damage to sacred monuments of art and religion is predicted. There will be religious troubles in the regions mentioned.

44

Par mer le rouge sera prins des pyrates,
La paix sera par son moyen troublee;
L'ire & l'aure commettra par sainct acte,
Au grand pontife sera l'armee doublee.

By sea the red one shall be taken by pirates,
The peace by that means shall be troubled,
He shall commit anger by a feigned act,
The high priest shall have a double army.

A cardinal, taken prisoner by pirates, shall cause a crisis between two nations and, in order to protect the Pope a double army will be granted to guard him.

45

Le grand Empire sera tost desole,
Et translate pres d'Arduenne silve;
Les deux bastards pres l'aisne de-
colle,
Et regnera Aeneodarb, nes de
milve.

The great Empire shall soon be
made desolate,
And shall be transplanted near the
Forest of Arden,
The two bastards shall have their
heads cut off by the eldest son,
And he that shall reign shall have
a reddish beard and a hawk's
nose.

The great Empire of Germany shall be broken up and its lands, especially near the borders of France, will be divided and ruled by many strangers.

46

Par chappeaux rouges querelles &
nouveaux scismes,
Quand on aura esleu le Sabinois,
On produira contre luy grands
sophismes,
Et sera Rome lesee par Albanois.

By red hats, quarrels and new
schisms,
When the Sabine shall be elected,
Great sophisms shall be produced
against him,
And Rome shall be damaged by the
Albanians.

The cardinals of Rome shall raise great quarrels and schisms when a man of Sabine (a region near Rome) is chosen Pope. Rome will further be endangered by the war-like advances of the Albanians.

47

Le grand Arabe marchera bien
avant,
Trahy sera par les Bisantinoise,
L'antique Rhodes luy viendra au
devant,
Et plus grand mal par austre Pan-
nonois.

The great Arab shall proceed a
great way,
He shall be betrayed by the Turks,
Ancient Rhodes shall come to
meet him,
Great evil by a south wind from
Hungary.

The Arab confederacy shall be betrayed by Turkey to the Hungarians.

48

Apres la grande affliction du sceptre,	After the great afflictions of the sceptre,
Deux ennemis par eux seront defaits,	Two enemies shall be overcome by themselves,
Classe d'Affrique aux Pannonois viedra naistre,	A fleet of Africa shall go toward the Hungarians,
Par mer & terre seront horribles faits.	By sea and land shall be horrid facts.

This has relation to the preceding stanza; due to a falling out between two enemies, the Hungarians will be the gainers.

49

Nul de l'Espagne, mais de l'antique France,	None out of Spain, but of the ancient France,
Ne sera esleu pour le tremblant nacelle;	Shall be elected to govern the tottering ship.
A l'ennemy sera faicte fiance,	The enemy shall be trusted,
Qui dans son regne sera peste cruelle.	Who to his kingdom shall be a cruel plague.

A Frenchman shall be chosen Pope, and he shall try to save the (ship of) state of the Church.

50

L'an d'eux les freres du lys seront en aage,	In the year that the brothers of the lilies shall be of age,
L'un d'eux tiendra la grande Romanis,	One of them shall hold the great Romany,
Trembler les monts, ouvert Latin passage,	The mountains shall tremble, the Latin passage shall be opened,
Pache marcher contre fort d'Armenie.	A Pascha shall march against the fort of Armenia.

One of France's generals will occupy Rome after crossing the Alps with a mighty army. At the same time an Oriental ally will assist the French by marching in from the Near East.

51

La gent de Dace, D'Angleterre & Polonne,	The people of Romania, England, and Poland,
Et de Bohesme seront nouvelle ligue;	And of Bohemia shall make a new league,
Pour passer outre d'Hercules la Colonne,	To go beyond the Pillars of Hercules,
Barcyns, Thyrrens dresser cruelle brigue.	Barcins and Thyrrens shall make a cruel plot.

Romania, England, Poland and Czecho-slovakia shall attempt a united invasion beyond Gibraltar, but will meet with great resistance.

52

Un Roy sera qui donrra l'opposite,	A King shall be, who shall be of the opposite,
Les exilez eslevez sur le Regne,	To the banished persons raised upon the Kingdom,
De sang nager la gent caste hypolite,	The chaste Hippolite nation shall swim in blood,
Et florira long temps soubs telle enseigne.	And shall flourish a great while under such a design.

Hippolytus, a son of Theseus and the Amazon Queen Antiope, lost his life when Poseidon, the Sea God, caused a sea monster to appear, who so frightened his horses that they overturned the chariot and Hippolytus was thrown out and killed.

53

La loy de Sol, & Venus contendans,	The law of the Sun and Venus contending,
Apparopriant l'esprit de prophetie,	Appropriating the spirit of prophecy,
Ne l'un ne l'autre ne seront entendans,	Neither one nor the other shall be heard,
Par Sol tiendra la loy du grand Messie.	By Sol the law of the great Messiah shall subsist.

The forces of light and darkness, struggling for domination over the spirit of man, shall both be superseded by the new law of the great Saviour.

54

Du pont Euxine & la grand Tar-
 taric,
Un Roy sera qui viendra voir la
 Gaule,
Transpercera Alane & l'Armenie,
Et dans Bisance lairra sanglante
 Gaule.

From the Black Sea and great Tar-
 taria,
A King shall come to see France,
He shall go through Alanea and
 Armenia,
And shall leave a bloody rod in
 Constantinople.

An Asiatic power shall come to France, by way of Armenia and Turkey.
Constantinople will be governed by one of his tools.

55

De la felice Arabie contrade,
Naistra puissant de loy Mahome-
 tique,
Vexer l'Espagne, conquester la
 Grenade,
Et plus par mer a la gent Lygus-
 tique.

Out of the country of greater
 Arabia,
Shall be born a strong master of
 Mohammedan law,
Who shall vex Spain and conquer
 Grenada,
And by sea shall come to the
 Italian nation.

From a country of Mohammedan law (Morocco), shall come one who
is a strong master of their law—the sword—who will cause grief to Spain
and conquer her. He shall be friendly to the Italians.

56

Par le trespas du tres vieillard
 pontife,
Sera esleu Romain de bon aage;
Qu'il sera dit que le siege debiffe,
Et long tiendra & de picquant
 courage.

By the death of the very old high
 priest,
Shall be elected a Roman of good
 age,
Of whom it shall be said, that he
 dishonors the seat,
And shall live long, and be of fierce
 courage.

Always deeply concerned with matters of the Church, Nostradamus
here discusses one of the many schisms then current among the clergy.

57

Istra du mont Gaulsier & Aventine,	One shall go out of the mountains Gaulsier and Aventine,
Qui par le trou advertira l'armee;	Who through a hole shall give notice to the army,
Entre deux rocs sera prins le butin,	Between two rocks shall be taken the prize,
De Sext. Mansol faillir la renommee.	And the glory of the Sun shall lose its renown.

The mountains of Gaulsier and Aventine, two of the seven hills of Rome, are here used symbolically by Nostradamus. The reference seems to be to one of the old struggles involving both the army and the church, in which a treacherous person within the church allows the army to take over some of its wealth.

58

De l'Aqueduct d'Uticense, Gardoing,	From the Aqueduct of Uticense and Gardoing,
Par la forest & mont inaccessible,	Through the forest and inaccessible mountains.
Emmy du pont sera tasche ou poing,	In the middle of the bridge shall be tied by the wrist,
Le chef Nemans qui tant sera terrible.	The chief Nemans, that shall be so terrible.

An incident in a future war, in France, is here obscurely described. The various places mentioned are probably points of attack.

59

Au chef Anglois a Nimes trop sejour,	The chief English shall stay too long at Nismes,
Dever l'Espagne au secours Aenobarbe,	A red-haired man shall go to the help of Spain,
Plusieurs mourront par Mars ouvert ce jour,	Many shall die by open war that day,
Quand en Artois faillir estoille en barbe.	When in Artois the star shall fail in the beard.

A play on words, this appears to have no deep significance, and the only clear reference concerns a bearded comet, or cometa barbatus as it is known in Latin.

60

Par teste rase viendra bien mal
  eslire,
Plus que sa charge ne porte passera;
Si grand fureur & rage fera dire,
Qu'a feu & sang tout sexe tran-
  chera.

By a shaven head shall be made
  an ill choice.
That shall go beyond his commis-
  sion,
He shall proceed with so great fury
  and rage,
That he shall put forth both sexes
  to fire and sword.

Six years after the death of Nostradamus, on St. Bartholomew's Day, August 24, 1572, a massacre of the Huguenots began in Paris. Spurred on by the high clergy of the Catholic Church, it spread to many provinces of France, and before it was checked many, many thousands of people were killed.

61

L'enfant du grand n'estant a sa
  naissance,
Subjuera les hauts monts Apen-
  nins,
Fera trembler tous ceux de la bal-
  ance,
Et des Monts Feurs jusques a Mont
  Cenis.

The child of the great one that was
  not at his birth,
Shall subdue the high Apennine
  Mountains,
Shall make all those under Libra
  to quake,
From Mount Feurs, as far as
  Mount Cenis.

A person, of illegitimate but noble birth, shall attain great heights as a military figure and shall cause havoc in both France and Italy by reason of his conquests.

62

Sur les rochers sang on verra pleuvoir,
Sol Orient, Saturn Occidental,
Pres Orgon guerre, a Rome grand
  mal voir,
Nefs parfondrees & prins le Tri-
  dental.

It shall rain blood upon the rocks,
The sun being in the east, and Saturn in the west,
War shall be near Orgon and a
  great evil at Rome,
Ships shall be cast away, and the
  trident be taken.

This quatrain carries on Nostradamus' repeated warnings of a future war between the Orient and Occident, and the horrible consequences thereof.

63

De vaine emprinse l'honneur in-
deue plainte,
Gallots errants, par Latins froid,
faim vagues;
Non loing du Tybre de sang terre
tainte,
Et sur humaine seront diverses
plagues.

Honor brings a complaint against
a vain undertaking,
Galleys shall wander through the
Latin seas, cold, hunger, wars,
Not far from Tiber, the earth shall
be dyed with blood,
And upon mankind shall be vari-
ous plagues.

Tiber is the river on which Rome is situated; and the rest of the verse
indicates incidents which shall come to pass.

64

Les assemblez par repos du grand
nombre,
Par terre & mer, conseil contre-
mande;
Pres de l'Autonne, Gennes, Nue
de l'ombre,
Par champs & villes le chef contrebande.

The assembly by the rest of the
great number
By land and sea shall recall their
council.
Near Autonne, Gennes, Cloud of
the shadow,
In fields and towns, the chief shall
be one against another.

Here we have a prognostication of the dissensions among the heads of
nations gathered ostensibly for a council of peace.

65

Subit venu l'effrayeur sera grande,
Des principaux de l'affaire cachez,
Et dame en braise plus ne sera veus,
Et peu a peu seront les grands
fachez.

One coming upon a sudden shall
cause a great fear,
To the principals that were hidden
and concerned in the business,
And the fiery lady shall be seen no
more,
And little by little the great ones
shall be angry.

Consternation shall seize the betrayers of the people when they per-
ceive the growing strength of the masses and their insistence upon a voice
in their destiny.

66

Soubs les antiques edifices estaux,
Non eslonguez d'aqueduct ruyne,
De Sol & Luna mont les luysants
   metaux,
Ardante lampe Trajen d'or burine.

Under the ancient edifices of the
   vestals,
Not far from a ruined aqueduct,
Are the bright metals of sun and
   moon,
A burning lamp of Trajan, of en-
   graved gold.

Near a ruined aqueduct will be found ancient articles of gold and silver, including a Roman lamp of gold, inscribed with Trajan's name.

67

Quand chef Perousse n'osera sa
   tunique,
Sens au couvert tout nud s'expolier,
Seront print sept faict aristocra-
   tique,
Le pere & fils morts par points au
   collier.

When the chief of Perouse shall
   not dare without a tunic,
To expose himself naked in the
   dark,
Seven shall be taken for setting up
   an aristocracy,
The father and son shall die by
   pricks in the collar.

Perugia is a city in Italy, which will be the seat of an unsuccessful attempt at setting up a revolution.

68

Dans le Danube & du Rhin viendra
   boire,
Le grand Chameau, ne s'en repen-
   tira;
Trembler du Rhosne & plus fort
   ceux de Loire,
Et pres des Alpes Coq les ruynera.

In the Danube and Rhine shall
   come to drink,
The great camel and shall not repent,
The Rhone shall tremble and more
   those of Loire,
And near the Alps the Cock shall
   ruin him.

A Turkish invasion shall reach Germany as far as the Rhine and Danube. France shall be in danger for a while, but shall finally triumph in a battle near the Alps.

69

Plus ne sera le grand en faux sommeil,
L'inquietude viendra prendre repos;
Dresser phalange d'or, azur & vermeil,
Subjuger Affrique la ronger jusque aux os.

The great one shall be no more in a false sleep,
The restlessness shall take rest,
He shall raise an army of gold and azure
He shall conquer Africa and gnaw it to the bone.

A great nation shall awake from its false sense of security and isolationism, and raise an immense amount of gold and a great navy. With its new-found strength it will invade the African shore.

70

Les regions suvjettes a la Balance,
Feront trembler les monts par grande guerre;
Captif tout sexe deu & toute Bisance,
Qu'on criera a l'aube terre a terre.

The regions under the sign of Libra,
Shall make the mountains quake with great war,
Slaves of all sexes, with all Constantinople,
So that in the dawn, they shall cry from land to land.

The European nations shall embark on a universal war, with the complete destruction of Constantinople promised.

71

Par la fureur d'un qui attendra l'eau,
Par la grand rage tout l'exercite esmeu,
Charge de nobles a dix-septe batteaux,
Au long du Rhosne tard messager venu.

By the fury of one looking forward to the water,
By his great rage the whole army shall be troubled,
There shall be seventeen boats full of noblemen,
Along the Rhone the messenger shall come too late.

The fury and rage of an invader driving his legions toward English shores, shall result in a great destruction of navies.

72

Pour le plaisir d'edict voluptueux,
On meslera la poison dans la loy,
Venus sera en cours si vertueux,
Qu obsuquera du Soleil tout aloy.

By the pleasure of a voluptuous
   edict,
The poison shall be mixed with the
   law,
Venus shall be in so great request,
That it shall darken all the alloy
   of the sun.

A voluptuous pleasure-loving era shall be made possible by corrupt laws.
Sin will prevail, and piety shall be obscured.

73

Persecutee de Dieu sera l'Eglise,
Et les saints temples seront expo-
   liez;
L'enfant la mere mettra nud en
   chemise,
Seront Arabes aux Polons railez.

The church of God shall be persecuted,
And the holy temples shall be
   spoiled,
The child shall turn out his mother
   nude in her shirt,
Arabians shall agree with Polo-
   nians.

The Catholic Church shall be persecuted and its temples despoiled.
Anti-Semitism shall be rampant among the Arabs and Poles.

74

De sang Troy en naistra coeur Germanique,
Qui de viendra en si haute puissance,
Hors chassera gent estrange Arabique,
Tournant l'Eglise en pristine pre-
eminence.

Of Trojan blood shall be born a
   German heart,
Who shall attain to so high a
   power,
That he shall drive away the East-
   ern people,
Restoring the church to pristine
   pre-eminence.

A German of great courage shall attain great eminence by destroying
the influence of Oriental power and re-establishing the Church.

75

Montera haut sur le bien plus a dextre,
Demourra assis sur la pierre carree;
Vers le midy pose a sa fenestre,
Baston tortu en main bouchee serree.

Mounting high on the good, more to the right,
He shall remain sitting upon the square stone,
Towards the South, being set on the left hand,
A crooked stick in his hand and his mouth shut.

This predicts and describes the hectic sessions of the National Assembly during the French Revolution, where the parties of the left and the right contended for the power.

76

En lieu libere tendra son pavillon,
Et ne voudra en citez prendre place;
Aix, Carpen, l'Isle, Volce, Mont Cavaillon
Par tout les lieux abolira la trasse.

He shall pitch his tent in the open air,
Refusing to lodge in the city,
Aix, Carpentres, Lille, Volce, Mont Cavaillon,
In those places, he shall abolish his trace.

All the places mentioned in this stanza are in Provence. The event referred to has no current interest.

77

Tous les degrez d'honneur Ecclesiastique,
Seront changez en Dial Quirinal;
En Martial Quirinal flaminique,
Puis un Roy de France le rendra Vulcanal.

All the degrees of Ecclesiastical honor
Shall be changed into a Quirinal Dial,
Into Martial Quirinal, Flaminus,
After that, a King of France shall make it Vulcanal.

This is another discussion of clerical affairs in the Catholic Church in Nostradamus' time.

78

Les deux unis ne tiendront longue-ment.	The two united shall not hold long,
Et dans treze ans au Barbare Sat-trappe;	Within thirteen years to the Barbarian Satrap,
Aux deux costez feront tel perde-ment,	They shall cause such loss on both sides, *catholic*
Qu'un benira la barque & sa cappe.	That one shall bless the boat and its covering.

Adolf Hitler and Von Hindenburg first became associated (historically) in 1920, the year that the Nazi Party was founded. Thirteen years later, just prior to Hindenburg's death, Hitler assumed full power, resulting in the ultimate ruin and destruction of the German State.

79

Le sacree pompe veindra baisse les aisles	The sacred pomp shall bow down her wings,
Par la venue du grand Legislateur;	At the coming of the great law giver,
Humble haussera, vexera les re-belles,	He shall raise the humble and vex the rebellious,
Naistra sur terre aucun semulateur.	No emulator of his shall be born.

The advent of Abraham Lincoln is plainly prophesied here.

80

L'Ogmion grand Bisance approch-era,	The Ogmion shall come near great Constantinople,
Chasses sera la Barbarique Ligue,	And shall expel the Barbarian League,
Des deux loix l'une l'unique lasch-era,	Of the two laws, the wicked one shall yield,
Barbare & France en perpetuelle brigue.	The Barbarian, and the French shall be in perpetual friction.

A King of France shall go to Constantinople, and shall break the Barbarian League; that is, Christian principles shall triumph over the Mohammedan law.

81

L'Oyseau Royal sur la cite Solaire,	The Royal Bird upon the city of
Sept mois devant fera nocturne augure,	the Sun,
Mur d'Orient cherra tonnerre esclaire,	Seven months together shall make a nocturnal augury,
Sept jours aux portes les ennemis a l'heure,	The Eastern wall shall fall, the lightning shall shine,
	Then the enemies shall be at the gate for seven days.

The Royal Bird (eagle) shall fly for many months over an Eastern city. When it unlooses its most deadly weapon (which shines with the brilliance of lightning) the Eastern wall will crumble.

82

Au conclud pache hors de la forteresse,	On the conclusion of the pact made, out of the fortress,
Ne sortira celuy en desespoir mis,	Shall not come he that was in despair,
Quand ceux d'Arbois, de Langres, contre Bresse,	When those of Arbois, of Langres, against Brescia,
Auront monts Dolle bouscade d'ennemis.	Shall put in Dolle an ambuschade of foes.

During a war a truce will be declared, but the commander of the besieged city shall refuse its terms.

83

Ceux qui auront entrepris subvertir,	Those that shall have undertaken to subvert,
Nompareil regne puissant & invincible,	The kingdom that has no equal in power and victories,
Feront par fraude, nuicts trois advertis	Shall cause by fraud, notice to be given for three nights together
Quand le plus grand a table lire Bible.	When the greatest shall be reading a Bible at the table.

A subversive movement within a great nation shall have its inception on a Sunday night.

84

Naistra du gouphre & cite emme-
suree,
Nay de parens obscurs & tene-
breux;
Quand la puissance du grand Roy
reveres,
Voudre destruire par Rouen &
Eureux.

One shall be born out of the gulf
and immeasurable city,
Born of parents obscure and dark,
Who, by means of Rouen and Eureux,
Will go about to destroy the power
of the great King.

A person of obscure and dark parentage is predestined to destroy the
power of a great King.

85

Par les Sueves & lieux circonvoi-
sins,
Seront en guerre pour cause des
neuus.
Gamp marins locustes & cousing,
Du Leman fautes seront bien des-
nuees.

Through Switzerland and the
neighboring places,
By reason of the clouds shall fall
to war.
The lobsters, locusts, and gnats,
The fault of Geneva shall appear
very naked,

The failure of the League of Nations and the advent of war are
prophesied.

86

Par les deux testes & trois bras se-
parez,
La cite grande par eau sera vexes,
Des grandes d'entr'aux par exil
esgarez,
Par teste Perse, Bisance fort
pressee.

Divided in two heads and parted
in three arms,
The great city shall be troubled
with waters,
Some great ones among them scattered by banishment,
By a Persian head, Turkey shall be
much oppressed.

Paris will be threatened by an inundation, and the great ones will be
forced to flee; during the same period there will be much unrest in the East.

87

L'an que Saturne sera hors de servage, Au franc terroir sera d'eau inonde; De sang Troyen sera son mariage, Et sera seur d'Espagnol circonder.	In the year that Saturn out of servitude, In the free country shall be drowned by water, With Trojan blood his marriage shall be, And he surely shall be surrounded by Spaniards.

The term "Trojan blood" refers to the French Nation. The meaning to be gathered from this stanza seems to be that, at the time of a great flood in France, a notable marriage will be made which will endanger French and Spanish relations.

88

Sur le sablon par un hydeux deluge, Des autres mers trouve monstre marin; Proche du lieu sera fait un refuge, Tenant Savone esclave de Turin.	Upon the sand through a hideous deluge Of other seas, shall be found a sea monster, Near to that place shall be made a sanctuary, Which shall make Savoy a slave to Turin.

Warfare between two Italian political factions is here predicted.

89

Dedans Hongrie par Boheme, Navarre, Et par bannieres feintes seditious; Par fleurs de lys pays portant la barre, Contre Orleans fera esmotions.	In Hungaria, through Bohemia and Navarre, And by banners feigned seditious, By Fleur de Lys, peace that carries the bar, Against Orleans shall make commotions.

The first two lines of this quatrain foretold the religious troubles that were to happen in Hungaria, Bohemia and Navarre. The last two tell of the Prince of Condé, whose coat of arms bears the flower and the bar, who seized Orleans for the Protestant party.

90

Dans les Cyclades, en Corinthe, &
  Larisse,
Dedans Sparte tout le Peloponese;
Si grand famine, peste, par faux
  connisse,
Neuf mois tiendra & tout le cher-
  rouesse.

In the Cyclades, in Corinth and
  Larissa,
In Sparta, and all the Pelopon-
  nesus,
Shall be so great a famine and
  plague
To last nine months in the south-
  ern peninsula.

All the Greek regions mentioned shall be afflicted with famine and plague.

91

Au grand marche qu'on dit des
  mesongers,
De tout torrent & champ Athe-
  nien,
Seront surprins par les chevaux
  legers,
Par Albanois, Mars, Leo, Sat, au
  versien.

In the great market called of the
  liars,
Which is all torrent and Athenian field,
They shall be surprised by the light
  horses,
Of the Albanese, Mars in Leo, Saturn in Aquarius.

Athens shall be overrun by the Nordics, here called Albanese by Nostradamus, after albus, Latin for white or blond.

92

Apres le siege tenu dix sept ans,
Cinq changeront en tel revolu
  terme,
Puis sera l'un esleu de mesme
  temps,
Qui des Romains ne sera trop con-
  forme.

After the seat possessed seventeen
  years,
Five shall change in such a space
  of time,
After that, one shall be elected at
  the same time,
Who shall not be very conformable
  to the Romans.

A Pope shall hold office for seventeen years. After that, within the space of seventeen years, five others shall be elected; and finally, a Pope shall be chosen who will not be approved by the Roman Clergy.

93

Sous le terroir de rond globe lunaire,
Lors que sera dominateur Mercure,
L'isle d'Escosse sera un luminaire,
Qui les Anglois mettra a deconfiture.

Under the territory of the round lunary globe,
When Mercury shall be lord of the ascendant,
The Island of Scotland shall make a luminary,
That shall put the English to a revolution.

Out of Scotland shall come a great light that will bring about a revolution in England.

94

Translatera en la grand Germanie,
Brabant & Flandres, Gand, Bruges, & Bologne;
La treue sainte le grand duc d'Armenie.
Assaillira Vienne & la Cologne.

He shall translate into the Great Germany,
Brabant, Flanders, Gand, Bruges and Bullen,
The truce feigned, the great Duke of Armenia,
Shall assault Vienna and Cologne.

Germany will attempt to assimilate Belgium and Holland, while a feigned truce with the great Eastern Power will be broken, and the end will be the destruction of Germany itself.

95

Nautique rame invitera les umbres
Du grand Empire, lors viendra conciter;
La mer Egee des lignes les encombres,
Empeschant l'onde Tyrrene de floter.

The nautical branch shall invite the shadows,
Of the great Empire, then it shall come to stir,
The Aegean Sea, with lines of encumbers,
Hindering the Tyrrenian Sea to roll.

The navy of a great Empire shall take the lead in a rebellion centering in the Mediterranean.

CENTURY V
31 - 155

96

Sur le milieu du grand monde la rose,	In the middle of the great world shall be the rose,
Pour nouveaux faits sang public espandu,	For new deeds, blood shall be publicly spilt,
A dire vray on aura bouche close,	To say the truth, every one shall close his mouth,
Lors au besoin viendra tard l'attendu.	Then at the time will be the one long looked for.

Nostradamus predicts the coming of a great world leader and, by a simple play on words as expressed in the first line, we have his name: rose and world (welt, in German) combine to make Roosevelt.

97

Le nay difforme par horreur suffoque,	The deformed shall through horror be suffocated,
Dans la cite du grand Roy habitable,	In the habitable city of the great King.
L'edit severe des captifs rovoque,	The severe edict against the banished shall be revoked,
Gresle & tonnerre Condon inestimable.	Hail and thunder shall do inestimable harm at Condon.

Condon is a city in old France, the rest is obvious.

98

A quarante-huit degre climatterique,	At the climacterical degree of eight and forty,
Afin de Cancer si grande secheresse,	At the end of Cancer, shall be such a drought,
Poisson en mer, fleuve, lac cuit hectique,	That fish in the sea, river, and lake shall be boiled hectic,
Bearn, Bigorre par feu ciel en detresse.	Bearn and Bigorre by heavenly fire shall be in distress.

Nostradamus here foretells of a period of great heat and drought, mostly in provinces in France.

99

Milan, Ferrare, Turin & Aquillee,
Capne, Brundis vexez par gent Cel-
tique,
Par le Lyon a Phalange aquilee,
Quand Rome aura le chef vieux
Britannique.

Milan, Ferrara, Turin and Aquilia,
Capne, Brundis, shall be vexed by
the French,
By the Lion and Troop of Aquelia,
When Rome shall have as chief,
old Britannia.

England shall conquer Italy assisted by the French Army, and the military Governor of Rome shall be an Englishman.

100

Le boute-feu par son feu attrape,
De feu du ciel par Tarcas & Co-
minge,
Foix, Aux, Mazeres, haut vieillard
eschappe,
Par ceux de Hasse, des Saxons &
Turinge.

The arsonist shall be overtaken by
his own fire,
Heavenly fire shall fall at Tartas
and Cominge,
Foix, Auch, Mazere, a tall old man
shall escape,
By means of those of Hesse, Saxony, and Thuringia.

The ones who set the world on fire, shall be overtaken by stern justice.
The Germans shall aid in the escape of one of the guilty ones.

A clear prophecy of the Eichman trial and indication that Hjalmar
Schact the master mind and financial genius who master minded the Nazi
fiasco shall escape the Nuremburg trials.

CENTURY VI

1

Au tour des Monts Pyrenees grand amas,
De gent estrange, secourir Roy nouveau;
Pres de Garonne du grand temple du Mas,
Un Romain chef le craindra dedans l'eau.

About the Pyrenean Mountains there shall be a great gathering
Of strange nations to succour a new King,
Near Garonne and the great temple of the Maas,
A Roman captain shall fear him in the water.

Assistance by a group of nations shall raise a new ruler to power near the Pyrenees Mountains. A Roman leader shall fear this new threat.

2

En l'an cinq cens octante plus & moins,
On attend le siecle bien estrange;
En l'an sept cens & trois (cieus en tesmoins)
Que plusieurs regnes un a cinq feront change.

In the year five hundred eighty more or less,
There shall be a strange age,
In the year seven hundred and three (witness heaven)
Many kingdoms, one to five shall be changed.

Nostradamus commences his count of time from A. D. 325, the date of the Council of Nicaea. In the above stanza, by using the figure 325 as a key, we find that (1)589 added to it, gives us the date 1914, one of the most important dates in the history of the world. Similarly, (1)703 added to 325 gives us 2028, in which year, Nostradamus tells us, there will be a complete change in the lineup of nations.

3

Fleuve qu'esprouve le nouveau nay
Celtique,
Sera en grande de l'Empire dis-
corde;
Le jeune prince par gent Ecclesias-
tique,
Ostera le sceptre coronal de con-
corde.

The river that makes trial of the
new-born Celtic,
Shall be at great variance with the
Empire,
The young prince shall be an Ec-
clesiastical person,
And have his sceptre taken off, and
the crown of concord.

The Rhine River shall be the scene of trial for a new Prince of France.

4

Le Celtique fleuve changera de
rivage,
Plus ne tiendra la cite d'Agripine;
Tout trasmue ormis le vieil langage,
Saturne, Leo, Mars, Cancer en ra-
pine.

The river Rhine shall change her
shores,
It shall touch no more the city of
Cologne,
All shall be transformed, except the
language,
Saturn, Leo, Mars, Cancer in ra-
pine.

The borders of Germany shall change so as to no longer include Cologne. A complete upheaval will take place in Germany after a period of
great unrest.

5

Si grand famine par une pestifere,
Par pluye longue le long du Pole
Artique;
Samarobryn cent lieux de l'hemis-
phere,
Vivront sans loy, exempt de poli-
tique.

So great a famine with a plague,
Through a long rain shall come
along the Arctic Pole,
Samarobryn a hundred leagues
from the hemisphere,
Shall live without law, exempt
from politics.

From the northern hemisphere shall come a devastating plague, followed by a period of anarchy throughout the affected countries.

6

Apparoistra vers le Septentrion,
Non loing de Cancer l'estoille che-
    velue;
Suse, Sienne, Boece, Eretrion,
Mourra de Rome grand, la nuit
    disperue.

Towards the North shall appear,
Not far from Cancer, a blazing star,
Suza, Sienna, Boetia, Eretrion,
There shall die at Rome a great
    man, the night being past.

A light in the sky will appear, and a powerful Italian, unable to live in its glare, shall die.

7

Norvege & Dace, & l'isle Britàn-
    nique,
Par les unis freres seront vexees;
Le chef Romain issu du sang Gal-
    lique,
Et les copis aux forest repoulsees.

Norway and Dacia, and the British
    Island,
Shall be vexed by the brothers
    united,
The Roman Captain issued from
    French blood,
His forces shall be beaten back to
    the forest.

A union of nations will beat back and conquer their common enemy.

8

Ceux qui estoient en regne pour
    scavoir,
Au Royal change deviendront a
    pouvris,
Uns exilez sans appuy, or n'auoir,
Lettres & lettres ne seront a grand
    pris.

Those that were in esteem for their
    learning,
Upon the change of a King will
    become poor,
Some banished, without help, hav-
    ing no gold,
Learned and learning shall not be
    much valued.

A period of oppression against scholars and scientists shall arise.

9

Aux temples saints seront faits grands scandales,	To the holy temples shall be done much scandals,
Comptez seront par honneur & louanges,	That shall be accounted for honors and praises,
D'un que l'on graue d'argent, d'or les medalles,	By one, whose medals are graven in gold and silver,
La fin sera en tourmens bien estranges.	The end of it shall be in very strange torments.

As an adherent of the Roman Catholic Church, Nostradamus could only look with disapproval on the Protestant party under the leadership of the future Henry IV. As the King of Navarre, he had medals and money stamped with his image for use in the holy temples and cathedrals. The last line proved prophetic, when on St. Bartholomew's Day, August 24, 1572, the Protestant Massacre occurred.

10

Un peu de temps les temples de couleurs,	Within a little while the temples of the colours,
De blanc & noir les deux entre-meslee;	White and black shall be intermixt,
Rouges & jaunes leur embleront les leurs,	Red and yellow shall take away their colours,
Sang, terre, peste, faim, feu, d'eau affolce.	Blood, earth, plague, famine, fire, water shall destroy them.

After a period of much travail all the races of the world shall lose their prejudices and be as one.

11

Des sept rameaux a trois seront reduits,	The seven branches shall be reduced to three,
Les plus aisnez seront surprins par mort,	The eldest shall be surprised by death,
Fratricider les deux seront seduits,	Two shall be said to kill their brothers,
Les conjures en dormant seront morts.	The conspirators shall be killed being asleep.

Seven brothers shall be reduced to three; of those one shall die suddenly and it will be suspected that he was killed by the other two. And they in turn shall meet violent deaths.

12

Dresser copies pour monter a l'Empire,	To raise an army, to ascend the Empire,
Du Vatican le sang Royal tiendra;	Of the Vatican, the Royal blood shall endeavor,
Flamans, Anglois, Espaigne aspire,	Flemings, English, Spain shall aspire,
Contre l'Italie & France contendre.	And shall contend against Italy and France.

There shall be a great commotion among the nations of Europe over the election of a Pope.

13

Un dubieux ne viendra loing du regne,	A doubtful man shall not come far from the reign,
La plus grand part le voudra soustenir,	The greatest part will uphold him,
Un captiole ne voudra point qu'il regne,	A capitol will not consent that he should reign,
Sa grande chaire ne pourra maintenir.	His great chair he shall not be able to maintain.

Napoleon, after great successes, was finally forced to abdicate.

14

Loing de sa terre roy perdra la bataille,	Far from his country the king shall lose a battle,
Prompt eschappe poursuivy suyuant prins,	Nimble, escaped, followed, following taken,
Ignare prins soubs la doree maille,	Ignorantly taken under the gilded coat of mail,
Soubs faint habit & l'ennemy surprins.	Under a feigned habit the enemy taken.

The Battle of Moscow was the turning point in the career of Napoleon; it was the beginning of the end.

15

Dessous la tombe sera trouve le prince,	Under the tomb shall be found the prince,
Qu'aura le pris par dessus Nuremberg;	That shall have a price above Nuremberg.
L'Espagnol Roy en Capricorn mince,	That Spanish King in Capricorn shall be thine,
Feinct & trahy par le grand Vitemberg.	Deceived and betrayed by the great Lutheran.

A prince shall commit suicide thus foiling the dictates of the Nuremberg judges. There will be a betrayal of a powerful Spaniard by a German ruler.

16

Ce que ravy sera du jeune Milve,	That which shall be taken from the young Kite,
Par les Normans de France & Picardie;	By the Normans of France and Picardy,
Les noirs du temple du lieu Negrisilve,	The black ones of the temple of the Black Forest,
Feront aux berg & feu de Lombardie.	Shall make a rendezvous and a fire in Lombardy.

The Normans shall succeed in overthrowing a young arrogant Prince, and to celebrate their victory they will build a temple in the Black Forest.

17

Apres les livres bruslez les asiniers,	After the books shall be burnt, the asses,
Constraints seront changer habits divers;	Shall be compelled several times to change their clothes,
Les Saturnins bruslez par les musniers,	The Saturnins shall be burnt by the millers,
Hors la plus part qui ne sera musniers.	Except the greater part, that shall not be discovered.

The millers (unlearned persons) shall attempt to annihilate the culture of the Saturnins (studious people) even to the wholesale burning of books. This prophecy was fulfilled in its entirety when the Nazis publicly banned and burned all books that were against their ideology.

CENTURY VI 185

18

Par les physiques le grand Roy de-
laisse,
Par fort non art ne l'Ebrieu est en
vie;
Luy & son genre au regne haut
pousse,
Grace donne a gent qui Christ envie.

The great King being forsaken by
the physician,
Shall be kept alive by power, and
not by the art of a Hebrew,
He, and his kindred shall be put at
the top of the kingdom,
Grace shall be given to a people
that envieth Christ.

A sick King, deserted by his physician, shall be cured by the help of
a Jew, and as a token of the King's gratitude, the Jews of that nation will
enjoy great privileges.

19

La vray flamme engloutira la dame,
Que voudra mettre les innocens a
feu,
Pres de l'assaut l'excercite s'en-
flamme,
Quand dans Seville monstre en
boeuf sera veu.

The true flame shall swallow up
the lady,
That went about to burn the guilt-
less,
Before the assault the army shall be
encouraged,
When in Seville, a monster like an
ox shall be seen.

A monster shall be seen in Seville, similar to the ancient Minotaur
who demanded a tribute of innocent children.

20

L'union feinte sera peu de duree,
Des uns changes reformez la plus-
part,
Dans les caisseaux sera gent en-
dures,
Lors aura Rome un nouveau leo-
part.

The feigned union shall not last
long,
Some shall be changed, others for
the most part reformed,
In the ships people shall be penned
up,
Then shall Rome have a new leopard.

After a short period of peace, there will again be trouble among the
clerical leaders of Rome, and a new Pope will come into power.

21

Quand ceux de Pole Artique unis ensemble,	When those of the Arctic Pole shall be united together,
En Orient grand effrayeur & crainte,	There shall be in the East, great fear and trembling,
Esleu nouveau sousteru le grand temple,	One shall be newly elected, that shall bear the brunt,
Rodes, Bisance de sang Barbare taints.	Rhodes, Constantinople, shall be dyed with Barbarian blood.

The people of northern Europe shall unite against those of the East. The actual battle shall take place near Turkey.

22

Dedans la terre du grand temple celique,	Within the ground of the great celestial temple,
Nepueu a Londres par paix faincte meurtry,	A nephew at London by a feigned peace shall be murdered,
La barque alors deviendra scismatique,	The boat at that time shall become schismatical,
Liberte faincte sera au corne & cry.	A feigned liberty shall be with hue and cry.

In St. Paul's Cathedral, London, the murdered body of a famous person will be found. It will cause great dissension among the churchmen since one of them will be suspected of the crime.

23

D'esprit de Roy munisememens descriees,	Despite the King, the coin will be brought lower,
Et seront peuples esmeus contre leur Roy,	The people shall rise against their King,
Paix, fait nouveau, sainctes loix empirees.	Peace being made, holy laws made worse,
Rapis onc fut en si tresdur arroy.	Paris was never in such a great disorder.

This is a remarkable account of the French Revolution, in proper chronological order—collapse of the financial structure, rising of the people, abandonment of religion and Paris in disorder.

24

Mars & le Sceptre se trouvera conjont,	Mars and the Sceptre, being conjoined together,
Dessous Cancer calamiteuse guerre;	Under Cancer shall be a calamitous war,
Un peu apres sera nouveau Roy oingt,	A little while after a new King shall be anointed,
Qui par long temps pacifiera la terre.	Who, for a long time, shall pacify the earth.

Nostradamus here speaks of a constellation called the Sceptre. Looking far into the future, he foretells of a time when this constellation shall be in conjunction with Mars, and the terrible war that will break out under this influence. And out of the debacle there will arise a new world leader and peace will reign for a long time afterward.

25

Par Mars constraire sera la Monarchie,	By Mars contrary shall the monarchy.
Du grand pescheur en trouble ruyneux;	Of the great fisherman, be brought into ruinous trouble,
Jeune, noire, rouge prendra la hierarchie,	A young, black red shall possess himself of the hierarchy,
Les proditeurs iront jour bruyneux.	The traitors shall undertake it on a misty day.

The Vatican shall be in a weakened position due to a ruinous war, and a young cardinal, backed by opponents of the reigning hierarchy, shall be made Pope.

26

Quartre ans le siege quelque peu bien tiendra,	Four years he shall keep the Papal seat pretty well,
Un surviendra libidineux de vie,	Then shall succeed one of a libidinous life,
Ravenne & Pise, Veronne soustiendront,	Ravenna, Pisa, shall take Verona's part,
Pour eslever la croix du Pape envie.	To raise up the Pope's cross to life.

A continuation of the preceding stanza, this predicts that the usurper will reign four years, being then succeeded by a notorious sensualist, whose main support shall come from those in the above-mentioned cities.

27

Dedans les isles de cinq fleuves a
un,
Par le croissant du grand Chyren
Selin;
Par les bruynes de l'air fureur de
l'un,
Six eschappez, cachez fardeaux de
lyn.

In the islands from five rivers to
one,
By the increase of the great emperor Henry,
By the frost of the air and the fury
of one,
Six shall escape, hidden within
bundles of flax.

Henri Pétain.

Again we have a play on words: Chyren meaning Henry, and Selin meaning King. Just what king or ruler Nostradamus refers to is not clear, and it is quite possible that he means by this obscurity to indicate some future world leader.

28

Le grand Celtique entrera dedans
Rome,
Menant amas d'exilez & bannis;
Le grand pasteur mettra a mort
tout homme
Qui pour le Coq estoit aux Alpes
unis.

The great Celtique shall enter into
Rome,
Leading with him a great number
of banished men,
The great shepherd shall put to
death every man,
That was united for the Cock, near
the Alps.

The campaign of Napoleon, which culminated in the French victory over Italy, is foretold.

29

La vefue saincte entendant les nouvelles,
De ses rameaux mis en perplex &
trouble,
Qui sera duict appraiser les querelles,
Par son pourchas des razes fera
comble.

The holy widow hearing the news,
Of her branches put in perplexity
or trouble,
That shall be skillful in appeasing
of quarrels,
By his purchase shall make a heap
of shaven heads.

Nostradamus here discusses a time of *interregnum*—the period after the death of a Pope until a new one is elected—and refers to the various parts of the Church in his usual obscure manner: by "the holy widow" he means the City of Rome; the "branches" are the clergymen; and the "shaven heads" refer to priests.

30

Par l'apparence de faincte sainctete,	By the appearance of a feigned holiness,
Sera trahy aux ennemis le siege,	The siege shall be betrayed to the enemies,
Nuict qu'on coidoit dormir en seurete,	In a night that everyone thought to be secure,
Pres de Braban marcheront ceux du Liege.	Near Brabant shall march those of Liege.

This appears to be a description of some trouble which occurred between the two regions mentioned.

31

Roy trouvera ce qu'il desiroit tant,	A King shall find what he so much longed for,
Quand le Prelat sera reprins a tort;	When a Prelate shall be censured wrongfully,
Responce au Duc le rendra mal content,	His answer to the Duke will make him discontented,
Qui dans Milan mettra plusieurs a mort.	Who in Milan shall put many to death.

Nostradamus discusses one of the many involved quarrels between the State and the Church.

32

Par trahisons de verges a mort battu,	By treason one shall be beaten with rods to death,
Puis surmonte sera par son desordre;	Then the traitor shall be overcome by his disorder,
Conseil frivole au grand captif sentu,	The great prisoner shall try a frivolous counsel,
Nez par fureur quand Berich viendra mordre.	When Berich shall bite another's nose through anger.

"When traitors fall out amongst themselves, honest men rejoice." Such is the sense of this stanza.

33

Sa main derniere par Alus sangui-
naire,
Ne se pourra plus la mer garentir;
Entre deux fleuves craindre main
militaire,
Le noir l'ireux le fera repentir.

His last hand bloody through all
U. S.
Shall not save him by sea,
Between two rivers he shall fear
the military hand,
The black and wrathful one shall
be repentant.

A prediction showing the role of the U. S. in the final phase of the
career of Mussolini seems to be indicated here.

34

De feu volant la machination,
Viendra troubler au grand chef
assiegez;
Dedans sera telle sedition,
Qu'en desespoir seront les profli-
gez.

The contraption of flying fire,
Shall trouble so much the captain
of the besieged,
And within shall be so much riot-
ing,
That the besieged shall be in de-
spair.

Although Nostradamus could only dimly sense the import of his prophetic words, we now know all too well the destruction and terror wrought
by the airborne weapons described in this quatrain.

35

Pres de Rion & proche Blanche-
laine,
Aries, Taurus, Cancer, Leo, la Vi-
ergge,
Mars, Jupiter, les Sol ardra grand
plaine,
Bois & cites lettres cachez au ci-
erge.

Near Rion and towards Blanche-
laine,
Aries, Taurus, Cancer, Leo, Virgo,
Mars, Jupiter, the Sun shall burn a
great plain,
Woods and cities, letters hidden in
a wax candle.

The first line of this verse is anagrammatic—the word "rion," spelled
backwards, becomes noir, black; "blanche" contains the letters blanc, meaning white. Therefore, we must surmise that when the above-mentioned
constellations are in conjunction there will be a fire of almost worldwide
proportions, the aftermath of which will be a definite division in the world
of "black" and "white."

36

Ne bien ne mal par bataille terrestre,
Ne parviendra aux confins de Perouse,
Rebeller Pise, Florence voir mal
estre,
Roy nuict blesse sur mulet a noire
housse.

Neither good nor evil by a loud
fight,
Shall reach to the borders of Pe-
rusia,
Pisa shall rebel, Florence shall be
in a bad way,
A King being on his mule shall be
wounded in the darkness.

All the cities named are in Italy; the balance should be easy to decipher.

37

L'oeuvre ancienne se parachevera,
Du toict cherra sur la grand mal
ruyne,
Innocent faict mort on accusera,
Nocent cache, taillis a la bruyne.

The ancient work shall be finished,
From the house tops shall fall great
misfortunes,
The innocent in fact, shall be accused after his death,
The guilty shall be hidden in a
wood in misty weather.

King Louis XVI attempted to escape from the rebels, but was apprehended in a forest hiding-place.

38

Aux profilgez de paix les ennemis,
Apres avou l'Italie supperee;
Noir sanguinaire, rouge sera com-
mis,
Feu sang verser, eau de sang col-
oree.

To the vanquished the enemies of
peace,
After they shall have overcome
Italy,
A bloody Black One shall be com-
mitted,
Fire and blood shall be discharged,
and water coloured with blood.

This is the prognostication of the rape of Italy by the Fascists under the
leadership of Mussolini.

39

L'enfant du regne par paternelle prince,	The child of the kingdom through his father's imprisonment,
Expolie sera pour delivrer;	Shall be deprived of his kingdom for the delivering of his father,
Aupres du Lac Trasimen l'azur prinse,	Near the Lake Trasimene shall be taken in a tower,
La trope hostage pour trop fort s'enyurer.	The troop that was in hostage being drunk.

Lake Trasimene, where Hannibal fought a famous battle with the Romans, is the only clear expression in this otherwise obscurely worded quatrain.

40

Grand de Magonce pour grand soif estaindre,	The great one of Mayence to quench a great thirst,
Sera prive de la grand dignite;	Shall be deprived of his high dignity,
Ceux de Cologne si fort le viendront plaindre,	Those of Cologne shall mourn him so much,
Que le Grand Groppe au Ryn sera jette.	That the Great Groppe shall be thrown into the Rhine.

The German populace shall feel the loss of their great prestige, and shall mourn the loss of their leader, Schickel-GROPPE (Hitler), even to the point of making his name synonymous with the German National Symbol, the River Rhine.

41

Le second chef du regne Dannemarc,	The second head of the Kingdom of Denmark,
Par ceux de Frise & l'isle Britannique,	By those of Holland, and the British Isles,
Fera despendre plus de cent mille marc,	Shall cause to be spent over 100 thousand marks,
Vain exploiter voyage en Italique.	Vainly trying to find a way into Italy.

A signification that Danish, Dutch, and English forces will attempt a costly and ultimately futile invasion of Italy.

42

A l'Ogmyon sera laisse le regne,
Du grand Selin qui plus sera de
faict,
Par l'Italie estendra son enseigne,
Regne sera par prudent contrefait.

Unto l'Ogmion shall be left the kingdom,
Of great Selyn, who shall do more than the rest,
Through Italy he shall spread his ensigns,
He shall govern by prudent forgeries.

A King of France shall dictate to the Vatican and exert great influence throughout Italy.

43

Long temps sera sans estre habitee,
Ou Seine & Marne autour vient arrouser,
De la Tamise & martiaux tentee,
Deceus les gardes en evidant repousser.

For a long time shall be uninhabited
Where the Seine and Marne come to water about,
From the Thames and martial people, they shall attempt
To deceive the guards into thinking to resist.

Because of traitors within her gates ruin will fall upon Paris, and the flight of the inhabitants will result in an almost deserted city.

44

De nuict par Nantes l'iris apparoistra,
Des Arcs Marins susciteront la pluye,
Arabique Goulfre grand classe parfondra,
Un monstre en Saxe naistra d'ours & truye.

By night in Nantes the rainbow shall appear,
Arches of the Sea shall cause rain,
The Arabian Gulf shall drown a great fleet,
A monster shall be in Saxony from a bear and a sow.

Incendiary bombs shall light up the nights in France; and in Germany, the British shall cause great destruction.

45

Le gouverneur du Regne bien sca- vant, Ne consentir voulant au fait Royal, Mellile classe par le contraire vent, Le remettra a son plus desloyal.	The governor of the Kingdom be- ing wise, Shall not consent to the King's will He shall ponder setting out a fleet by the contrary wind, Which he shall put into the hands of the most disloyal.

The reference here is obviously to the Battle of Trafalgar, that decisive naval victory of the British over the French and Spanish fleets; there is also an indication of the dissension between Napoleon and Admiral Villeneuve over the disposition of the French fleet.

46

Un juste sera en exil anvoye, Par pestilence aux confins de Non seggle, Response au rouge le fera desvoyer, Roy retirant a la Rane & l'Aigle.	A just person shall be banished, By plague to the borders of Non- Seggle, The answer to the red one shall make him deviate, Retiring himself to the Frog and the Eagle.

Russia, formerly allied against France, shall be privately assured that her best interests lie in deserting her partner and joining France and her allies.

47

Entre deux monts les deux grands assemblees, Delaiseront leur simulte secrette; Bruxelles & Dolle par Langres ac- cablees, Pour a Malignes executer leur peste.	Between two mountains the two great ones shall meet, They shall forsake their secret en- mity, Brussels and Dolle shall be crushed by Langres, To put their plague in execution at Maline.

A long-forgotten incident is here described, and I think it needs no further interpretation than the verse indicates.

48

La sainctete trop saincte & seduc- tive, Accompagnee d'une langue diserte; La cite vieille & Palme trop has- tive, Florence & Sienne rendront plus desertes.	The feigned and seducing holiness, Accompanied with a fluent tongue, Shall cause the old city and the too hasty Parma, Florence and Sienna to be more desert.

The sanctimonious mouthings of a fluent demagogue shall influence many people in Rome and other important Italian cities, and cause them to abet him in his nefarious schemes.

CENTURY X
46 PAGE 327

49

De la partie de Mammer grand pontife, Subjuguera les eonfins du Dan- ube, Chasser les croix par fer raffe ne riffe, Captifs, or, bagues, plus de cent mille rubles.	By the project of Mammon, high priest, They shall subjugate the borders of the Danube, They shall pursue crosses of iron, topsy-turvy, Slaves, gold, jewels, more than a hundred thousand rubles.

The Swastika, crooked-cross emblem of the Nazis, is clearly foreseen by Nostradamus; also the financial origin of their unholy crimes against humanity.

50

Dedans le puits seront trouvez les os, Sera l'incest commis par la maras- tre; L'estat change, on querre bruit les los, Et aura Mars ascendant pour son astre.	In the well shall be found the bones, Incest shall be committed by the stepmother, The state being changed, there shall be a great stir about the bones, And she shall have Mars for her ascending planet.

A stepmother shall have a child by her son-in-law, and will commit infanticide, throwing the body in a well. When the bones are discovered a great furor will take place.

51

Peuple assemble voir nouveau spectacle	People assembled to see a new show,
Princes & Roys par plusieurs assistans,	Princes and Kings, with many assistants,
Pilliers faillir, murs, mais comme miracle,	Pillars shall fail, walls also, but as a miracle,
Le Roy sauve & trente des instans.	The King saved, and thirty of the standers-by.

This pertains to the Congress of Vienna, which convened after the defeat of Napoleon and effected many changes among the nations of Europe.

52

En lieu du grand qui sera condamne,	Instead of the great one that shall be condemned,
De prison hors, son amy en sa place;	And put out of prison, his friend being in his place,
L'espoir Troyen en six mois joint mort nay,	The Trojan hope in six months united, still-born,
Le Sol a l'Vurne seront prins fleuves en glace.	The Sun in Aquarius, then rivers shall be frozen.

To the Trojan hope, viz., the King of France, after being married six months, shall be born a child, delivered before its time.

53

Le grand Prelat Celtique a Roy suspect,	The great Celtic Prelate suspected by his King,
De nuict par cours sortira hors du regne,	Shall in haste by night go out of the government.
Par Duc fertille a son grand Roy Bretagne,	By means of a Duke, fruitful to his King, Great Britain,
Bisance a Cypres & Tunes insuspect.	Turkey to Cyprus, and Tunis shall be unsuspected.

A Prelate of Celtic origin shall be removed from power by his King. Great Britain shall be the gainer.

54

Au poinct du jour second chant du coq,	At the break of day, at the second crowing of the cock,
Ceux de Tunes, de Fez, & le Bugie,	Those of Tunis, and Fez and Bugia,
Par les Arabes captif le Roy Maroq,	By means of the Arabians, shall take prisoner the King of Morocco
L'an mil six cens & sept de Liturgie.	In the year 1607 by liturgy.

Here again we have recourse to Nostradamus' key figure (as noted in quatrain 2, Century VI). By using this number, 325, and adding to it the figure 1607 referred to above, we get 1932. In this instance, the date is approximate, since the inference gathered from the quatrain clearly applies to conditions leading up to the Spanish Civil War which began in 1936.

55

Au Chelme Duc, en arrachant l'esponce,	The Chelme Duke, on throwing the sponge,
Voille Arabesque voir, subit descouverte;	Shall see Arabian Sails suddenly discovered,
Tripolis, Chio, & ceux de Trapesonce,	Tripoli, Chios, and those of Trapesan,
Duc Prins, Marnegro, & sa cite deserte.	The Duke shall be taken, Marnegro, and the city shall be deserted.

The regions mentioned are near or in Turkey. Chelme is a German word signifying a rogue. The meaning here seems to be that there shall be conflict between this wicked Duke and the rulers of these various cities.

56

La crainte armee de l'ennemy Narbon,	The feared army of the enemy Narbonne
Effrayera si fort les Hesperiques;	Shall so much terrify the Spaniards,
Parpignan vuide par L'aveugle d'Arbon,	That Parpignan shall be left empty by the blind d'Arbon,
Lors Barcelon par mer donra les piques.	Then Barcelona by sea shall give the weapons.

Parpignon, a border town between France and Spain, shall be captured by the French. Barcelona shall come to the rescue by way of the sea.

57

Celuy qu'estoit bien avant dans le regne,	He that was a great way in the kingdom,
Ayant chef rouge proche la hierarchie;	Having a red head and near the hierarchy,
Aspre & cruel, & se fera tant craindre,	Harsh and cruel, shall make himself so dreadful,
Succedera a Sacree Monarchie.	That he shall succeed to the Sacred Monarchy.

A Cardinal of great power—backed by much influence—shall make himself so indispensable to the Vatican, that he will be awarded the Papacy.

58

Entre les deux monarques eslongnez,	Between the two monarchs that live far from each other.
Lors que Sol par Selin cler perdue;	When the Sun shall be eclipsed by Selene,
Simulte grande entre deux indignez,	Great enmity shall be between the two,
Qu'aux Isles & Sienne la liberte rendue.	So that liberty will be restored to the Isles and Sienna.

When the Sun is eclipsed by the Moon, Sienna shall have its liberty restored.

59

Dame en fureur par rage d'adultere,	A lady in fury by rage of an adultery,
Viendra a son prince conjurer non de dire,	Shall come to her prince and conjure him to say nothing,
Mais bref cogneu sera le vitupere,	But soon shall the shameful thing be known,
Que seront mis dixsept a martyre.	So that seventeen shall be put to death.

An explicit statement that should be clear to all.

60

Le prince hors de son terroir Celtique,
Sera trahy, deceu par interprete;
Rouan, Rochelle, par ceux d'Armorique,
Au Port de Blaye deceus par moine
& prestre.

The Prince being out of his Celtic
country,
Shall be betrayed and deceived by
an interpreter.
Rouen, Rochelle, by those of Gascony,
At the Port of Bordeaux shall be
deceived by a monk and priest.

A false interpretation of a political message shall cause an uproar
throughout France.

61

Le grand tapis plie ne monstrera,
Fors qu'a demy la pluspart de l'his-
torie;
Chasse du regne loing aspre apparoistra.
Qu'au fait bellique chacun le viendra eroire.

The great carpet folded shall not
show,
But by half the greatest part of the
history,
The exiles of the kingdom shall
appear sharp afar off.
In warlike matters everyone shall
believe.

The true historical facts concerning an exiled leader, who maintained
his powerful influence even during his banishment, shall be forever concealed from posterity.

62

Trop tard tous deux, les fleurs seront perdues,
Contre la loy serpent ne voudra
faire;
Des ligueurs forces par gallops con-
fondues,
Savone, Albigne, par Monech
grand martyre.

Both the flowers shall be lost too
late,
Against the law the serpent shall
do nothing,
The forces of the leaguers, by gallops, shall be confounded,
Savoy, Albigne, by Monaco shall
suffer great martyrdom.

Nostradamus here expresses his hatred for heretics by referring to them
as serpents. By "gallops" he means horsemen, and the meaning to be drawn
from this stanza is that the heretics of the above-named towns shall be
persecuted and driven out.

63

La dame seule au regne demeuree,
L'unique estaint premier au lict d'honneur,
Sept ans sera de douleur exploree,
Quis longue vie au regne par grand heur.

The lady shall be left to reign alone,
The unique one being extinguished, first in the bed of honour,
Seven years she shall weep for grief,
After that she shall live long in the reign by grandeur.

Catherine de Medici outlived her husband, Henry II of France, by many years. After his death she went into deep mourning for seven years.

64

On ne tiendra pache aucun arreste,
Tous recevans iront par tromperie;
De paix & trefue, terre & mer proteste;
Par Barcelone classe prins d'industrie.

No binding agreement shall be kept,
Those that admit of it deal in trumpery,
There shall be no protestations by land and sea,
Barcelona shall take a fleet by ingenuity.

An armed truce with trickery on all sides shall beset the nations, and Spain shall be the gainer.

65

Gris & bureau, demie ouverte guerre,
De nuict seront assailliz & pillez;
Le bureau prins passera par la serre,
Son temple ouvert, deux aux plastres grillez.

Between the grays and the bureaus shall be half open war,
By night they shall be assaulted and plundered,
The government being taken shall put in custody,
His temple shall be opened, two shall be put in the grate.

Conflict between lower classes and bureaucrats is foreshadowed ending with the overthrow of a government.

66

Au fondement de la nouvelle secte,	At the founding of a new sect,
Seront les os du grand Romain trouvez,	The bones of the great Roman shall be found,
Sepulchre en marbre apparoistra converte.	The Sepulchre shall appear covered with marble,
Terra trembler en Avril, mal enfovez.	The earth shall quake in April, they shall be ill-buried.

A new sect of friars, while digging the foundation for a church, unearthed human bones which they believed to be the remains of a famous old Roman. The last line has no particular connection with this tale, signifying that there will be an earthquake during the month of April, at which time many graves will be opened and their contents revealed.

67

Au grand Empire par viendra tout un autre,	To the great Empire quite another shall come,
Bonte distant plus de felicite;	Being distant from goodness and happiness,
Regi par un issu non loing du peautre,	Governed by one of base parentage,
Corruer Regnes grande infelicite.	The Kingdom shall fall, a great unhappiness.

The future fate of all empires is here explicated.

68

Lors que soldats fureur seditieuse,	When the seditious fury of the soldiers,
Contre leur chef feront de nuict fer livre,	Against their chief shall make the iron shine by night,
Ennemy d'Albe soit par main furieuse,	The enemy d'Albe shall by a furious hand,
Lors vexer Rome & principaux seduire.	Then vex Rome and seduce the principal one.

The Duke of Alba, commander of the Spanish Army in the war against the Roman forces of the Pope, unmercifully forced the war to a successful conclusion for his master, Emperor Charles V.

69

La grand pitie sera sans long tarder,
Ceux qui donoient seront con-
    traints de prendre,
Nuds affamez de froid, soif, soy
    bander,
Passer les monts en faisant grand
    esclandre.

What a great pity will it be before
    long,
Those that did give, shall be con-
    strained to receive,
Naked, famished with cold, to mu-
    tiny,
To go over the mountains making
    great disorders.

A land of plenty shall soon be in want and the people will revolt.

70

Un chef du monde le grand Chy-
    ren sera;
Plus outre, apres ayme, craint, re-
    doute;
Son bruit & los les cieux sur pas-
    sera,
Et du seul titre Victeur, fort con-
    tent.

A chief of the world, the great
    Henry shall be,
At first, beloved, afterwards feared,
    dreaded,
His fame and praise shall go be-
    yond the heavens,
And shall be contented with the
    title of Victor.

The nations will organize a super-government covering the entire
world. The president will be named Henry.
    "Chyren" by transposition of letters is an anagram for "Henryc," the
then current form of Henry.

71

Quand on viendra le grand Roy
    parenter,
Avant qu'il ait du tout l'ame ren-
    due,
On le verra bien tost apparenter,
D'Aigles, Lions, Crois, Couronne
    vendue.

When they shall come to celebrate
    the obsequies of the great King,
A day before he be quite dead,
He shall be seen presently to be
    allied,
With Eagles, Lions, Crosses,
    Crowns of Rue.

A continuation of the previous stanza; at the end of Henry's reign,
he shall be exposed as being allied with predatory interests, bringing
much sorrow and suffering to mankind.

72

Par fureur faincte d'esmotion divine,
Sera la femme du grand fort violee;
Judges voulants damner telle doctrine,
Victime au peuple ignorant immolee.

By a feigned fury of divine inspiration,
The wife of the great one shall be ravished,
Judges willing to condemn such a doctrine,
A victim shall be sacrificed to the ignorant people.

Marie Antoinette, wife of Louis XVI of France, was condemned to death by the judges of the revolution and guillotined in the presence of a howling mob.

73

En cite grand un moyne & artisan,
Pres de la porte logez & aux murailles;
Contre modene secret, cave disant,
Trahis pour faire sous couleur d'espousailles.

In a great city a monk and an artisan
Dwelling near the gate and walls,
Against woman secrets, beware further,
A treason shall be plotted under pretense of marriage.

A monk, an artisan and a woman shall share a secret, relating to a treasonable act; womanlike she shall tell and so betray it.

74

La dechassee au regne tournera,
Ses ennemis trouvez des conjurez;
Plus que jamais son temps triomphera,
Trois & septante a mort trop asseurez.

The expelled shall come again to the kingdom,
Her enemies shall be found to be conspirators,
More than ever his time shall triumph,
Three and seventy appointed by death.

Exiled anti-Nazi liberals shall again return to the countries of Europe and many of their persecutors shall be marked for death.

75

Le grand Pilot sera par Roy mande,
Laisser la classe, pour plus haut lieu
attaindre;
Sept ans apres sera contrebande,
Barbare armee viendra Venise
craindre.

The great Pilot shall be sent for
by Royal mandate,
To leave the fleet, and be preferred
to a higher place,
Seven years after he shall be countermanded,
A barbarian army shall put Venice
to fear.

A great leader, long absent from public life, shall be recalled to pilot
his country's destiny during a time of great stress. The latter part of the
stanza indicates his final fall from grace in the face of overwhelming
public opposition.

76

La cite antique d'Antenoree forge,
Plus ne pouvant le tyran supporter;
Le manche fainct au temple couper
gorge,
Les siens le peuple a mort viendra
bouter.

The ancient city founded by Antenor,
Not being able to bear the tyrant
any longer.
The feigned handle in the temple
cut a throat,
The people will come to put his
servants to death.

The city founded by Antenor, who came to Italy with Aeneas, is Padua.
Being a university city, it will not be able to stand the antics of a
tyrant any longer. He shall have his throat cut, and his companions will
also be put to death.

77

Par la victoire du deceu fraudu-
lente,
Deux classes une, la revolte Ger-
mains,
Le chef meurtry & son fils dans la
tente,
Florence, Imole pourchassez dans
Romaine.

By the deceitful victory of the de-
ceived,
One of the two fleets shall revolt to
the Germans,
The chief and his son murdered
in their tent,
Florence, Imole, persecuted in
Romania.

The Germans shall be deceived into thinking that they have won a
victory. Trouble in Italy shall hasten their disillusionment and contribute
to their final defeat.

78

Crier victoire du grand Selin croissant,
Par les Romains sera l'Aigle clame,
Ticcin, Milan & Gennes ny consent,
Puis par eux mesmes Basil grand
  reclame.

They shall cry at the victory of the
  great Selin's crescent,
By the Romans the Eagle shall be
  claimed,
Ticin, Milan and Genoa consent
  not,
Then by themselves the great Basil
  shall be claimed.

The Romans, defeated in a battle with the Turks, will request aid from
other Italian cities. Being refused by them, they will then appeal to the
great King (Basil from the Greek word *Basileus*).

79

Pres de Tesin les habitants de
  Logre,
Garonne & Saone, Siene, Tar &
  Gironde,
Outre les monts dresseront pro-
  montoire,
Conflict donne, Pau granci, sub-
  merge onde.

Near the Tesin the inhabitants of
  Logre,
Garonne and Saone, Siene, Tar
  and Gironde,
Shall erect a promontory beyond
  the mountains,
Conflict given, the Po passed over,
  some shall be drowned.

The Italians shall attempt to build an empire beyond their own borders.
Eventually they will be defeated in this purpose, and shall suffer great losses.

80

De Fez le Regne parviendra a ceux
  d'Europe,
Feu leur cite, & lame trenchera;
Le grand d'Asie terre & mer a
  grand troupe,
Que bleux, pars, croix a mort de-
  chassera.

The Kingdom of Fez shall come to
  those of Europe,
Fire and sword shall destroy their
  city,
The great one of Asia, by land and
  sea with a great army,
So that blues, greens, crosses to
  death he shall drive.

"A strange prophecy if it prove true," said a 17th century disciple of
Nostradamus. And time so proves it—that this is the prediction of the
Spanish Civil War, of the uprisings which began in Morocco and spread
to Spain; and even indicates the aid that was given the Loyalists by Russia
and Franco by Germany.

81

Pleurs, cris, & plaincts, hurlemens, effrayeurs,	Tears, cries and complaints, howlings, fear,
Coeur inhuman, cruel, noir, & transy.	An inhuman heart, cruel black and astonished,
Leman, les Isles, de Gennes les majeurs,	Geneva, the Islands of the great ones of Genoa,
Sang espancher, tochsain, a nul mercy.	Shall spill blood, the bell shall ring and no mercy given.

During the course of a war that shall involve most of the earth's surface, a battle of great importance will be fought with the Dodecanese Islands as the prize.

82

Par les deserts de lieu, libre, & farouche,	Through the deserts of a place free and ragged,
Viendra errer nepueu du grand Pontife;	The nephew of the Pope shall come to wander,
Assomme a sept avec ques lourde souche,	Knocked in the head by seven with a heavy club,
Par ceux qu'apres occuperont le cyphe.	By those who after shall obtain the cipher.

A nephew of the Pope shall be exiled to a desert, where he shall be attacked by seven men, one of which will afterwards gain the Papacy.

83

Celuy qu'aura tant d'honneur & carresses,	He that shall have had so many honors and welcomes,
A son entree en la Gaule Belgique,	At his going into French Belgium,
Un temps apres fera tant de rudesses,	A while after shall commit so many rudenesses,
Et sera contre a la fleur tant bellique.	And shall be against the warlike flower.

This concerns the Duke of Alencon who was sent into the Low Countries as Governor for Henry III, King of France. So entranced was he by the beauty and riches of Antwerp, that he attempted to seize the city, but he was overcome by the citizens and most of his followers were destroyed.

84

Celuy qu'en Sparte Claude ne veut
  regner,
Il fera tant par voye seductive;
Que de court, long, le fera araigner,
Que contre Roy fera sa perspective.

He that Claudius will not have to
  reign in Sparta,
The same shall do so much by a
  deceitful way,
That he shall cause him to be ar-
  raigned short and long,
As if he had made his prospect
  upon the King.

One shall be hindered from reigning, by the machinations of another.

centory XII
36 — 348

85

La grand cite de Tharse par Gau-
  lois,
Sera destruite, captifs tous a Tur-
  ban,
Secours par mer, du grand Portu-
  galois,
Premier d'este le jour de sacre
  Urban.

The great city of Tharse taken by
  the French,
All who wore the turban shall be
  made slaves,
Help by sea from the great Portu-
  guese,
The first day of summer and the
  installation of Urban.

What is meant by the taking of Tarsus, the birthplace of the Apostle
Paul, is not clear to me. The rest of the stanza refers to the persecution
and enslavement of non-Christians during the reigns of various early
Popes (indicated by "Urban," the name taken by eight different Popes,
the last of whom held the office from 1623 to 1644).

86

Le grand Prelat un jour apres son
  songe
Interprete au rebours de son sens;
De la Gascongne luy surviendra un
  monge,
Qui fera eslire le grand Prelat de
  Sens.

The great Prelate the next day
  after his dream,
Interpreted contrary to his sense,
From Gascony shall come to him
  a monk,
That shall cause the great Prelate
  of Sens to be elected.

A lowly monk shall come to a princely churchman, and, following his
advice, the Prelate will be elected to a high office.

87

L'election faicte dans Francfort,
N'aura nul lieu, Milan s'opposera;
Le sien plus proche semblera si
grand fort,
Qu'outre le Rhin es mareschs chas-
sera.

The election made at Frankfort,
Shall be void, Milan shall oppose
it;
He of the Milan party shall be so
strong,
As to drive the other beyond the
marshes of the Rhine.

At Frankfort in Germany, the ancient German rulers were elected.
Milan is the place where the Italian Fascist leaders first became powerful.
The rest is plain.

88

Un regne grand demourra desole,
Aupres del Hebrose seront assem-
blees;
Mont Pyrenees le rendront console,
Lors que dans May seront terres
tremblees.

A great king shall be left desolate,
Near the River Hebrus an assembly
shall be made,
The Pyrenean Mountains shall
comfort him,
When in May shall be an earthquake.

A reference to an ancient incident, this concerns a King who, after
being defeated in battle near the River Hebrus (the ancient name for
the River Maritza), loses his kingdom and is forced to flee to the shelter
of the Pyrenees Mountains.

89

Entre deux cymbles pieds & mains
estachez,
De miel face oingt, & de laict sub-
stante;
Geuspes & mouches seront amour
fachez,
Poccilateurs faucer, cyphe tente.

Between two boats one shall be
tied hand and foot,
His face anointed with honey, and
be nourished with milk,
Wasps and bees shall make much
of him mad,
For being treacherous cup bearers,
and poisoning the cup.

A description of a form of ancient torture meted out to poisoners—put
between two troughs called boats, their bodies were daubed with honey,
so that wasps and bees could torment them to death.

90

L'honnissement puant abominable,
Apres le faict sera felicite;
Grand excuse, pour n'estre favor-
   able,
Qu'a paix Neptune ne sera incite.

The stinking and abominable de-
   filing,
After the deed shall be successful,
The great one excused for not being favorable,
That Neptune might be persuaded
   to peace.

This refers to an infamous pact, agreed upon by several nations, ostensibly for the preservation of peace. The Munich Pact and the temporary
acclamation of the role played by Chamberlain are clearly indicated.

91

Le conducteur de la Guerre Navale,
Rouge effrene, severe, horrible
   grippe,
Captif eschappe de l'aisne dans la
   baste;
Quand il naistra du grand un fils
   Agrippe.

The leader of the Naval War,
Red, rash, severe, horrible execu-
   tioner.
Being slave, shall escape, hidden
   among the harness,
When shall be born to the great
   one, a son named Agrippa.

Cornelius Agrippa, 1486–1535, a German soldier, philosopher and
alchemist, is here alluded to.

92

Princesse de beaute tant venuste,
Au chef menee, le second faict
   trahy;
La cite au glaive de poudre face
   aduste,
Par trop grand meurtre le chef du
   Roy hay.

A Princess of an exquisite beauty,
Shall be brought to the chief, the
   second fact betrayed,
The city shall be given to fire and
   sword,
By too great a murder, the chief
   man of the King shall be hated.

The sequence of events is plain, the only difficulty is in the naming of
the city.

93

Prelat avare, d'ambition trompe,
Rien ne fera que trop cuider
viendra,
Ses messagers, & luy bien attrape,
Tout au rebours voir qui le bois
fendra.

A covetous Prelate, deceived by
ambition,
Shall do nothing but covet too
much,
His messengers and he shall be
trapped,
When they shall see one cleave the
the wood the contrary way.

Cardinal Richelieu's overweening ambition led him to be the greatest
figure of his day; a prophetic picture of Richelieu and his intrigues is given
here by Nostradamus.

94

Un Roy ire sera aux sedifragues,
Quand interdicts seront hernois de
guerre,
La poison taincte au succre par les
fragues,
Par eaux meurtris, morts disant
serre serre.

A King shall be irate against the
treaty breakers,
When the warlike armour shall be
forbidden,
The poison with sugar shall be put
in the strawberries,
They shall be killed and die, saying, "close, close."

After a trial, held against the treaty breakers, they shall be executed saying, "We came very close."

95

Par detracteur calomnie a puis nay;
Quand istront faict enormes &
martiaux;
La moindre part dubieuse a l'aisne,
Et tost au regne seront faicts par-
tiaux.

The youngest son shall be slan-
dered by a detractor,
When enormous and martial deeds
shall be done,
The least part shall be doubtful to
the eldest,
And soon after they shall both be
equal in the government.

A quarrel between two brothers (princes) will lead to the verge of
civil war. Their differences will be conciliated and both will play an equal
share in the government of their country.

96

Grand cite a soldats abandonnee,
Onc ny eut mortel tumult si
proche,
O qu'elle hideuse calamite s'approche,
Fors une offense n'y sera pardon-
nee.

A great city shall be abandoned to
the soldiers,
There never was a mortal tumult
so near,
Oh! what a hideous calamity approaches,
Except one offense, nothing shall
be pardoned.

A great city shall be pillaged by a barbarian horde; the only ones spared shall be those of the same race.

97

Cinq & quarante degrez ciel bruslera,
Feu approcher de la grand cite
neuve,
Instant grand flamme esparse sau-
tera,
Quand on voudra des Normans
faire preuve.

The heaven shall burn at five and
forty degrees,
The fire shall come near the great
new city,
In an instant a great flame dis-
persed shall burst out,
When they shall make a trial of
the Normans.

A cataclysmic fire shall engulf the greatest and newest of the world's big cities.

98

Ruyne aux Volsques de peur si fort
terribles,
Leur grand cite taincte, faict pestilent;
Piller sol, lune, & violer leurs
temples;
Et les deux fleuves rougir de sang
coulant.

Ruin shall happen to the Vandals
that will be terrible,
Their great city shall be tainted, a
pestilent deed;
They shall plunder sun and moon,
and violate their temples,
And two rivers shall be red with
running blood.

The atomic bombing of Hiroshima is foretold by Nostradamus. Its location, between two rivers, is given, as well as the mention of the temples of the Japanese.

99

L'ennemy docte se tournera confus,
Grand camp malade, & de faict par
embusches,
Mont Pyrenees & Pernus luy seront faict refus,
Proche du fleuve descouvrant antiques ruches.

The learned enemy shall go back
confounded,
A great camp shall be sick and in
effect through ambush,
The Pyrenean Mountains shall
refuse him,
Near the river discovering the
ancient hives.

An educated yet barbarous nation shall be defeated in its attempt to
foist its culture on other peoples, and its leaders shall be refused sanctuary
wherever they try to flee.

100

Fille de l'Aure, asyle du mal sain,
Ou jusqu'au ciel se void l'ampthi-
teatre;
Prodige veu, ton mal est fort prochain,
Seras captive, & des fois plus de
quatre.

Daughter of Laura, sanctuary of
the sick,
Where to the heavens is seen the
amphitheatre;
A prodigy being seen, the danger
is near,
Thou shalt be taken captive above
four times.

An ingenious stanza, it contains many things. The reference to "Daughter of Laura" concerns the city of Nismes in Languedoc, famous for its
amphitheatre and for being the birthplace of Laura, mistress of the poet
Petrarch. The last two lines contain a warning of approaching civil war
in France, clearly an indication of the far-in-the-future French Revolution.

LEGIS CAUTIO CONTRA INEPTOS CRITICOS

Qui legent hos versus, mature censunto;
Prophanum vulgus & inscium ne attrectato.
Omnesque Astrologi, Blenni, Barbari procul sunto,
Qui aliter faxit, is rite sacer esto.

INVOCATION OF THE LAW AGAINST INEPT CRITICS

Those who read these verses, let them consider with mature mind,

Let not the profane, vulgar and ignorant be attracted to their study.

All Astrologers, Fools and Barbarians draw not near,

He who acts otherwise, is cursed according to rite.

[Various quatrains within the following Century were found to duplicate those occurring in the previous Centuries, and therefore have been deleted. The numbering of the quatrains has been maintained according to the original sequence.]

1

L'arc du thresor par Achilles deceu,
Aux procrees sceu la quadrangu-
laire;
Au faict Royal le comment sera
sceu,
Corps veu pendu au veu du popu-
laire.

The arch of the treasure by Achilles deceived,
Shall show to posterity the quadrangle,
In the royal deed the comment
shall be known,
The body seen hung in full view
of the people.

Marshal d'Ancre, Treasurer of France, and favorite of the Queen Regent, Marie de Medici, was exposed by Achilles de Harlay, President of Paris, and convicted for the mishandling of funds. By order of Louis XIII, he was killed in the quadrangle of the Louvre and his body was later hanged in a public place.

2

Par Mars ouvert Arles ne donra
guerre,
De nuict seront les soldats eston-
nez;
Noir, blanc, a l'Inde dissimule en
terre,
Sous la saincte ombre traistre verrez & sonnez.

Arles shall not proceed by open
war,
By night the soldiers shall be astonished,
Black, white, and blue dissembled
on the ground,
Under the feigned shadow will be
proclaimed traitors.

Arles, a city in France, shall be the scene of a mutiny.

214

3

Apres de France la victoire navale,
Les Barchinons, Sallinons, les Phocens,
Lierre d'or, l'enclume serre dedans
   la balle,
Ceux de Toulon au fraud seront
   consents.

After the naval victory of the
   French,
Upon those of Tunis, Salle, and
   the Phocens,
Keg of gold, the anvil shut up in
   a ball,
Those of Toulon to the fraud shall
   consent.

A naval victory of the French over those of the Barbary Coast shall
be attained by means of a novel weapon, an anvil and a ball, shut up in
a keg of gold.

4

Le Duc de Langres assiege dedans
   Dole,
Accompagne d'Ostin & Lyonnois;
Geneve, Auspourg, joinct ceux de
   Mirandole,
Passer les monts conter les Ancon-
   nois.

The Duke of Langres shall be be-
   sieged in Dole,
Being in company with those of
   Autun and Lion,
Geneva, Augsburg, those of Miran-
   dola,
Shall go over the mountains against
   those of Ancona.

France, Italy, Switzerland, and Germany shall be involved in a military
expedition.

5

Vin sur la table en sera respandu,
Le tiers n'aura celle qu'il preten-
   doit;
Deux fois du noir de Parme des-
   cendu,
Perouse a Pise ce qu'il cuidoit.

Wine shall be spilt upon the table,
By reason that a third person shall
   not have her,
Twice, the black one, descended
   from Parma,
Shall do to Perugia and Pisa what
   he intended.

The all-powerful Black One in Italy shall dominate and ravage Italian
centers of culture at will.

6

Naples, Palerme, & tout la Sicile,
Par main barbare sera inhabitee,
Corsique, Salerne & de Sardeigne,
  l'Isle,
Faim, peste guerre, fin de maux
  intemptee.

Naples, Palermo and all Sicily,
By barbarous hands shall be de-
  populated,
Corsica, Salerno and the Island of
  Sardinia,
In them shall be famine, plague,
  war and endless evils.

A picture, as foreseen by Nostradamus, of conditions in Italy in the closing years of World War II.

7

Sur le combat des grands chevaus
  legers,
On criera le grand croissant con-
  fond,
De nuict tuer moutons, habits de
  bergers,
Abismes rouges dans le fosse profond.

At the fight of the great light
  horsemen,
They shall cry out, confound the
  great crescent,
By night they shall kill sheep
  dressed as shepherds,
Red abysms shall be in the deep
  ditch.

A nocturnal sally by the Turks shall cause much damage to defenseless populations.

8

Flora, fuis, fuis le plus proche Ro-
  main,
Au Fesulan sera conflict donne;
Sang espandu, les plus grands prins
  a main,
Temple ne sexe ne sera pardonne.

Flora, fly, fly from the nearest Roman,
In the Fesulan shall be the fight,
Blood shall be spilt, the greatest
  shall be taken,
Neither temple nor sex shall be
  spared.

Flora is the Goddess of Flowers and Agriculture, and Fesulan is a place in Italy. Nostradamus warns the inhabitants of Fesulan that there will be some trouble during a Festival in honor of the Goddess Flora.

9

Dame a l'abscence de son grand capitaine,	A lady in the absence of her great captain,
Sera priee d'amour du Viceroy,	Shall be entreated of love by the Viceroy,
Faincte promesse & mal'heureuse estraine,	A pretended promise and unhappy New Year's gift,
Entre les mains du grand Prince Barroys.	In the hand of the great Prince of Bar.

Bar was a principality adjoining Lorraine, which Henry IV gave as a marriage gift to his sister Catherine, when she married the Duke of Lorraine's son. The rest of this quatrain indicates some unhappiness connected with this match.

10

Par le grand Prince limitrophe du Mans,	The great Prince dwelling near Le Mans,
Preux & vaillant chef de grand exercite;	Stout and valiant, general of a great army,
Par mer & terre de Gallois & Normans,	Of Britons and Normans by sea and land,
Caspre passer Barcelonne pille Isle.	Ravaging Cape Barcelona and plunder the Island.

Le Mans is a city in France, and a French general from this vicinity shall lead an army of Britons and Normans to ravage Barcelona.

11

L'enfant Royal contemnera la mere,	The Royal Infant shall despise his mother,
Oeil, pieds blessez, rude, inobeissant,	Eye, feet wounded, rude, disobedient,
Nouvelle a dame estrange & bien amere,	News to a lady very strange and bitter,
Seront tuez des siens plus de cinq cens.	There shall be killed about five hundred.

In 1615, when Louis XIII, King of France, was about fifteen years of age, he was persuaded to make war against his own mother, Marie de Medici, then Regent of the Kingdom. In the ensuing battle about five hundred of the Queen's soldiers were slain.

12

Le grand puisnay fera fin de guerre,
Aux dieux assemble les excusez,
Cahors, Moissac iront long de la serre,
Rusec, Lectore, les Agenoise rasez.

The great young brother shall make an end of the war,
In two places he shall gather the excused,
Cahors, Moissac, shall go out of his clutches,
Russec, Lectore and those of Agen shall be cut off.

All the places mentioned are in the Province of Guyenne, France; and the incident mentioned concerns an inter-city war involving all these regions.

13

De la cite marine & tributaire,
La teste raze prendra la satrapie;
Chasser sordide qui puis sera contraire,
Par quatorze ans tiendra la tyrannie.

Of the maritime city and tributary,
The shaven head shall take the government,
He shall turn out a vile man who shall oppose him,
During fourteen years he will keep away the tyranny.

A positive assertion concerning Cardinal Richelieu, who actually took over a secular branch of the government, and made himself Governor of Havre de Grace.

14

Faux exposer viendra topographie,
Seront les cruches des monuments ouvertes;
Pulluler secte, sainte philosophie,
Pour blanches, noires, & pour antiques vertes.

They shall show topography falsely,
The urns of the monuments shall be open,
Sects shall multiply and holy philosophy,
Shall give black for white, and green for gold.

A corrupt period in history is foretold, when too many sects will spring up, creating great conflict in the church.

15

Devant cite de l'insubre countree,
Sept ans sera le siege devant mis;
Le tres grand Roy y fera son entree,
Cite puis libre hors de ses ennemis.

Before a city of the lower country,
Seven years of siege shall be laid,
The most great King shall make his entry into it,
Then the city shall be full being out of the enemies' hands.

A city in the Low Country will be under siege for seven years, after which it will be liberated and the former inhabitants, who had fled from their enemy, will return to enjoy the new freedom.

16

Entree profonde par la grand Royne faicte;
Rendra le lieu puissant inaccessible;
L'armee des trois Lyons sera deffaicte,
Faisant dedans cas hideux & terrible.

The deep trench made by the Queen,
Shall make the place powerful and inaccessible,
The army of the three lions shall be defeated,
Doing within a hideous and terrible thing.

An army, owing allegiance to an alliance of three predatory monarchs, shall be defeated but not before committing hideous crimes against captured civilians.

17

Le Prince rare en pitie & clemence,
Apres avoir la paix aux siens baille,
Viendra changer par mort grand cognoissance,
Par grand repos le regne travaille.

The Prince, rare in pity and clemency,
After he shall have given peace to his subjects,
Shall by death change his great knowledge,
After great rest the kingdom shall be troubled.

This concerns Henry IV, peace-loving King of France, who was assassinated on May 14, 1610, by Ravaillac. After his death there was much trouble in the Kingdom caused by the dissension among the Princes.

18

Les assiegez couleront leurs paches,
Sept jours apres feront cruelle issue,
Dans repoulez, feu sang, sept mis
a l'hache,
Dame captive qu'avoit la paix issue.

The besieged shall color their articles,
Seven days after they shall make a
cruel issue,
They shall be beaten back, fire,
blood, seven put to the axe,
The lady shall be prisoner who
tried to make peace.

A description of an event which will be the turning point in a war.

19

Le fort Nicene ne sera combatu,
Vaincu sera par rutilant metal,
Son faict sera un long temps de-
batu,
Au citadins estrange espouvantal.

The Nicene fort shall not be fought
against,
By shining metal it shall be overcome,
The doing of it shall a long time
be debated,
It shall be a strange fearful thing
to the citizens.

Nice, endangered by invaders, shall buy her way to peace by the use
of shining metal (gold).

20

Ambassadeurs de la Toscane lan-
gue,
Avril & May Alpes & mer passer,
Celuy de veau exposera l'harangue,
Vie Gauloise en voulant effacer.

The ambassadors of the Tuscan
tongue,
In April and May, shall go over the
Alps and the sea,
One like a calf, shall make a speech,
Attempting to defame French cus-
toms.

On May 7, 1938, Mussolini, in a mutual admiration session with the
Fuehrer, in Berlin, flamboyantly stated, "Germany and Italy have left
behind them the Utopias to which Europe has entrusted her destiny. It
is this law which Nazi Germany and Fascist Italy has obeyed, obeys, and
will obey."

21

Par pestilente inimitie Volsique,
Dissimulee chassera le tyran;
Au pont de Sorgues se fera la traf-
fique,
De mettre a mort luy & son adher-
ent.

By a pestilent Italian enmity,
The dissembler shall expel the
tyrant,
The bargains shall be made at Sorgues bridge,
To put him and his adherent to
death.

Premier Pierre Laval, cohort of Mussolini, was eventually expelled, captured and executed, thus fulfilling the prophecy.

22

Les Citoyens de Mesopotamie,
Irez encontre amis de Tarraconne,
Jeux, Ris, banquets, toute gent en-
dormie,
Vicaire au Rhosne, prins cite, ceux
d'Ausone.

The citizens of Mesopotamia,
Being angry with the friends of
Tarrogona,
Sport, laughter, banquets, every-
body being asleep,
The vicar being in Rhone, the city
taken by those of Bordeaux.

This concerns a region of France which lies between two rivers, and its long since forgotten quarrel with the citizens of Bordeaux.

23

Le Royal Sceptre sera contrainct de
prendre,
Ce que ses predecesseurs voint en-
gage;
Puis que l'aigneau on fera mal entendre,
Lors qu'on viendra le palais sacca-
ger.

The Royal Sceptre shall be constrained to take
What his predecessors had mort-
gaged,
After that they shall misinform the
lamb,
When they shall come to plunder
the palace.

Clearly this refers to a palace scandal, but it is worded so obscurely that it is too difficult to discern what royal family is involved.

24

L'ensevely sortira du tombeau,	The buried shall come out of his grave,
Fera de chaines lier le fort du pont,	The fort of the bridge shall be tied with chains,
Empoisonne avec oeufs de Barbeau,	Poisoned with the roe of a Barbel,
Grand de Lorraine par le Marquis du Pont,	Shall a great one of Lorraine be, by the Marquis Dupont.

The first part of this verse has no importance or relationship to the prophecy, which concerns the poisoning of the Duke of Lorrain by the Marquis Du Pont.

25

Par guerre longue tout l'exercite espuiser,	By a long war, all the army drained dry,
Que pour soldats ne trouveront pecune,	So that to raise soldiers, they shall find no money,
Lieu d'or, d'argent, cuir on viendra cuser,	Instead of gold and silver, they shall stamp leather,
Gaulois aerain, signe croissant de Lune.	The French copper, marked with the signs of the crescent moon.

Before the discovery of the West Indies, and the consequent expansion and exploitation of the colonies, many European countries were forced to use substitutes for the usual gold and silver coins.

26

Fustes galees autour de sept navires,	Flying boats and galleys round about seven ships,
Sera livree une mortelle guerre;	Shall be in the livery of deadly war,
Chef de Madrid, recevra coup de vires,	The chief of Madrid shall receive blows of oars,
Deux eschapees, & cinq menees a terre.	Two shall escape, and five carried to land.

A Spanish Admiral shall suffer great losses in a naval battle. Of his entire fleet only two ships shall manage to escape. The rest will be taken as prizes, among them the ship which the Admiral personally commanded.

27

Au coin de vast la grand cavalerie,	In a corner of the wasted, the great cavalry,
Proche a Ferrare empeshce au bagage,	Near Ferrara, shall be busy about the baggage,
Pompe a Turin feront tel volerie,	Pomp at Turin, they shall make such a robbery,
Que dans le fort raviront leur hostage.	That in the fort they shall ravish their hostage.

During a war the people of the country will sustain great losses and suffer greatly, while their leaders will lead lives of luxury in a fortified city.

28

Le captaine conduira grande proye,	The captain shall lead a great prey,
Sur la montagne des ennemis plus proche,	Upon the mountain, that shall be nearest to the enemies,
Environne, par feu fera telle voye.	Being encompassed with fire, he shall make such a way,
Tous eschappez, or trente mis en broche.	All shall escape, except thirty that shall be spitted.

A leader, surrounded by enemy soldiers, shall contrive to lead his men out of danger, except thirty who will be taken and tortured by their captors.

29

Le grand duc d'Albe se viendra rebeller,	The great Duke of Alba shall rebel,
A ses grands peres fera le tradiment;	To his grandfathers he shall make the plot,
Le grand de Guise le viendra debeller,	The great Guise shall vanquish him,
Captif mene & dresse monument.	Led prisoner, and a monument erected.

The Duke of Alba was sent to Rome by Charles V of Spain, to lend his aid to others of the Spanish Party in that city.

30

Le sac s'approche, feu, grand sang espandu,	The sack draws near, fire, abundance of blood spilt,
Pau, grand fleuve, aux bouvirs l'entreprinse,	Pau, a great river, an enterprise by churls,
De Gennes, Nice, apres long attendu,	Of Genoa, Nice after they shall have stayed long,
Foussan, Turin, a Savillan la prinse.	Fossan, Turin, the prize shall be at Savillan.

For four years, 1555–59, there was constant fighting among various cities in Italy, especially those near the River Pau (Po).

31

De Langeudoc, & Guienne plus de dix,	From Languedoc and Guienne more than 10,000
Mille voudront les Alpes repasser;	Would be glad to repass the Alps,
Grans Allobroges marcher contre Brundis,	Great Allobroges shall march against Brundis,
Aquin & Bresse les viendront recasser.	Aquin and Bresse shall beat them back.

A French army passing over the Alps into Italy will regret this maneuver.

32

Du Mont Royal naistra d'une casane,	Out of Montreal shall be born in a cottage,
Qui duc, & compte viendra tyranniser,	One that shall tyrannize over duke and earl,
Dresser copie de la marche Millane,	He shall raise an army in the land of the rebellion,
Favence, Florence d'or & gens espuiser.	He shall empty Favence and Florence of their gold.

A Canadian leader, of lowly birth, shall be raised to great power and eventually assume command over men of the nobility.

33

Par fraude, regne, forces expolier,
La classe obsesse, passages a l'es-
pie;
Deux faicnts amis se viendront
t'allier,
Esueiller haine de long temps assoupie.

By fraud a kingdom and army shall
be despoiled,
The fleet shall be possessed, passages shall be made to spies,
Two feigned friends shall agree
together,
They shall raise up a hatred that
had long been dormant.

The alliance between Hitler and Mussolini is predicted. The infiltration by propaganda, the rousing of Anti-Semitism and their "divide and conquer" technique are described.

34

En grand regret sera la gent Gauloise,
Coeur vain, leger croira temerite;
Pain, sel, ne vin, eau, venin ne cer-
voise,
Plus grand captif, faim, froid, ne-
cessite.

In great regret shall the French
nation be,
Their vain and light heart shall believe rashly,
They shall have neither bread, salt,
wine nor beer,
Moreover, they shall be prisoners
and shall suffer hunger, cold and
need.

This continuation of the preceding stanza tells of conditions in France under the heel of the Axis invader.

35

Le grand poche viendra plaindre,
pleurer,
D'avoir esleu, trompez seront en
l'aage,
Guiere avec eux ne voudra demeu-
rer;
Deceu sera par ceux de son langage.

The great pouch shall bewail and
bemoan,
Having elected one, they shall be
deceived,
His age shall not stay long with
them,
He shall be deceived by those of
his own language.

This continues the previous prediction of conditions in France, under Hitlerism; and goes on to outline the sabotaging, by the French underground movement, of the Vichy regime under Marshal Petain.

36

Dieu, le ciel tout le divin verbe a
   l'onde,
Porte par rouges sept razes a Bizance,
Contre les oingts trois cens de Trebisonde,
Deux loix mettront, & horreur,
   pluis credence.

God, Heaven all the divine world
   in water,
Carried by red ones, seven shaved
   heads at Stamboul,
Against the anointed, three hundred of Trebizond,
They shall put two laws, and horror, and afterwards believe.

A great disputation is to take place in Constantinople, seven priests against three hundred unbelievers.

37

Dix envoyez, chef de nef mettre a
   mort,
D'un adverty, en classe guerre ouverte;
Confusion chef, l'un se picque &
   mord,
Le ryn, stecades nefs, cap dedans
   la nerte.

Ten shall be sent to put the captain of the ship to death,
He shall have notice by one, the
   fleet shall be in open war,
Great confusion shall be, by pricks
   and bites,
The Rhine, dung boats, within the
   north cape.

A mutiny shall take place within the German Navy.

38

L'aisne Royal sur coursier voltigeant,
Picquer viendra si rudement courir;
Cueulle, lipee, pied dans l'estrain
   pliegnant,
Traine, tire, horriblement mourir.

The eldest Royal, prancing upon a
   horse,
Shall spur, and run fiercely,
Open mouth, the foot in stirrup,
   complaining,
Drawn, pulled, die horribly.

The eldest son of a King shall die a horrible death as the result of being thrown from a horse.

39

Le conducteur de l'armee Fran-
coise,
Cuidant perdre le principale phalange;
Par sus pave de l'Avaigne & d'ar-
doise,
Soy parfondra par Gennes gent
estrange.

The leader of the French army,
Hoping to rout the principal pha-
lanx,
Upon the pavement of Avaigne
and slate,
Shall sink in the ground by Genoa,
a strange nation.

A French General shall meet with disaster in his attempt to attack
the strongest flank of the enemy. The land being strange to him, he shall
lead his men into swampy territory and they shall flounder and sink into
the ground, and thus be routed.

40

Dedans tonneaux hors oingts d'-
huile & gresse,
Seront vingt un devant le port fermez,
Au second guet par mort feront
prouesse,
Gaigner les portes, & du guet as-
sommez.

In empty tuns slippery with oil
and grease,
Before the harbor, one and twenty
shall be shut,
At the second watch by death they
shall do great feats of arms,
To win the gates, and be killed by
the watch.

By a stratagem, twenty-one men shall attempt to sneak through the
gates of an enemy harbor but shall fail and be killed.

41

Les os des pieds & des mains enserrez,
Par bruit maison long temps inhabitee,
Seront par songes concavant de-
terrez,
Maison salubre & sans bruit habitee.

The bones of the feet and hands
in shackles,
By a noise a house shall be a long
time deserted,
By a dream the buried shall be
taken out of the ground,
The house shall be salubrious, and
inhabited without noise.

A ghost shall inhabit a house, wherein a skeleton is shackled. After
decent burial of the remains the house shall again be at rest.

42

Quand Innocent tiendra le lieu de Pierre,	When Innocent shall hold the place of Peter,
Le Nizaram Sicilian se verra,	The Sicilian Nizaram shall see himself,
En grands honneurs, mais apres il cherra,	In great honors, but after that he shall fall,
Dans le bourbier d'une civil guerre.	Into the dirt of a civil war.

This prognostication is remarkable for its clarity of wording and the exactness of its fulfillment. Setting the period of time, our first reference is to Innocent X who was elected Pope in 1644. His noted contemporary, the French Cardinal Mazarin (anagrammatically referred to here as Nizaram) was of Italian origin. Under the sponsorship of Richelieu he became a citizen of France and eventually the successor of the great Cardinal. He was one of the most powerful figures of his time and led the fortunes of France during the closing years of the Thirty Years' War.

43

Lutece en Mars, Senateurs en credit,	Lutetia in Mars, Senators shall be in credit,
Por une unit Gaule sera troublee,	In a night France shall be troubled,
Du grand Croesus l'Horoscope predit,	The Horoscope of the Great Croesus predicts,
Par Saturnus, sa puissance exilee.	That by Saturn his power shall be put down.

Lutetia is the Latin word for Paris. After the death of Henry IV, King of France, the Parliament of Paris began to check on the activities of various noblemen, among them the Marquis d'Ancre. His fate is described in Quatrain 1, Century VII.

44

Deux de poison saisis nouveaux Venus,	Two by poison provided by the new Venus,
Dans la cuisine du grand Prince verser;	To pour in the kitchen of the great Prince,
Par le souillard tous deux au faict cogneus,	By the scullion the fact shall be known,
Prins qui cuidoit de mort l'aisne vexer.	And be taken, that thought by death to vex the elder.

A woman shall provide poison, in a plot to do away with a great Prince. A cook's boy shall discover the plot when tasting the King's dish.

73

Renfort de sieges manubis & man-
iples,
Changez le sacre & passe sur le
Pronsne,
Prins & captifs n'arreste les priz
triples,
Plus par fonds mis, esleve, mis au
trosne.

Recruit of sieges, spoils and prizes,
Holy day shall be changed and
passed over the Pronsne,
Taken, made captive and not held
in the triple field,
Moreover, one from the bottom
shall be raised to the throne.

A period of military unrest will take place, resulting in the raising of a little Corporal to the throne.

80

L'Occident libres les Isles Britan-
niques,
Le recogneu passer le bas, puis
haut,
Ne content trist Rebel, corff, Esco-
tiques,
Puis rebeller par plui & par nuict
chaut.

The West shall be free, and the
British Isles,
The discovered shall pass low, then
high,
Scotch Pirates shall be, who shall
rebel,
In a rainy and hot night.

John Paul Jones, called by the British "the Scotch Pirate and Rebel," is here referred to by Nostradamus, as is the fact that the West (America) shall be free.

82

La stratageme simulte sera rare,
La mort en voye rebelle par con-
tree,
Par le retour du voyage Barbare,
Exalteront la protestante entree.

The simulated stratagem shall be
scarce,
Death shall be in a rebellious way
through the country,
By the return from the Barbarian
voyage,
They shall exalt the Protestant entrance.

A political stratagem shall result in the triumph of the Protestants.

83

Vent chaut, conseil, pleurs, timidite,
De nuict au lit assailly sans les armes,
D'oppression grande calamite,
L'Epithalame converty pleurs & larmes.

Hot wind, counsel, tears, fearfulness,
He shall be assaulted in his bed by night without arms,
From that oppression shall be raised a great calamity,
The Epithalamium shall be converted into tears.

The Epithalamium, a nuptial song or poem in praise of the bride or bridegroom, is referred to here. The connected event can be gathered from the text of the stanza.

EPISTLE TO HENRY II

To the most invincible, most high, and most Christian King of France, Henry the Second: Michael Nostradamus, his most obedient servant and subject, wishes victory and happiness.

By reason of that singular observation, O most Christian and victorious King, my face, which had been cloudy a great while, did present itself before your immeasurable Majesty. I have been ever since perpetually dazzled, continually honoring and worshipping that day, in which I presented myself before it, as before a singular and humane Majesty. Now seeking after some occasion whereby I might make appear the goodness and sincerity of my heart and extend my acquaintance toward your most excellent Majesty, and seeing that it was impossible for me to declare it by effects, as well as because of the darkness and obscurity of my mind, even for the enlightening it did receive from the face of the greatest Monarch in the world. It was a great while before I could resolve to whom I should dedicate these three last Centuries of my Prophecies, which make the complete thousand. After I had a long time considered, I have with a great temerity made my address to your Majesty, being no way daunted by it, as the great author Plutarch related in the Life of Lycurgus, that, seeing the offerings and gifts that were sacrificed in the temples of their heathen gods, many came no more, lest the people should wonder at the expense.

Notwithstanding, seeing your royal splendor joined with an incomparable humanity, I have made my address to it, not as to the Kings of Persia, of

---

This dedicatory letter was used by Nostradamus as the preface to his second edition which contained new prophecies.

The following notation appeared, on the page preceding the above epistle, in the 1672 edition (: The Prophecies or Prognostications of Michael Nostradamus, translated and annotated by Theophilus de Garencieres.

Friendly Reader,

Before you read the following epistle, I would have you be warned of a few things: One is, that according to my opinion, it is very obscure and intelligible (sic) in most places, being without any just connection, and besides the obscurity of the sense, the crabbedness of the expression is such, that had not the importunity of the Bookseller prevailed, I would have left it out, but considering the respect due to Antiquity, the satisfaction we owe to curious persons, who would perhaps have thought the Book imperfect without it, we let it go, trusting to your candor and ingenuity.

whom to come near it was forbidden, but as to a most prudent and wise prince. I have dedicated my nocturnal and prophetical calculations, written rather by a natural instinct and poetical furor than by any rules of poetry; and the most part of it written and agreeing with the years, months and weeks, of the regions, countries and most of the towns and cities in Europe; touching also something of Africa, and of a part of Asia, by the change of regions that come near to those climates, and compounded in a natural fashion. But some may answer (who hath need to blow his nose) that the rhyme is as easy to be understood, as the sense is hard to get at. Therefore, O most humane King, most of the prophetical stanzas are so difficult, that there is no way to be found for the interpretation of them. Nevertheless, being in hope of setting down the towns, cities, and regions, wherein most of those shall happen, especially in the year 1585, and in the year 1606, beginning from this present time, which is the 14th of March, 1557.

Going further to the fulfilling of those things, which shall be in the beginning of the seventh millenary, according to my astronomical calculation and other learning which I could reach (at which time the adversaries of Christ and of His Church shall begin to multiply), all has been composed and calculated in days and hours of election, and well disposed, and all as accurately as was possible for me to do. And the whole "*Minerva libera et non invita,*" * calculating almost as much of the time that is come, as of that which is past, comprehending it in the present time, and what by the course of the said time shall be known to happen in all regions punctually as it is here written, adding nothing superfluous, although it be said "*Quod de futuris non est determinata omnino veritas.*" ** It is very true, Sir, that by my natural instinct given me by my progenitors, I did think I could foretell anything; but having made an agreement between this said instinct of mine, and a long calculation of art, and by a great tranquility and repose of mind, by emptying my soul of all care, I have foretold most part of these ex *tripode œneo* (by the brass tripod), though there be many who attribute to me some things that are no more mine than what is nothing at all. Only the eternal God, who is the searcher of men's hearts, being pious, just, and merciful, is the true Judge of it; Him I beseech to defend me from the calumny of wicked men, who would as willingly question how all your ancient progenitors, the Kings of France, have healed the disease called the Kings-evil; how some other nations have cured the biting of venomous beasts; others have had a certain instinct to foretell things that are to come, and of others too tedious to be here inserted. Notwithstanding those in

---

* "When Minerva was free and favorable."
** "There can be no truth entirely determined for certain which concerns the future."

whom the malignancy of the wicked spirit shall not be suppressed by length of time, I hope that after my decease my work shall be in more esteem than when I was alive.

However, if I should fail in the calculation of times, or should not please some, may it please your most imperial Majesty to forgive me, protesting before God and His Saints, that I do not intend to insert anything in writing in this present Epistle that may be contrary to the true Catholic faith, while consulting the astronomical calculations, according to my learning. For the space of times of our fathers that have been before us are such, submitting myself to the correction of the most learned, that the first man Adam was before Noah, about one thousand two hundred and forty-two years, not computing the time according to the Gentile records, as Varro did, but only according to the Sacred Scriptures, taking them as a guide to my astronomical calculations, and to the best of my understanding. After Noah and the universal flood, about a thousand and fourscore years, came Abraham, who was a supreme astrologer, according to most men's opinion, and did first invent the Chaldean letters; after that came Moses, some five hundred and fifteen or sixteen years after. And between the time of David and Moses there passed about five hundred and seventy years. After which, between the time of David and that of our Saviour and Redeemer Jesus Christ, born of the Virgin Mary, there passed (according to some chronographers) a thousand three hundred and fifty years.

Some may object, that this calculation is not true; because it differs from that of Eusebius. And from the time of human redemption, to that of the execrable seduction of the Saracens, have passed six hundred and four and twenty years or thereabouts. From that time hitherto, it is easy to gather what times are past. If my computations be not good among all nations, however, all has been calculated by the course of the celestial bodies joined with emotion infused in me at certain loose hours, the emotion which has been handed down to me by my ancient progenitors. But the danger at this time (most excellent King) requires that such secret events should not be manifested except by an enigmatical sentence, having but one sense and only one intelligence, without having mixed with it any ambiguous or amphibological calculation. But rather under a cloudy obscurity, through a natural infusion, coming near to the sentence of one of the thousand and two Prophets, that have been since the Creation of the world, according to the calculation and Punic Chronicle of Joel: "*Effundum spiritum meum super omnem carnem, et prophetabunt filii vestri, et filiae vestrae.*" * But such a prophecy did proceed from the mouth of the Holy Spirit, who was the supreme and eternal power, which being

---

* See Joel ii.28.

come with that of the celestial bodies, has caused some of them to predict great and wonderful things.

For my part I challenge no such thing in this place, God forbid. I confess truly, that all comes from God, for which I give Him thanks, honor, and praise, without having mixed anything of that divination which proceeds à fato, but à Deo, à natura (which proceeds from fate, but from God, and nature). And most of it is joined with the motion and course of the celestial bodies, much as if seeing in a lens, and through a cloudy vision, the great and sad events, the prodigious and calamitous accidents that shall befall the worshippers. First upon the temples of God, and secondly upon those who draw their support from earth, this draws near, with a thousand other calamitous accidents, which shall be known in the course of time.

For God will take notice of the long barrenness of the great Dame, who afterwards shall conceive two principal children. But, being in danger, she will give birth with risk at her age of death in the eighteenth year, and not able to go beyond thirty-six, shall leave behind her three males and one female, and he will have two who never had any of the same father. The differences between the three brothers shall be such, though united and agreed, that the three and four parts of Europe will tremble. By the lesser in years shall the Christian monarchy be upheld and augmented; sects shall rise and presently be put down again; the Arabians shall be put back; kingdoms shall be united and new laws made. Concerning the other children, the first shall possess the furious crowned Lions, holding their paws upon the escutcheons. The second, well attended by the Latins, will go so deep among the Lions, that a second trembling and furious descent will be made, to get upon the Pyrenees Mountains. The ancient monarchy shall not be transferred, and the third inundation of human blood shall happen; also for a good while Mars shall not be in Lent.

The daughter shall be given for the preservation of the Church, the dominator of it falling into the Pagan sect of the new unbelievers, and she will have two children, one from faithfulness, and the other from unfaithfulness, by the confirmation of the Catholic Church. The other, who to his confusion and late repentance, shall go about to ruin her, shall have three regions over a wide extent of leagues, that is to say, the Roman, the German, and the Spanish, and it will take a military hand to adequately take care of the area stretching from the 50th to the 52nd degree of latitude. And all those remote regions north above the 48th degree, who by vain fright shall quake, and then those of the west, south and east shall tremble because of their power, and the power of that what shall be done cannot be undone by warlike power. They shall be equal in nature, but much different in faith.

After this the barren Dame, of a greater power than the second, shall be admitted by two people, by the first made obstinate by him that had power over the others; by the second, and by the third, that shall extend his circuit to the east of Europe; there his forces will stop and be overcome, but by sea he will make his excursions into Trinacria and the Adriatic with his myrmidons. Germany shall fall, and the Barbarian Sect shall be wholly driven from among the Latins. Then the great Empire of Antichrist shall begin in the Attila, and Xerxes come down with an innumerable multitude of people, so that the coming of the Holy Ghost, proceeding from the 48th degree, shall transmigrate, driving away the abomination of the Antichrist, who made war against the royal person of the great vicar of Jesus Christ and against His Church, and His Kingdom, and reign per tempus, et in occasione temporis (for a time, and to the end of time). And before this shall precede a solar eclipse, the most dark and obscure that was since the creation of the world, till the death and passion of Jesus Christ, and from Him until now. There shall be in the month of October, a great revolution made, such that everybody will think that the earth has lost its natural motion and has gone down into perpetual darkness. In the spring before and after this, shall happen extraordinary changes, reversals of kingdoms, and great earthquakes; all this accompanied with the procreation of the New Babylon, a miserable prostitute large with the abomination of the first holocaust. And this shall last only seventy-three years and seven months.

Then from that stock that has been so long time barren, proceeding from the 50th degree, one will issue who will renovate all the Christian Church. Then shall be a great peace, union and concord, between some of the children of races long wandering and separated by diverse kingdoms; and such peace shall be made that the instigator and promoter of military function by diversity of religions, shall be tied to the bottom of the deep, and united to the kingdom of the furious who shall counterfeit the wise. The countries, towns, cities and provinces that had deserted their first ways to free themselves, captivating themselves more deeply, shall be secretly angry at their liberty and religion lost, and shall begin to strike from the left, to return once more to the right.

Then restoring the holiness, so long beaten down with their former writings, afterwards will come the great dog, the irresistible mastiff (war) who shall destroy all that was done before. Churches shall be built up again as before, the clergy shall be restored to its former state, until it falls back again into whoredom and luxury, and commits a thousand crimes. And being near to another desolation, when she shall be in her higher and more sublime dignity, there shall rise powers and military hands, who shall take away from her the two swords, and leave only the resemblance, after which, tired of the crookedness that is about them, the people will cause these things to straighten. Not willing to submit

unto them by the end opposite to the sharp hand that touches the ground
they shall provoke. To the branch long barren, will proceed one who
shall deliver the people of the world from that meek and voluntary
slavery; putting themselves under the protection of Mars, depriving Jupiter
of all his honors and dignities, for the free city established and seated
in another little Mesopotamia. And the chief governor shall be thrust
out of the middle, and set in the high place of the air, being ignorant of
the conspiracy of the conspirators, with the second Thrasibulus, who long
before did prepare for this thing. Then shall the impurities and abomina-
tions be objected with great shame, and made manifest to the darkness
of the veiled light, and shall cease toward the end of the change of his
kingdom, and the chief men of the Church shall be put back from the
love of God and many of them shall apostatize from the true faith.

Of the three sects (Lutheran, Catholic, and Mahometan), that which
is middlemost, by the actions of its worshippers, shall be thrown into
ruins. The first, wholly in all Europe, and the most part of Africa undone
by the third, by means of the poor in spirit, who by madness elevated
shall, through libidinous luxury, commit adultery. The people will rise
and maintain it, and shall drive away those that did adhere to the legis-
lators, and it shall seem, from the kingdoms spoiled by the Eastern men,
that God the Creator has loosed Satan from his infernal prison, to cause
to be born the great Dog and Dohan (Gog and Magog), who shall make
so great and abominable a breach in the Churches, that neither the reds
nor the whites, who are without eyes and without arms, shall not judge
of it, and their power shall be taken away from them.

Then shall there be a greater persecution against the Church than
ever was, and in the meantime shall be so great a plague, that two parts
of three in the world shall fail, so much so that no one shall be able to
know the true owners of fields and houses, and there shall happen a
total desolation to the clergy, and martial men shall usurp what shall
come from the City of the Sun, and from Malta, and from the Islands
of Hières, and the great chain of the port shall be open which takes its
name from a sea ox (Bosphorus).

A new incursion shall be made from the sea coasts, willing to deliver
the Castulan Leap from the first Mahometan taking, and the assaulting
shall not altogether be in vain, an´ that place where the habitation of
Abraham was, shall be assaulted by those who shall have reverence for
the Jovials. The great eastern city of Achem shall be encompassed and
assaulted on all sides by a great power of armed men. Their sea forces
shall be weakened by the western men, and to that kingdom shall happen
great desolation, and the great cities shall be depopulated, and those that
shall come in shall be comprehended within the vengeance of the wrath
of God. The Holy Sepulchre, held in great veneration for so long a time,

shall remain a great while open to the universal aspect of the heavens, sun and moon. The sacred place shall be converted into a stable for cattle small and large, and put to profane uses. O what a calamitous time shall be then for women with child! For then the principal Eastern *Jews* Ruler, being for the most part moved by the Northern and Western men, shall be vanquished and put to death, beaten, and all the rest put to flight, and the children he had by many women put in prison. Then shall be fulfilled the prophecy of the Royal Prophet. "*Ut audiret gemitus compeditorum, et solveret filios interemptorum.*" *

What great oppression shall be made then upon the princes and governors of kingdoms, and especially on those that shall live eastward and near the sea, their languages intermixed with all nations. The language of the Latin nations mixed with Arabic and North African communication. All the Eastern kings shall be driven away, beaten and brought to nothing, not altogether by means of the strength of the kings of the North, and *secret society* the drawing near of our age, but by means of three secretly united, seeking for death by ambushes one against another. The renewing of the trium- virate shall last seven years, while the fame of such a sect shall be spread all the world over, and the sacrifice of the holy and immaculate host shall be upheld. And then shall the lords be two in number, victorious in the North against the Eastern ones, and there shall be such a great noise and warlike tumult that all the East shall quake for fear of those two brothers of the North who are yet not brothers. And because, Sir, by this discourse, I put all things confusedly in these predictions as to the time concerning the event of them; for the account of the time which follows, very little is conformable, if at all, to that I have done before, being by astronomic rule and according to the Sacred Scriptures, in which I cannot err.

I could have set down in every quatrain the exact time in which they shall happen, but it would not please everybody, and much less the inter- pretation of them, till, Sir, your Majesty has granted me full power so to do, that my calumniators may have nothing to say against me. Never- theless, reckoning the years since the creation of the world to the birth of Noah, there passed 1506 years, and from the birth of Noah to the building of the ark at the time of the universal flood, 600 years passed (whether solar years, or lunar, or mixed), for my part according to the Scriptures, I hold that they were solar. And at the end of those 600 years Noah entered into the ark to save himself from the flood, which flood was universal upon the earth and lasted a year and two months; and from the end of the flood to the birth of Abraham did pass 295 years; and from the birth of Abraham to that of Isaac did pass 100 years;

---

* "Let the sighing of the prisoner come before thee, to release the children of death" (Ps. lxxviii. 11).

from Isaac to Jacob, sixty years; and from the time he went into Egypt until he came out of it, did pass 130 years; and from the time that Jacob went into Egypt until his posterity came out of it did pass 430 years; and from the coming out of Egypt to the building of Solomon's Temple in the fortieth year of his reign did pass 480 years; and from the building of the Temple to Jesus Christ, according to the computation of the chronographers, did pass 490 years. And thus by this calculation, which I have gathered out of the Holy Scriptures, the whole comes to about 4173 years and eight months more or less. But since the time of Jesus Christ hitherto, I leave it because of the diversity of opinion. Having calculated these present prophecies in accordance to the order of the chain which contains the revolution, and all by astronomical rule, and according to my natural instinct; after some time, and including in it the time Saturn takes to turn to come in on the 7th of the month of April until the 25th of August; Jupiter from the 14th of June to the 7th of October; Mars from the 27th of April till the 22nd of June; Venus from the 9th of April to the 22nd of May; Mercury from the 3rd of February to the 24th of the same; afterwards from the 1st of June to the 24th of the same; and from the 25th of September to the 16th of October, Saturn in Capricorn, Jupiter in Aquarius, Mars in Scorpio, Venus in Pisces, Mercury within a month in Capricorn, Aquarius in Pisces, the moon in Aquarius, the Dragon's head in Libra, the tail opposite to her sign. Following a conjunction of Jupiter and Mercury, with a quadrin aspect of Mars to Mercury, and the head of the Dragon shall be with a conjunction of Sol and Jupiter; the year shall be peaceful without eclipse.

Then the beginning of that year shall see a greater persecution against the Christian Church than ever was in Africa, and it shall be in the year 1792,* at which time everyone will think it a renovation of the age. After that the Roman people shall begin to stand upright again, and to put away the obscure darkness, receiving some of its former light, but now without great divisions and continual changes. Venice, after that, with great strength and power will lift up her wings so high that she will not be much inferior to the strength of ancient Rome. And at that time great Byzantine sails, joined with the Italians by the help and power of the North, shall hinder them so that those of Crete shall not keep their faith. The ships built by the ancient martial men will keep company with them under the waves of Neptune. In the Adriatic there shall be a great discord, what was united shall be put asunder, and what was before a great city shall become a house, including the Pampotan and Mesopotamia of Europe, in (19)45, and others to 41, 42, and 47. And

---

* Date of French Revolution.

in that time and those countries the infernal power shall rise against the Church of Jesus Christ. This shall be the second Antichrist, which shall persecute the said church and its true vicar by the means of the power of temporal kings, who through their ignorance shall be seduced by tongues more sharp than any sword in the hands of a madman.

The said reign of Antichrist shall not last but till the ending of him who was born of Age, and of the other in the city of Plancus (Lyons), accompanied by the elect of Modena, Fulcy by Ferrara, maintained by the Adriatic, Liguriens, and the proximity of the great Trinacria (Sicily). Afterwards the Gallic Ogmion shall pass the Mount Jovis (Barcelona), followed with such a number that even from afar off the Empire shall be presented with its grand law, and then and for some time after, shall be profusely spilled the blood of the innocents by the guilty raised on high. Then by great floods the memory of those things contained in such instruments, shall receive incalculable loss, even to the letters themselves. This will happen to the Northerns. By the Divine Will Satan will be bound once more, and universal peace shall be among men, and the Church of Jesus Christ shall be free from all tribulation, although the Azostains (debauchees) would desire to mix with the honey their pestilent seduction. This shall happen about the seventh millenary, when the sanctuary of Jesus Christ shall no more be trodden down by the unbelievers that shall come from the North. The world will then be near its great conflagration, although by the calculations of my prophecies, the course of time goes much further.

In the epistle that some years ago I dedicated to my son Caesar Nostradamus, I have openly enough declared some things without prognosticating. But here, Sir, are comprehended many great and wonderful events, which those that come after us shall see. And during the said astrological computation, in harmony with the Sacred Scriptures, the persecution of the clergy shall have its beginning in the power of the Northern Kings joined by the Eastern ones. And that persecution shall last eleven years, or a little less, at which time the chief Northern king shall fail, which years being ended, shall come in his stead a united Southern one, who shall yet more violently persecute the clergy of the Church for the space of three years by the apostolical seduction of one that shall have absolute power over the militant Church of God. The holy people of God and keepers of His law, and all order of religion, shall be grievously persecuted and afflicted, so much that the blood of the true ecclesiastical men shall flow all over. One of these horrid kings shall be praised by his followers for having spilt more human blood of the innocent clergymen than anybody has done to wine. The said king shall commit incredible crimes against the Church; human blood shall run through public streets and Churches, as water coming from an impetuous rain. Next, rivers shall be red with blood. In a sea fight the sea shall be red, so that one king will say to another, "Bellis rubuit navalibus aequor." * After that in the same year, and those following, shall happen the most horrible pestilence, caused by the famine preceding, and so great tribulations as ever did happen since the first foundation of the Christian Church throughout all the Latin regions, some marks remaining in some countries under Spain.

Then the third Northern king (Russia?), hearing the complaint of the people of his principal title, shall raise up so great an army, shall go through the limits of his last ancestors and progenitors, that they will all be set up again in their first state. The great Vicar of the Cope shall be restored in his former estate, but desolate and altogether forsaken, shall then go back to the sanctuary that was destroyed by Paganism, when the Old and New Testament will be thrust out and burnt. After that shall the Antichrist be the infernal prince. And in this last era all the kingdoms of Christianity and also of the unbelievers shall quake for the space of years, and there shall be more grievous wars and battles; towns, cities, castles and other buildings shall be burnt, desolated and destroyed with a great effusion of vestal blood, married women and widows ravished, sucking children dashed against the walls of towns, and so many evils shall be committed by the means of the infernal prince, Satan, that almost the entire world shall be undone and desolate.

Before these events many unusual birds shall cry through the air, crying, "Huy, huy." ("Now, now.") A little while after they shall vanish. After this shall have lasted a good while, there shall be renewed a reign of Saturn and a golden age. God the Creator shall say, hearing the affliction of His people, Satan shall be put and tied in the bottom of the deep, and there shall begin an age of universal peace between God and man. The ecclesiastical power shall return in force and Satan shall be bound for the space of a thousand years, and then shall be loosed again.

All these figures are justly fitted by the Sacred Scriptures to the celestial things, that is to say, Saturn, Jupiter and Mars, and others joined with them, as may be seen more at large in some of my quatrains. I would have calculated it more deeply, and coordinated one with the other, but seeing, O most excellent King, that some stand ready to censure me, I shall now withdraw my pen to its nocturnal repose.

"Multa etiam, O Rex potentissime proeclara, et sane in brevi ventura, sed omnia in hac tua Epistola, innectere non possumus, nec volumus, sed ad intellegenda quoedam facta, horrida fata pauca libanda sunt, quamvis tanta sit in omnes tua amplitudo et humanitas homines, deosque pietas, ut

----

* "The sea blushed red with the blood of naval fights."

solos amplissimo et Christianissimo Regis nomine, et ad quem summa totius religionis auctoritas deferatur dignus esse videare." * But I shall only beseech you, O most merciful King, by your singular and prudent goodness, to understand rather the desire of my heart, and the earnest desire I have to obey your most excellent Majesty, ever since my eyes were so near to your royal splendor, than the greatness of my word can attain to or deserve.

Faciebat   Michael Nostradamus
Solonoe Petrae Provincae

From Salon this 27th June, 1558

---

* "So many things, O most potent King of all, of the most remarkable kind are to happen soon, that I neither would nor could incorporate them all into this epistle; but in order to intelligently comprehend certain facts, a few horrible fated events must be set down in extract, although your amplitude and humanity toward mankind is so great, as is your piety to God, that you alone seem worthy of the great title of the most Christian King, and to whom the highest authority in all religion should be deferred."

1

Pau, nay, loron plus feu qu'a sang
sera,
Laude nager, fuir grand aux surrez,
Les aggassas entree refusera,
Pampon, Durance, les tiendra en-
serrez.

Pau, nay, loron, more in fire their
blood shall be,
Seen to swim, great ones shall run
to their surreys,
The aggassas shall refuse the entry,
Pampon, Durance shall keep them
enclosed.

This seemingly obscure and unintelligible quatrain conceals a complex
play on words by means of which Nostradamus predicts the advent of
Napoleon, viz., nay-pau-loron.

2

Condon & Aux & autour de Mi-
rande,
Je voy du ciel feu qui les environne,
Sol, Mars, conjoint au Lion, puis
Marmande,
Foudre, grand guerre, mur tombe
dans Garonne.

Condon and Aux, and about Mirande,
I see a fire from heaven that sur-
rounds them,
Sol, Mars, in conjunction with the
lion, and then Marmande
Lightning, great war, wall falls into
the Garonne.

Cities in France are named, all of which will suffer much military destruction.

3

Au fort chasteau de Vigilanne & Resviers,	In the strong castle of Vigilanne and Resviers,
Sera serre le puisnay de Nancy;	Shall be kept close the youngest son of Nancy,
Dedans Turin seront ards les premiers,	Within Turin, the first shall be burnt up,
Lors que de dueil Lyon sera transy.	When Lyons shall be overwhelmed with sorrow.

Contemporary politics, that loomed large at the time but which have since lost their significance, are here recorded.

4

Dedans Monech le Coq sera receu,	Within Monaco the Cock shall be received,
Le Cardinal de France apparoistra,	The Cardinal of France shall appear,
Par Logarion Romain sera deceu,	By Logarion Roman shall be deceived,
Foiblesse a l'Aigle, & force au Coq naistra.	Weakness to the Eagle, and strength to the Cock shall grow.

Monaco, then an Italian possession, admitted the French for the first time, persuaded by the policy of Cardinal Richelieu, the Gallic Cock being the gainer thereby.

5

Apparoistra temple luisant orne,	A brilliantly adorned temple shall appear,
La lampe & cierge a Borne & Bretueil,	The lamp and wax candle of Borne and Bretueil,
Pour la Lucerne le canton destorne,	For Lucerne the canton is turned,
Quand on verra le grand Coq cercueil.	When the great Cock shall be seen in his coffin.

After the death of a French King the glory of France will be at its zenith.

6

Charte fulgure a Lyon apparente
Luysant, print Malte, subit sera
  estrainte,
Sardon, Mauris traitera decevante,
Geneve a Londres a Coq trahison
  fainte.

A thundering light at Lyons appearing,
Brightly, Malta instantly shall be
  put out,
Sardon shall treat Mauris deceit-
  fully,
From Geneva to London, the Cock
  a pretended treason.

Tremendous aerial bombardments shall devastate France and extend
even to Malta and Sardinia. The French shall pretend to be unfaithful
to Geneva and London.

7

Verceil, Milan donra intelligence,
Dedans Tycin sera fait la paye,
Courir par Seine eau, sang feu par
  Florence,
Unique choir d'haut en bas faisant
  maye.

Verceil, Milan shall give intelligence,
In the Ticin shall the peace be
  made,
Run through Seine water, blood,
  fire through Florence,
Only one shall fall from top to
  bottom making friends.

Italian cities in northern Italy shall make peace with the French;
only one person shall suffer by this act.

8

Pres de Linterne dans de tonnes
  fermez,
Chivaz fera pour l'Aigle la menee,
L'esleu casse, luy ses gens enfermez,
Dedans Turin rapt espouse em-
  menee.

Near Linterne, enclosed within the
  farms,
Chivas shall drive the plot for the
  Eagle,
The elect dismissed, he and his
  men shut up,
Within Turin, the bride raped
  and carried away.

Linterne and Chivas are small towns in Italy. In a plot to gain power,
the local government will be overcome and the prize seized.

9

Pendant que l'Aigle & le Coq a
Savone
Seront unis, Mer, Levant & Hon-
grie,
L'armee a Naples, Palerme, Mar-
que d'Ancone,
Rome, Venise, par barbe horrible
crie.

While the Eagle and Cock at Sa-
vonna
Shall be united, Sea, Levant and
Hungary,
The army at Naples, Palermo,
Mark of Ancona,
Rome, Venice, cry because of a
horrid barb.

The American Eagle and the French Cock shall be in a united campaign against the Italians, Hungarians, etc., and the Italian armies shall
be in great distress because of a new and punishing weapon used against
them.

10

Puanteur grande sortira de Lausanne,
Qu'on ne scaura l'origine du fait,
L'on mettra hors tout la gent loing-
taine,
Feu veu au ciel, peuple estranger
deffait.

A great stink shall come forth from
Lausanne,
So that no one shall know the ori-
gin of it,
They shall put out all the foreign-
ers,
Fire seen in heaven, a strange peo-
ple defeated.

The presages contained in this quatrain are now faits accomplis, written
with a bloody pen on the pages of History. The Conference of Lausanne
is predicted and the signing of many diplomatic instruments, including
the Treaty of Peace itself. Cynically Nostradamus refers to the "stink that
shall come forth from Lausanne," indicating the cynicism of the partici-
pants; he even shows the blind faith with which these documents were
accepted by the people of the world. He foretells that the "peace" shall
be short-lived; that minorities shall be persecuted; that the fires of war
shall be rekindled and again sweep over the earth.

11

Peuple infiny paroistra a Vicence,
Sans force feu brusler la basilique,
Pres de Lunage deffait grande de
Valence,
Lors que Venise par mort prendra
pique.

Infinite number of people shall appear at Vincenza,
Without force, fire shall burn in
the basilick,
Near Lunage the great one of Va-
lencia shall be defeated,
When Venice by death shall be
piqued.

Basilick is the name of an old Italian fort which was heavily fortified
by cannon. The sense of this verse then is that Italy will be engaged in
a war.

12

Apparoistra aupres de Buffalore
L'haut & procere entre dedans Milan,
L'Abbe de Foix avec ceux de Sainct Maure,
Feront la forbe habillez en vilain.

Near the Bufalore shall appear
The high and tall, come into Milan,
The Abbot of Foix with those of Saint Maure,
Shall make the deceit, being clothed like a villain.

Foix and St. Mauve are towns in France. This concerns a debate among the clergymen of these communities.

13

Le croise frere par amour effrenee,
Fera par Praytus Bellerophon mourir,
Classe a mil ans la femme forcenee,
Beu le bruvage, tous deux apres perrir.

The crossed brother through unbridled love,
Shall cause Bellerophon to be killed by Praytus,
Fleet to thousand years, the women frantic,
The drink being drunk, both after that shall perish.

Bellerophon was a hero of Greek mythology. He fell from his steed Pegasus and perished, while attempting to fly to heaven.

14

Le grand credit, d'or, d'argent, l'abundance,
Aveuglera par libide l'honneur;
Cogneu sera d'adultere l'offense,
Qui parviendra a son grand deshonneur.

The great credit, of gold, of silver, great abundance,
Shall blind honor by lust,
The offense of the adulterer shall be known,
Which shall come to his great dishonor.

A period of inflation accompanied by laxity of morals shall sweep the civilized world.

15

Vers Aquilon grands efforts par hommasse	Towards the North great endeavours by a masculine woman,
Presque l'Europe & l'univers vexer,	To trouble Europe, and almost all the world,
Les deux eclipses mettre en telle chasse,	The two eclipses shall be put to flight,
Et aux Pannons vie & mort renforcer.	And shall reinforce life, and death to the Poles.

Catherine the Great, 1729–96, Empress of Russia, is here indicated. She was a disciple and friend of the Encyclopaedists, especially of Voltaire, and although she started out with the intention of following their principles in the matters of domestic reform, it was short-lived and completely shattered by the advent of the French Revolution. During her reign she engineered the shameless partitions of Poland, to the great detriment of that nation.

16

Au lieu que Jieson feit sa nef fabriquer,	In the place where Jason carried his ship to be built,
Si grand deluge sera & si subite,	So great a flood shall be and so sudden,
Qu'on n'aura lieu ne terres s'ataquer,	That there shall be neither place nor land to save themselves,
L'onde monter Fesulan Olympique.	The waves shall climb upon the Olympic Fesulan.

Mount Olympus, the mythical home of the gods, is where Jason built his ship, for the Argonauts' voyage. The sense of this stanza is that an inexorable movement shall engulf all those in authority and a new order be created.

17

Les bien aisez subit seront desmis,	Those that were at ease shall be put down,
Le monde mis par les trois freres en trouble,	The world shall be put in trouble by three brothers,
Cite marine saisiront ennemis,	The maritime city shall be seized by its enemies,
Faim, feu, sang, peste, & de tous maux le double.	Hunger, fire, blood, plague, and double of all evils.

Social conditions are to change; world wide repercussions with an abundance of misfortunes shall beset all, due to the machinations of three brothers.

18

De Flore issue de sa mort sera
cause,
Un temps devant par jeusne & vi-
elle bueyre,
Car les trois lys luy feront telle
pause,
Par son fruit sauve comme chair
crue mueyre.

Issued from Flora, shall be the
cause of her death,
A time before, by fasting and stale
drink,
For the three lilies, shall make her
such a pause,
Saved by her fruit, as raw flesh
dead.

The three lilies represent the Fleur de Lys, symbol of France. After
a period of want and suffering France will be succored by the sacrifices of
her patriots.

19

A soustenir la grand cappe troublee,
Pour l'esclaireir les rouges marcheront,
De mort famille sera presque acca-
blee,
Les rouges rouges, le rouge assom-
meront.

To maintain up the great troubled
cloak,
The red ones shall march to clear
it,
A family shall be almost crushed
to death,
The red reds, shall knock down
the red one.

A conspiracy of cardinals against the Pope is here described.

20

Le faux message par election feinte,
Courir par urban rompue pache ar-
reste,
Voix aceptees, de sang chapelle
tainte,
Et a un autre l'empire contraincte.

The false message, by a fraudulent
election,
Shall be stopped from going about
the town,
Voices shall be bought, and a
chapel tinted with blood,
By another, who contests the rule.

By bribery a fraudulent rumor shall be perpetrated, and a bloody
struggle will arise in the church.

21

Au port de Agde trois fustes entreront,	In the Port of Agda, three ships shall enter,
Portant infection avec foy & pestilence,	Carrying with them infection and pestilence,
Passant le pont mil milles embleront,	Going beyond the bridge, they shall carry away thousands.
Et le pont rompre a tierce resistance.	At the third resistance the bridge shall be broken.

Agda, a city in France, shall be the entering point for foreign propaganda, eventually conquering the country thereby.

22

Gorsan, Narbonne, par le sel advertir,	Gorsan, Narbonne, by the salt shall give notice,
Tucham, la grace Parpignan trahie,	To Tucham, the grace Perpignan betrayed,
La ville rouge n'y voudra consentir,	The red city will not give consent to it,
Par haulte Voldrap gris vie faillie.	By high Voldrap, gray life ended.

French cities are named; by an edict from the "red city" (Rome) help will be given to their inhabitants.

23

Lettres trouvees de la Royne les coffres,	Letters found in the Queen's coffers,
Point de subscrit sans aucun nom d'autheur,	No superscription, no name of author,
Par la police seront cachez les offres,	By the police shall be concealed the offers,
Qu'on ne scaura qui sera l'amateur.	So that no one shall know who shall be the lover.

The affair of The Diamond Necklace, involving Cagliostro, the master swindler, Cardinal Rohan, and the Queen of France, is here indicated.

24

Lieutenant a l'entree de l'huys
Assommera la grand de Perpignan,
En se cuidant sauver a Montper-
tuis,
Sera deceu bastard de Lusignan.

The lieutenant shall at the entrance
of the door,
Knock down the great one of Perpignan,
Thinking to save himself at the
mountain straits,
And the bastard of Lusignan shall
be deceived.

Perpignan, at the frontier between Spain and France, shall be the scene of many disgraceful events.

25

Coeur de l'amant ouvert d'amour
furtive,
Dans le ruisseau fera ravir la Dame,
Le demy mal contrefera lascive,
Le pere a deux privera corps de
l'ame.

The lover's heart, being by a furtive love
Shall cause the lady to be ravished
in the brook,
The lascivious shall counterfeit
half a discontent.
The father shall deprive them both
of their souls.

A father, discovering his mistress and his son in a compromising situation, shall kill both of them.

26

De Carones trouvez en Barcelonne,
Mys descouvers, lieu terrouers &
ruyne,
Le grand qui tient ne voudra Pam-
plonne,
Par l'abbaye de Montferrat bruyne.

From Carons found in Barcelona,
Found discovered, in place of soil
and ruin,
The great that hold, will not Pam-
pelone,
By the abbey of Montserrat, a fine
rain.

This evidently refers to the discovery of some sort of plant, which eventually becomes one of the staple foods of the poor people of Europe.

27

La voye Auxelle l'un sur l'autre
    fornix,
Du muy de ser hor mis brave &
    genest,
L'escript d'Empereur le Phoenix,
Veu en celuy ce qu'a nul autre
    n'est.

The way Auxelle, one arch upon
    another,
Being brave and gallant put out the
    iron vessel,
The writing of the Emperor, the
    Phoenix,
In it shall be seen, what nowhere
    else is.

The return of Napoleon from Elba is here compared to the rising of
the phoenix from its ashes.

28

Les simulachres d'or et d'argent
    enflez,
Qu'apres le rapt, lac au feu furent
    jettez,
Au descouvert estaincts tous &
    troublez,
Au marbre escripts, perscripts in-
    teriettez.

The idols swollen with gold and
    silver,
Which after the rape were thrown
    into the lake and fire,
Being discovered after the putting
    out of the fire,
Shall be written in marble, pre-
    cepts being inserted.

An incident of antiquity is described here: the stealing of gold and
silver idols from a temple, their desecration by fire and water, and the
subsequent erection of a marble monument inscribed in their honor.

29

Au quart pilier l'on sacre a Saturne,
Par tremblant terre & deluge
    fendu,
Sous l'edifice Saturin trouves urne,
D'or Capion, ravy & puis rendu.

At the fourth pillar where they
    sacrifice to Saturn,
Shaken by an earthquake and a
    flood,
A funeral urn shall be found under
    that Saturnin edifice,
Full of gold, stolen, and then re-
    turned.

A funeral urn, in which the ancient Romans kept the ashes of their great
ones, shall be uncovered by an upheaval, but gold will be found in it
instead.

30

Dedans Tholose non loing de Belu-
zer,
Faisant un puis loing, palais d'es-
pectacle
Thresor trouve un chacun ira vexer,
Et en deux locs tout & pres des
vesacle.

Within Toulouse not far from Be-
luzer,
Digging a well, for the palace of
spectacle,
A treasure found that shall vex
everyone,
In two parcels and near the Basacle.

In Toulouse, in the industrial part of the city called the Basacle, a
Pandora's box will be found.

31

Premier grand fruict le Prince de
Pesquiere;
Mais puis viendra bien & cruel
malin,
Dedans Venise perdra sa gloire
fiere,
Et mis a mal par plus joyue Celin.

The first great fruit the Prince of
Pescaire,
But he shall become very cruel and
malicious,
He shall lose his fierce pride in
Venice,
And shall be put to evil by the
young Turks.

Pescaire, a town near Naples, will be the birthplace of a statesman.
Rising to power at an early age, he will become arrogant and over-confident.
At the height of his career he will be killed in a duel with a Turk.

32

Garde toy roy Gaulois de ton ne-
pveu,
Qui fera tant que ton unique fils,
Sera meurtry a Venus faisant voeu,
Accompagne denuict que trois &
six.

Take heed, O French King, of thy
nephew,
Who shall cause that thine only
son,
Shall be murdered making a vow
to Venus,
Accompanied with three and six.

Napoleon III, nephew of Napoleon Bonaparte, is referred to here;
the significance being the complete disintegration of Napoleonic prestige
under his reign.

33

Le grand naistra de Veronne & Vincense,	The great one of Verona and Vincenza shall be born,
Qui portera un surnon bien indigne,	Who shall bear a very unworthy name,
Qui a Venise voudra faire vengeance,	Who shall endeavor at Venice to avenge himself,
Luy mesme prins homme du guet & signe.	But he shall be taken by a policeman.

Another reference to Mussolini, this retells the sordid details of his ignoble fate.

34

Apres victoire du Lion au Lion,	After the victory of the Lion against the Lion,
Sur la montagne de Jura Secatombe,	Upon the mountain of Jura, Hecatombe,
Delues, & brodes septiesme million,	Of them decorated, the seventh million,
Lyon, Ulme a Mausol mort & tombe.	Lyons, Ulme fall dead at Mausol.

The mention of places in Switzerland, France, Germany, and the word "lion" taken as meaning Great Britain, we believe that these things in connection with the phrases "seventh million" and "fall dead" refer to the world wars and their casualties.

35

Dedans l'entree de Garonne & Blaye,	Within the entrance of Garonne and Blaye,
Et la forest non loing de Damazan,	And the forest not far from Damazan,
Du Marsaves gelees, puis gresle & bize,	Of Marsaves frosts, then hail and north wind,
Dordonnois gelle par erreur de Mezan.	Dordonois frozen by the error of Mezan.

This describes an unusually bad winter in Europe—rivers frozen solid, terrible winds and hailstorms raging throughout the land.

36

Sera commis contre Oinde a Duche,	The Duche shall be committed against Oinde,
Se Saulne, & sainct Aubin & Beloeuvre,	Of Saulne and Saint Aubin and Beloeuvre,
Paver de marbre, de tous loing espluche,	To have with marble and of towers well picked,
Non Bleteran resister & chef d'oeuvre.	Not Bleteran to resist, and master stroke.

In these latter-day prophecies, we find a few obscure and unintelligible verses. This quite apparently is one of them.

37

Le forteresse aupres de la Thamise,	The fortress near the Thames,
Cherra par lors, le Roy dedans serre,	Shall fall, then the King that was kept within
Aupres du pont sera veu en chemisee,	Shall be seen near the bridge in his shirt,
Un devant mort, puis dans le fort barre.	One dead before, then in the fort kept close.

The execution of Charles I of England is here predicted. He was beheaded in the city of London on January 30, 1649.

38

Le Roy de Bloys dans Avignon regner,	The King of Blois in Avignon shall reign,
Un autre fois le peuple emonopole,	Another time the people do murmur,
Dedans le Rhosne par murs fera baigner,	He shall cause in the Rhone to be bathed through the walls,
Jusques a cinq, le dernier pres de Nolle.	As many as five, the last shall be near Nole.

A King of France shall occupy Avignon, a city in France belonging to a Pope. Some of the inhabitants, objecting to this seizure, shall be thrown over the city walls into the river.

39

Qu'aura este par prince Bizantin,
Sera tollu par prince de Tholose,
Lay foy de Foix, par le chef Tho-
   lentin,
Luy faillira ne refusant l'espouse.

What shall have been by a Byzantine prince,
Shall be taken away by the prince
   of Tholose,
The faith of Foix by the chief Tho-
   lentin,
Shall fail him, not refusing the
   spouse.

The French shall occupy territory in the Near East, formerly ruled by
the Mohammedans.

40

Le sang du juste par Taur & la
   Dorade,
Pour se venger contre les Saturnins
Au nouveau lac plongeront la
   Mainade,
Puis marcheront contre les Alba-
   nins.

The blood of the just by Taur and
   Dorade,
To avenge themselves against the
   Saturnins,
In the new lake shall plunge the
   Mainade,
Then shall march against the Al-
   banins.

It is an almost impossible task to attempt to place geographically the
cities and people named, since they bear no resemblance to any known
historical references. The event evidently pertains to a quarrel and a revenge.

41

Esleu sera Renard ne sonnant mot,
Faisant le saint public, vivant pain
   d'orge,
Tyrannizer apres tant a un cop,
Mettant la pied des plus grands
   sur la gorge.

A fox shall be elected that said
   nothing,
Making a public saint, living with
   barley bread,
Shall tyrannize after upon a sudden
And put his foot upon the throat
   of the greatest.

A prediction regarding a Pope to be elected, who, reputedly a saint,
after attaining power shall be a great tyrant.

42

Par avarice, par force & violence,	By avarice, and force and violence,
Viendra vexer les siens chefs d'Orleans,	Shall come to vex his own chief of Orleans,
Pres Sainct Memire assault & resistance,	Near St. Memire, assault and resistance,
Mort dans sa tente, diront qu'il dort leans.	Dead in his tent, they shall say, he sleepeth there.

At St. Memire, a French town, a mutiny against the tyrannical local government chiefs shall result in the murder of one of them. To protect the murderer, the inhabitants shall, for a long time, attempt to conceal the body from the authorities.

43

Par le decide de deux choses bastars,	By the decision of two things, bastards,
Nepveu du sang occupera le regne,	Nephew of the blood shall occupy the government,
Dedans lectoure seront les coups de dards,	Within Lectore shall be blows of darts,
Nepveu par pleira l'enseigne.	Nephew through fear shall fold up his ensigns.

A forecast of conditions in France, during a period of unrest, when low-born persons shall seize power.

44

Le procree naturel l'Ogmion,	The natural begotten of Ogmion,
De sept a neuf du chemin destorner,	From seven to nine shall be put out of the way,
A roy de longue & amy au my hom,	To king of long, and friend to half man,
Doit a Navarre fort de Pau prosterner.	Ought to Navarre prostrate the fort of Pau.

An illegitimate son of a great monarch shall attempt to murder the king.

45

La main escharpe & la jambe bandee,	The hand on a scarf and the leg bandaged,
Louis puisne de palais partira,	The younger Louis shall depart from the palace,
Au mot du guet la mort sera tardee,	At the watchword his death shall be protracted,
Puis dans le temple a Pasques saignera.	Then afterwards at Easter he shall bleed in the temple.

The younger, meaning the last great one of the line of Kings named Louis (Louis XVI), shall be executed.

46

Pol Mensolee mourra trois lieues du Rhone,	Paul Mensolee shall die leagues from the Rhone,
Fuis les deux prochains Tarare destrois;	Avoid the two straits near the Tarara,
Car Mars fera le plus horrible throsne,	For Mars shall keep such a horrible throne,
De coq & d'aigle, de France freres trois.	Of cock and eagle, of France three brothers.

Paul Mensolee is warned to avoid the roads to Mt. Tarare, as they are infested with thieves and murderers.

47

Lac Trasmenian portera tesmoignage,	Trasmenian Lake shall bear witness,
Des conjurez sarez dedans Perouse,	Of the conspirators shut up in Perugia,
Un despolle contrefera le sage,	A Des Polle shall simulate the prudent,
Tuant Tedesq de Sterne & Minuse.	Killing Germans of Sterne and Minuse.

A reference to the victory of Hannibal at Lake Trasimenus near the town of Perugia, Italy.

48

Saturne en Cancer, Jupiter avec
Mars,
Dedans Fevrier, Caldondon, salva-
terre,
Sault, Castallon, assailly de trois
pars,
Fres de Verbiesque, conflit mor-
telle guerre.

Saturn in Cancer, Jupiter with
Mars,
In February Caldondon, ground
saved,
The Republic assaulted on three
sides,
Near Verbiesque, fight and mortal
war.

The oft-repeated warning of a great war is here contained.

49

Satur au beuf, Jove en l'eau, Mars
en fleiche,
Six de Fevrier mortalite donra,
Ceux de Tardaigne a Bruge si
grand breche,
Qu'a Ponterose chef Barbarin
mourra.

Saturn in bull, Jupiter in water,
Mars in arrow,
The sixth of February shall give
mortality,
Those of Tardaigne shall make in
Bruges so great a breach,
That the chief Barbarin shall die
at Ponterose.

The event indicated shall occur under the influence of these planets,
when Saturn is in Taurus, Jupiter in Aquarius, and Mars in Sagittarius.
By the death of the chief Barbarin is meant the death of Pope Urban VIII.

50

La pestilence l'entour de Capadille,
Une aurte faim pres de Sagone
s'appreste
Le chevalier bastard de bon senille,
Au grand de Thunes fera tranche la
teste.

The plague shall be round about
Capadillo,
Another famine cometh near to
that of Sagunce,
The knight bastard of the good
old man,
Shall cause the great one of Tunis
to be beheaded.

Plague and famine shall cause great suffering in both Italy and Spain.
Political unrest will set in during this time of stress.

51

Le Bizantin faisant oblation,
Apres avoir Cordube a soy reprinse;
Son chemin long, repos pampla-
tion,
Mer passant proy par la Cologne
prinse.

The Byzantin, making an offering,
After he hath taken Cordova to
himself again,
His road long, rest, contemplation,
Crossing the sea hath a prey by
Cologne.

The reference here is to the abdication of Charles V, King of Spain.
He retired to a small house on the grounds of a monastery and spent the
last years of his life in study and contemplation.

52

Le roy de Bloys Avignon regner,
D'Amboise & seme viendra le long
de Lyndre,
Ongle a Poitiers sainctes aisles
ruyner
Devant Bony.

The King of Blois shall reign in
Avignon,
He shall come from Amboise and
Seme, along the Linden,
A nail at Poitiers shall ruin his holy
wing,
Before Bony.

One must delve deeply into this quatrain to gather its full meaning.
It depicts the phenomenal rise of Napoleon, and even refers to the un-
precedented procedure of the Pope's journey to Paris to crown Napoleon
as Emperor.

53

Dedans Bologne voudra laver ses
fautes,
Il ne pourra au temple du soleil,
Il volera faisant chose si hautes,
En hierarchie n'en fut oneq un
pareil.

Within Boulogne, he shall want to
wash himself of his faults,
In the church of the sun, but he
shall not be able,
He shall fly, doing things too high,
That in the hierarchy was never
the like.

This predicts that Cardinal Richelieu, who attained greater secular
heights than any other man of the church, shall wish to go on a holy
pilgrimage, but shall defer it too long and shall be prevented from doing
so by his death.

54

Soubs la couleur de traicte mariage,
Fait magnanime par grand Chyren
 Selin,
Quintin, Arras recouvrez au voy-
 age,
D'Espagnols fait second banc
 Macelin.

Under the pretense of a treaty of
 marriage,
A magnanimous act shall be done
 by Henry the Great,
St. Quentin and Arras, recovered
 in the journey,
Of Spaniards shall be made a
 second Macelin bench.

A King of France, Henry the Great, through a pretended treaty of
marriage, shall acquire new territories. The word Macelin is from the
Latin word Macellum which means shambles. And the meaning here is
that there will be a war and subsequent havoc in Spain.

55

Entre deux fleuves se verra enserre,
Tonneaux a caques unis a passer
 outre,
Huict ponts rompus chef a tant
 enferre,
Enfans parfaicts sont jugulez en
 coultre.

Between two rivers he shall find
 himself shut up,
Tuns and casks put together to
 pass over,
Eight bridges broken, the chief at
 last in prison,
Perfect children shall have their
 throats cut.

A commander of an army, about to launch an attack, shall be tem-
porarily stopped by the destruction of all bridges across the river near
which the enemy is encamped. Causing a pontoon bridge to be built,
he and his men will cross over and by a surprise attack will overcome
and capture the enemy.

56

La bande foible le terre occupera,
Ceux du haut lieu feront horribles
 cris,
Le gros troupeau d'estre coin
 troublera,
Tombe pres D. nebro descouvert
 les escrits.

The weak party shall occupy the
 ground,
Those of the high places shall make
 horrible cries,
It shall trouble the great flock in
 the right corner,
He falleth near D. nebro discov-
 ereth the writings.

The continuing struggles between "left" and "right" political parties
are here predicted. The obscurely worded last line leads us to believe
that Nostradamus purposely wished to withhold his views as to the ultimate outcome.

57

De souldat simple parveindre en empire,	From a simple soldier, he shall come to have supreme command,
De robe courte parviendra a la longue,	From a short gown he shall come to a long one,
Vaillant aux armes, en eglise ou plus pire,	Valiant in arms, no worse man in the church,
Vexer les prestres comme l'eau faict l'esponge.	He shall vex the priests, as water does a sponge.

A perfect picture of Oliver Cromwell: From a simple soldier he rose to be Lord Protector; from a student in the university he became a graduate of Oxford; and as for vexing the clergy, there was no one of his day who caused them more trouble.

58

Regne en querelle aux freres divise,	A kingdom in dispute and divided between the brothers,
Prendre les armes & le nom Britannique,	To take the arms and the Britannic name,
Tiltre d'Anglican sera tard advise,	And the English title, he shall advise himself late.
Surprins de nuict, mener a l'air Gallique.	Surprised in the night and carried into the French air.

This predicts the abdication of King Edward VIII, and the accession to the throne of his brother, Duke of York, who became George VI.

59

Par deux fois haut, par deux fois mis a bas,	Twice set up high, and twice brought down,
L'Orient aussi l'Occident foiblira,	The East also the West shall weaken,
Son adversaire apres plusieurs combats,	His adversary after many fights,
Par mer chasse au besoing faillira.	Expelled by sea, shall fail in need.

The role of Germany in World Wars I and II is predicted. Both times the goal of that country was world domination, and both times she was defeated by the combined efforts of East and West.

CENTURY IX
50 60 page 294

60

Premier an Gaule, premier en
    Romanie,
Par mer & terre aux Anglois &
    Paris,
Merveilleux faits par celle grand
    mesnie,
Violant, Terax perdra le Norlaris.

The first in France, the first in
    Romania,
By sea and land to the English and
    Paris,
Wonderful deeds by that great
    company,
By ravishing, Terax shall ruin Nor-
    laris.

    The rapidity of the Nazi expansion (the "blitz" technique) both East
and West during the dark days of World War II, the wonderful yet vain resistance of the conquered peoples, the ravishing of the countries—all is
here prognosticated.

61

Jamais par le decouvrement du jour
Ne parviendra au signe sceptrifere
Que tous ses siege ne soient en
    sejour,
Portant au coq don du Tag amisere.

Never by the discovering of the day
He shall attain to the scepter bear-
    ing sign,
Till all his martial trials be settled,
Carrying to the cock, a gift from
    Der Tag of misery.

    Three factors in this verse—the use of the alien word "Tag," the
warning of war, and the reference to the "Cock" (France)—lead us to
believe that here is a prognostication of the now infamous words "Der
Tag," which was Germany's rallying cry for the day of vengeance and
hoped-for triumph over the democracies.

62

Lors qu'on verra expiler le sainct
    temple,
Plus grand du Rhosne & sacres
    prophaner,
Par eux naistra pestilence si ample,
Roy faict injuste ne fera con-
    damner.

When one shall see spoiled the
    holy temple,
The greatest of the Rhone, and
    sacred things profaned,
From them shall come so great a
    pestilence,
That the King being unjust shall
    not condemn them.

    When the city of Lyons, the greatest on the Rhone River, is invaded
and pillaged, a pestilence will descend upon the city, destroying both inhabitants and invaders.

63

Quand l'adultere blesse sans coup aura	When the adulterer wounded without a blow,
Meurdry la femme & le fils par despit,	Shall have murdered the wife and son by spite,
Famme assoumes l'enfant estranglera;	The woman knocked down, shall strangle the child,
Huict captifs prins s'estouffer sans respit.	Eight taken prisoners, and stifled without tarrying.

A tragic story is told here, of an adulterer who, through his philandering, contracts a contagious disease and in turn infects his wife and child. Being upbraided by his wife, he attempts to murder her and his son and then flees from the scene. She, dying, strangles her child. Without attempting to investigate the facts of the case, eight innocent persons are hanged for these two murders.

64

Dedans les Isles les enfans transportez,	In the Islands the children shall be transported,
Les deux de sept seront en desespoir;	The two of seven shall be in despair,
Ceux du terrouer en seront supportez,	Those of the company shall be supported by
Nom pelle prins, des ligues fuy l'espoir.	Nompelle taken, avoid the hope of the league.

Two royal children (of a family of seven) shall be exiled from their country, and despite the attempts of a current movement to recall them, they shall not return for many years.

65

Le vieux frustre du principal espoir,	The old man frustrated of his chief hope,
Il parviendra au chef de son empire;	He shall attain to the head of the empire,
Vingt mois tiendra le regne a grand, pouvoir,	Twenty months he shall keep the kingdom with great power,
Tiran, cruel en delaissant un pire.	Tyrant, cruel, and leaving a worse one.

Louis XVIII, long frustrated in his ambition to rule France, finally gained the throne in 1814 (at the age of 59) after the downfall of Napoleon.

66

Quand l'escriture D. M. trouvee,
Et cave antique a lamp descouverte,
Loy, Roy & Prinse Ulpian esprou-
vee,
Pavillon Royne & Duc sous la
couverte.

When the writing D. M. shall be
found,
And an ancient cave discovered
with a lamp.
Law, King, and Prince Ulpian tried,
Tent, Queen and Duke under the
cover.

Nostradamus here predicts the event of the re-discovery of his writings and the great new meanings that will be found contained in them.

67

Par. Car. Nersas, a ruine grand dis-
corde,
Ne l'un ne l'autre n'aura election,
Nersas du peuple aura amour &
concorde,
Ferrare, Collone grand protection.

Par. Car. Nersas, to ruin great discord
Neither one nor the other shall be
elected,
Nersas shall have of the people love
and concord,
Ferrara, Colonna shall have great
protection.

A great variance of opinion shall lead to strife over the election of a Pope, and as a result the two leading candidates will be defeated and a hitherto unknown will gain that high honor.

68

Vieux Cardinal par le jeune deceu,
Hors de sa charge se verra desarme,
Arles ne monstres double soit
aperceu,
Et l'Aqueduct & le Prince em-
baume.

An old Cardinal, by a young one
shall be deceived,
And shall see himself out of his
position,
Arles do not show, a double
strength perceived,
And the Aqueduct, and the em-
balmed Prince.

Intrigue and vying for power shall flourish among Princes of the Church, and French cities will take sides in the struggle.

69

Aupres du jeune se vieux Ange
 baisser,
Et le viendra sur monter a la fin;
Dix ans esgaux aux plus vieux
 rabaisser,
De trois deux l'un huictiesme Seraphin.

Near the young one the old angel
 shall bow,
And shall at last overcome him,
Ten years equal, to make the old
 one stoop,
Of three, two, one, the eighth a
 Seraphin.

An old man (referred to as an angel) shall humbly defer to a young man, even through he is aware that he is being cheated. After ten years the old one shall turn upon and overcome the young villain. (The mythical allusions in the last line seem to have no particular meaning.)

70

Il entrera vilain, meschant, infame
Tyrannisant la Mesopotamie
Tous amis faict d'adulterine dame,
Terre horrible noir de physiogno-
 mie.

He shall come in villain, wicked,
 infamous,
To tyrannize Mesopotamia,
He maketh all friends by an adul-
 terous lady,
Foul, horrid, black, in his physi-
 ognomy.

The country near Babylon shall be terrorized by a person of the Negro race.

71

Croistra le nombre si grand des
 Astronomes,
Chassez, bannis & livres censurez,
L'an mil six cens & sept par sacre
 glomes,
Que nul aux sacres ne seront as-
 seurez.

The number of Astronomers shall
 grow so great,
Driven away, banished, books cen-
 sured,
The year one thousand six hundred
 and seven years by Glomes,
That none shall be secure in sacred
 places.

Nostradamus dates all events from A. D. 325 (Council of Nicaea); thus 1607 plus 325 equals 1932. On January 30, 1933 Hitler became Chancellor of Germany, ushering in the era of the burning of books, the banishment of men of science, religion and art, the crushing of all culture that did not concur with Nazi doctrines.

72

Champ Perusin O l'enorme deffaite
Et le conflict tout aupres de
Ravenne,
Passage sacre lors qu'on fera la
feste,
Vainqueur vaincu, cheval manger
l'avenne.

Perugian field, O the enormous defeat,
And the fight about Ravenna,
Sacred passage when the feast shall
be celebrated,
The victorious vanquished, the
horse to eat up his oats.

Perugia and Ravenna are cities in Italy, where a decisive battle will be
fought on a holiday.

73

Soldat barbare le grand roy frappera,
In justement non eslongne de
mort,
L'avare mere du faict cause sera,
Conjurateur & regne en grand
remort.

A barbarous soldier shall strike the
king,
Unjustly, not far from death,
The covetous mother shall be the
cause of it,
The conspirator and kingdom in
great remorse.

The meaning is so plain, that to interpret it would be superfluous.

74

En terre neuve bien avant Roy
entre,
Pendant subges luy viendront faire
acueil,
Sa perfidie aura tel recontre,
Qu'aux citadins lieu de feste &
receuil.

In a new land, well after a King
enters,
Whilst his subjects shall come to
welcome him,
His perfidy shall find such an accident,
To the citizens it shall be received
instead of feasts.

An unpopular ruler shall die while on tour in a conquered land. The
citizens shall be joyful thereat.

75

Le pere & fils seront meurdris en-
semble,
Le prefecteur dedans son pavillon
La mere a Tours du fils ventre aura
  enfle,
Cache verdure de fueilles papillon.
	The father and son shall be mur-
	dered together,
	The governor shall be so in his tent,
	At Tours the mother shall be got
	  with child by her son,
	Conceal the greenness with butter-
	fly leaves.

This depicts murder, violence and incest in the city of Tours—and the fruit of the incest shall be strangled at birth and secretly buried, the small grave covered with grass and leaves and left forever unmarked.

76

Plus Macelin que Roy en Angle-
terre,
Lieu obscur nay par force aura
  l'empire,
Lasche, sans foy, sans loy, seignera
  terre,
Son temps s'approche si pres que
  je souspire.
	More Macelin than King in Eng-
	land,
	Born in obscure place, by force
	  shall rule the empire,
	Of loose morals, without faith,
	  without law, the ground shall
	  bleed.
	His time is drawing so near that I
	  sigh.

Macelin is from the Latin word Macellum, meaning shambles. A ruler of England is to come, who will be one of the world's worst tyrants and will bring about the near ruin of his country.

77

L'Antechrist trois bien trois anni-
chilez,
Vingt & sept ans sang durera sa
  guerre,
Les heretiques morts; captifs exilez,
Son corps humain eau rougie,
  gresler terre.
	By Anti-Christ, three shall be
	  brought to nothing,
	His war shall last seven and twenty
	  years,
	The heretics dead, prisoners exiled,
	  exiled,
	Blood, human body, water made
	  red, earth shrunk.

1917 – 1944 – communism.

In 1918, defeated Germany (Anti-Christ) laid the foundations for her dream of world conquest, which came to an end exactly as Nostradamus predicted, twenty-seven years later in 1945.

78

Un Bragamas avec la langue torte
Viendra des dieux rompre le sanc-
    tuaire,
Aux heretiques il ouvrira la porte,
En suscitant l'eglise militaire.

A Bragamas with his harmful
    tongue,
Shall come and break the God's
    sanctuary,
He shall open the gates to heretics,
By raising the militant church.

The word "Bragamas" denotes a braggard, and the meaning of the
verse is that he shall cause great harm to God's sanctuary (the Roman
Catholic Church) by his boastful and false claims of great power.

79

Qui par fer pere perdra, nay de
    Nonnaire,
De gorgon sur la fera sang per-
    fetant,
En terre estrange fera si tout de
    taire,
Qui bruslera luy mesme & son
    entante.

He who by iron shall destroy his
    father, born in Nonnaire,
Shall in the end carry the blood of
    the gorgon,
Shall in a strange country make all
    so silent,
That he shall burn himself, and his
    double talk.

The reference here is to a man of ruthlessness and cunning who, by
these traits, shall gain power over a great country. Suppressing all individ-
ual opinion and freedom of speech, he shall rule with an all-powerful hand.

80

Des innocens le sang de vefue &
    vierge,
Tant de maux faicts par moyen de
    grand Roge,
Saints simulachres trempez en ar-
    dant cierge,
De frayeur crainte ne verra nul que
    boge.

The blood of the innocent widow
    and virgin,
Much evil committed by the means
    of that great rogue,
Holy images, dipped in burning
    wax candles,
For fear, nobody shall be seen to
    stir.

A band of marauders shall roam the countryside, despoiling the innocent. Church property shall be unsafe and the populace shall be in great
fear.

81

Le neur empire en desolation
Sera change du pole aquilonaire,
De la Sicile viendra l'emotion,
Troubler l'emprise a Philip, tribu-
taire.

The new empire in desolation,
Shall be changed from the North-
ern Pole,
The commotion shall come from
Italy,
To trouble the undertaking, tribu-
tary to Phillip.

The empire of Germany shall be laid waste by invaders from both the north and south. Spain, her spiritual ally, shall be troubled at the same time.

82

Ronge long, sec, faisant du bon
vallet,
A la parfin n'aura que son congie.
Poignant poyson, lettres au collet,
Sera saisi, eschappe, en dangie.

Long devourer, dry, cringing and
fawning,
In conclusion shall have nothing,
but leave to be gone,
Piercing poison and letters in his
collar,
Shall be seized, escape and in
danger.

This depicts the downfall, capture and escape of a tyrant, before whom people had cringed in fear for many years. Although he is never apprehended, he lives out his years in constant fear and danger and dies a miserable death.

83

Le plus grand voile hors du port de
Zara,
Pres de Bisance fera son entreprise,
D'ennemy perte & l'amy ne fera,
Le tiers a deux fera grand pille &
prise.

The greatest sail out of the port of
Zara,
Near Turkey shall make his under-
taking,
There shall be no loss of foes or
friends,
The third shall make a great pillage
upon the two.

The Venetians (Zara) shall take the Island of Tenedos, near Constantinople, without loss of life on either side.

84

Paterne aura de la Sicile crie,
Tous les aprests due Goulphre de
  Trieste,
Qui s'entendra jusques a la Trina-
  cria,
De tant de voiles, fuy, fuy, l'hor-
  rible peste.

Paterno shall have out of Sicily
  screaming,
All the preparations of the Gulf
  of Trieste,
That shall be heard as far as Trinacria,
Of so many sails, fly, fly, the horrible plague.

There seems to be a misspelling here in the word Paterno. We believe
it refers to Palermo, and warns of a plague that shall strike around that
vicinity.

85

Entre Bayonne & a Saincte Jean de
  Lux,
Sera pose de Mars le promottoire;
Aux Hanix d'Aquilon, Nanar hos-
  tera Lux,
Puis suffoque au lict sans adjutoire.

Between Bayonne and St. Jean of
  Lux,
Shall be put down the promoting
  of Mars,
From the Hunix of the North,
  Nanar shall take away Lux,
Then shall be suffocated in bed
  without help.

After many years of war between France and Spain, peace was declared and a marriage arranged between the King of France and the Infanta
of Spain. The last two lines have no significance and we believe they were
put in merely to make up the rhyme.

86

Par Arnani, Tholose, Ville Fran-
  que,
Bande infinie par le Mont Adrian,
Passe riviere, hutin par pont la
  planque,
Bayonne entrer tous Bichoro criant.

By Arnani, Toulouse and Ville-
  franche,
An infinite number of people by
  Mont Adrian,
Cross rivers, noise upon the bridges
  and planks,
Come all into Bayonne crying
  Bichoro.

"Bichoro" is an old French word for Victory. Bayonne, on the border
of Spain, shall be successfully invaded by the French.

87

Mort conspiree viendra en plein effect,	A conspired death shall come to an effect,
Charge donnee & voyage de mort,	Charge given, and a journey of death,
Esleu, cree, receu, par siens deffaict,	Elected, created, received, by his own defeated,
Sang d'innocence devant soy par remort.	Blood of innocence before him by remorse.

A conspiracy against an elected one is here foreshadowed.

88

Dans le Sardaigne un noble Roy viendra,	Into Sardinia shall come a noble King,
Qui ne tiendra que trois ans le Royaume,	Who shall hold the Kingdom only three years,
Plusieurs couleurs avec soy conjoindra,	He shall join many colors to his own,
Luy mesme apres soin matriscome.	Himself afterwards, care, sleep, repentance come.

A King of Sardinia shall not be in power long, in spite of his strong mercenary army.

89

Pour ne tomber entre mains de son oncle,	That he might not fall into the hands of his uncle,
Qui les enfans par regner trucidez,	That had murdered his children for to rule,
Orant au peuple mettant pied sur Peloncle,	Taking away from the people, and putting his foot on the bald-headed one,
Morts & traisne entre chevaux barbez.	Killed and drawn among horses.

A bald-headed tyrant shall be killed in a dishonorable manner after having misruled the country.

90

Quand des croisez un trouve de
sens trouble,
En lieu du sacre verra boeuf
cornu,
Par vierge porc son lieu lors sera
double
Par Roy plus ordre ne sera soustenu.

When of the crossed, one of a
troubled mind,
In a sacred place, shall see a horny
ox,
By virgin swine then shall his place
be double,
By King henceforth, order shall not
be sustained.

A madman, whose symbol is a strange cross, shall be aided in his schemes of conquest by unmitigated scoundrels (pure swine), but his power will be short-lived.

91

Parmy les champs de Rodanes en-
trees,
Ou les croisez seront presque unis,
Les deuz Brassiers en Pisces ren-
contrees,
Et un grand nombre par deluge
punis.

Through the fields where the
Rhone meanders,
Where the crossed shall be almost
united,
The two Brassiers met in Pisces,
And a great number punished by
a flood.

This quatrain continues from the preceding one, indicating the near-success of the plots of the "madman" and his cohorts and predicting their final overthrow.

92

Loin hors du regne mis en hazard
voyage,
Grand ost duyra, pour soy l'occupera,
Le Roy tiendra les siens captif,
ostage,
A son retour tour pays pillera.

Far from the kingdom a hazardous
journey undertaken,
He shall lead a great army, which
he shall make his own,
The King shall keep his prisoners
and pledges,
At his return he shall plunder all
the country.

A General shall mutiny against a King. In retaliation, the King shall hold his relatives hostage; but on the General's return he shall pillage the country.

93

Sept mois sans plus obtiendra pre-
lature
Par son decez grand scisme fera
naistre,
Sept mois tiendra un aurte la pre-
ture,
Pres de Venise paix union renaistre.

Seven months and no more he shall
obtain the prelacy,
By his decease he shall cause a
great schism,
Another shall be seven months governor,
Near Venice peace and union shall
grow again.

A sharp division of opinion will occur on the death of a Pope after only seven months in office. It will be further aggravated by the death of a governor who also held office for only seven months. When both offices are again filled, to the satisfaction of the dissenting parties, peace will reign once more.

94

Devant le lac ou plus cher fut gette,
De sept mois, & son ost desconfit,
Seront Hispans par Albannois
gastez,
Par delay perte en donnant le con-
flit.

Before the lake, wherein most dear
was thrown,
Of seven months and his army dis-
comfited,
Spaniards shall be spoiled by
Albanians,
By delaying, loss in giving the
battle.

The League of Nations at Lake Geneva is meant here. Spain shall delay giving battle to the English and be the loser thereby.

95

Le seducteur sera mis dans la fosse,
Et estache jusques a quelque
temps,
Le clerc uny, le chef avec sa crosse,
Pycante droite attraira les contens.

The deceiver shall be put into the
dungeon,
And bound fast for a while,
The clergy united, the chief with
his cross emblem,
Pointing upright, shall draw in the
contented.

Those of the party of the Cross shall be supported by the rich. Dissenters shall be thrown into jail in order to keep them from spreading their doctrines of heresy.

96

La Synagogue sterile sans nul fruit,
Sera receue entre les infideles,
De Babylon la fille du persuit,
Misere & triest luy trenchera les aisles.

The Synagogue barren, without fruit,
Shall be received among the infidels,
In Babylon, the daughter of the persecuted,
Miserable and sad shall cut her wings.

There will be a period of great persecution of the Jews, and their Synagogues will become empty and desolate because of it.

97

Aux fine du var changer le pempotans,
Pres du rivage, le trois beaux enfans naistre,
Ruyne au peuple par aage competans
Regne au pays charger plus croistre.

At the finish of the war, to change the glory,
Near the shore shall three fair children be born,
Ruin to the people, by competent age,
To change that country's Kingdom and see it grow no more.

The entire course of a Kingdom shall be changed by the appearance of three brothers, who shall enter into and take over the branches of government.

98

Des gens d'Eglise sang sera espanche,
Comme de l'eau en si grand abondance
Et d'un long temps ne sera restranche,
Veue au clerc ruine & doleance.

The blood of churchmen shall be spilt,
As water in such great abundance,
And for a long time shall not be stayed,
Ruin and grievance shall be seen to the clergy.

This refers to the various religious wars that plagued France and during which numerous clergymen were killed. We believe that it might also indicate the Thirty Years' War, which was primarily a religious conflict.

99

Par la puissance de trois Roys tem-
porels,
En autre lieu sera mis le Saint
Siege;
Ou la substance de l'esprit cor-
porel,
Sera remis & receu pour vray siege.

By the power of three temporal
Kings,
The Holy See shall be put in an-
other place,
Where the substance of the cor-
poreal spirit,
Shall be restored, and admitted for
a true seat.

A coalition of three temporal rulers shall attempt to change the location of the Holy City.

100

Pour l'abundance de l'arme re-
spandue,
Du haut en bas, par le bas au plus
haut,
Trop grande foy par jeu vie perdue,
De soif mourir par abondant deffaut.

Through the abundance of the
army scattered,
High will be low, low will be high,
Too great a faith, a life lost in jest-
ing,
To die by thirst, through abundance of want.

Nations will increase their military might and great armies will be scattered throughout the world. The people, burdened with the increased taxes for the maintenance of these armies, will finally rebel, and world-wide revolution will follow.

Automation and the discovery of new sources of energy will make it possible to reduce all of our power requirements to a point where Labor will not have to be employed more than twelve hours per week. This will eliminate the chief cause of the wars of agression that have plagued the world since the industrial revolution for the diminishing natural resources but will also create a new and powerful Politico-Labor group that will hold the balance of power.

In the United States this shall manifest itself in a new third party built on the foundations of the Union Labor movement.

1*

| Seront confus plusieurs de leurs attente, | Many shall be confounded in their expectation, |

Seront confus plusieurs de leurs attente,
Aux habitants ne sera pardonne,
Qui bien pensoient perseverer l'attente,
Mais grand loisir ne leur sera donne.

Many shall be confounded in their expectation,
The people shall not be pardoned,
Who thought to persevere in their resolution,
But there shall not be given them a great leisure for it.

The collaborationists shall not escape; they shall be sought out and prosecuted.

2

Plusieurs viendront, & parleront de paix,
Entre Monarques & Seigneurs bien puissans,
Mais ne sera accorde de si pres,
Que ne se rendent, plus qu'autres obeissans.

Many shall come and talk of peace,
Between Monarchs and Lords very powerful,
But it shall not be agreed to it so soon,
If they do not show themselves more obedient than others.

We are just on the verge of the fulfillment of this prophecy; relations between powerful industrialists and leaders of the labor organizations shall not be settled soon, unless a greater spirit of cooperation develops.

3

Las quelle fureur, helas quelle pitie,
Il y aura entre beaucoup de gens!
On ne vit onc une telle amitie,
Qu'auront les loups a courir diligens.

See! what fury, alas what pity,
There shall be betwixt many people,
There never was seen such a friendship,
As the wolves shall have in being diligent to run.

Under the guise of political organizational activity, various elements of society shall be set at each other's throats.

* These six stanzas have heretofore been included with Century VIII.

4

Beaucoup de gens viendront parle-
menter,
Aux grands seigneurs qui leur
feront la guerre,
On ne voudra en rien les escouter,
Helas! si Dieu n'enuoye paix en
terre.

Many peoples shall come to speak,
To great lords that shall make war
against them,
They shall not be admitted to a
hearing,
Alas! If God does not send peace
upon earth.

This needs no explanation.

5

Plusieurs secours viendront de tous
costez,
De gens loingtains qui voudront
resister;
Ils seront tout a coup bien hastez,
Mais ne pourront pour celte heure
assister.

Many helps shall come on all sides,
Of peoples far off, that would want
to resist,
They shall be upon a sudden all
very hasty,
But for the present they shall not
be able to assist.

At a time of need, when a great emergency threatens, the nations of the
world will promise to aid the needy, but will not be in a position to give
immediate help.

6

Las quel plaisir ont Princes estrang-
ers!
Garde toy bien qu'en ton pays ne
vienne,
Il y auroit de terribles dangers,
En maints contrees, mesme en la
Vienne.

Ha! Pleasure take foreign Princes,
Guard thyself lest any should come
into thy country,
There should be terrible dangers,
In several countries, and chiefly in
Vienna.

A clear warning to the nations of the world to profit by the example
of Austria, and to arm themselves against subversive foreign propaganda.

CENTURY IX

1

Dans la maison du traducteur de Boure,
Seront les lettres trouvees sur la table,
Borgne, roux blanc, chenu tiendra de cours,
Qui changera au nouveau Connestable.

In the house of the translator of Boure,
The letters shall be found upon the table,
Blind of one eye, red, white, hoary, shall keep its course,
Which shall change at the coming of the new constable.

A disseminator of subversive propaganda will be exposed upon the election of a new local governor.

2

Du haut du Mont Aventin voix ouye,
Vuides, vuidez de tous les deux costez,
Du sang des rouges sera l'ire assomie,
D'Arimin, Prato, Columna debotez.

From the top of Mount Aventine, a voice was heard,
Get you gone, get you gone on all sides,
With the blood of the red one, the passions shall be glutted,
From Arimini and Prato, the Colonnas shall be driven away.

Mt. Aventine is one of seven hills of Rome. A fratricidal struggle shall take place in Italy resulting in the ruin of the Colonna family.

3

La magna vaqua a Ravenne grand trouble,
Conduicts par quinze enserrez a Fornase;
A Rome naistra deux monstres a teste double,
Sang, feu, deluge, les plus grands l'espase.

The magna vaqua great trouble at Ravenna,
Conducted by fifteen, shut up at Fornase,
At Rome, shall be born two monsters with a double head,
Blood, fire, flood, the greater ones astonished.

The expression "magna vaqua" is a derisive term, meaning a great nothing. The significance of the quatrain lies in the prediction of the monstrous Rome-Berlin Axis, and the indication of its short but bloody period of existence.

4

L'an ensuyvant descouverts par deluge,
Deux chefs esleuz, le premier ne tiendra,
De fuyr ombre a l'un d'eux le refuge,
Saccagee case qui premier maintiendra.

The year following being discovered by a flood,
Two chiefs elected, the first shall not hold,
To fly from shade, to one shall be a refuge
That house shall be plundered which shall maintain the first.

A follow-up of the preceding stanza, this predicts the flight of Mussolini to Germany, after the crumbling of his power, and the eventual ruin of both him and Hitler.

5

Tiere doibt du pied au premier semblera
A un nouveau Monarque de bas haut
Qui Pise & Luiques tyran occupera,
Du precedent corriger le deffault.

The third toe shall be like the first,
To a new high monarch come from a low estate,
Who being a tyrant shall occupy Pisa and Lucca,
To correct the faults of him that preceded him.

One of low estate, pretending to improve conditions in Italy, shall seize power and become a dictator.

6

Par la Guyenne infinite d'Anglois
Occuperont par nom d'Angle
    Aquitaine,
Du Languedoc, I, palme Bour-
    delois,
Qu'ils nommeront apres Barboxi-
    taine.

There shall be in Guyenne an in-
    finite number of English,
Who shall occupy it by the name
    of Aquitanian England,
On Languedoc, near the land of
    Bordeaux,
Which afterwards they shall call
    Barboxitain.

The prediction here is that the English will invade and occupy the west coast of France near Bordeaux.

7

Qui ouvrira le monument trouve,
Et ne viendra le serrer prompte-
    ment,
Mal luy viendra, & ne pourra
    prouve,
Si mieux doit estre Roy Breton ou
    Normand.

He that shall open the found
    sepulchre,
And shall not close it again
    promptly,
Evil will befall him, and he shall
    not be able to prove
Whether is best, a British or Nor-
    man King.

The discovery and opening of the tomb of Tutankhamen brought sudden and mysterious death to the discoverer and to members of his family.

8

Puisnay Roy fait son pere mettre a
    mort,
Apres conflict de mort tres in hon-
    este;
Escrit trouve soupcon, donra
    remort,
Quand loup chasse pose sur la
    couchette.

A Younger King causeth his father
    to be put
To a dishonest death, after a battle,
Writing being found shall give sus-
    picion and remorse,
When a hunted wolf shall pose on
    the cot.

A young prince, during the action of a battle, shall turn and, unseen by others, shall kill his father. However, after a short time, documents will turn up in which his murderous intentions are clearly outlined, and he shall be overthrown.

9

Quand lampe ardente de feu inextinguible Sera trouvee au Temple des Vestales, Enfant trouve, feu, eau passant par crible; Nismes eau perir, Tholose cheoir les hales.	When a lamp burning with an unquenchable fire, Shall be found in the Temple of the Vestals, A child shall be found, water running through a sieve, Nismes to perish by water, the city hall shall fall at Toulouse.

There was a custom among the Vestal Virgins of ancient Rome, pertaining to the punishment of those among them who had forfeited their honor. They were buried alive in a cave, with some bread and water and a lamp with an infinitesimal amount of oil. Beyond this reference, this quatrain holds no greater meaning.

10

Moine, Moinesse d'enfant mort expose, Mourir par ourse ravy par verrier, Par Foix & Panniers le camp sera pose, Contre Tholose, Carcas, dresser sorrier.	Monk and Nun having exposed a dead child, To be killed by a bear and be carried away by a glazier, The camp shall be pitched at Foix and Panniers, Against Toulouse, Carcassone shall be against them.

Neglect of the teaching of spiritual values shall cause innocent children to fall prey to false doctrines.

11

Le just a tort a mort l'on viendra mettre Publiquement, & du milieu estaint; Si grand peste en ce lieu viendra naistre, Que les jugeans fouyr seront contraints.	The just shall be put to death wrongfully, Publicly, and being taken out of the midst, So great a plague, shall break into that place, That the judges shall be compelled to run away.

This has some relation to the preceding stanza, involving an extension of those conditions mentioned.

12

Le tant d'argent de Diane & Mercure, Les simulachres au lac seront trouvez; Le figulier cherchant argille neuve, Luy & les siens, d'or seront abbreuvez.	The so much silver of Diana and Mercury, The statues shall be found in the lake, The potter seeking for a new clay, He and his, shall be filled with gold.

A smooth-tongued demagogue, ever seeking new victims under the pretense of reform, shall be shown to have betrayed and looted all.

13

Les exilez autour de la Solongne Conduicts de nuict pour marcher en l'Auxois, Deux de Modene truculent de Bologne, Mis, descouverts par feu de Burancois.	The exiles in the tower of Sologne, Being conducted by night to go into Auxois, Two of Modena, the cruel of Bologna, Shall be discovered by the fire of Burancois.

Pertaining to a local incident of Nostradamus' time, this merely describes the escape and eventual capture of some criminals.

14

Mis en planure chauderon d'infecteurs, Vin, miel, & huyle, & bastis sur fourneaux, Seront plongez, sans mal dit malfacteurs, Sept, fum, extaint au canon des Bordeaux.	On the plain shall be put a great dyers vat, Filled with wine, honey and oil and built on a furnace, In it shall be plunged without evil, those called malefactors, Seven, summoned, at the law of Bordeaux.

Boiling in oil, a favorite punishment reserved for counterfeiters in ancient France, shall be meted out to seven persons at Bordeaux.

15

Pres de Parpan les rouges detenus,
Ceux du milieu parfondrez menez
  loing;
Trois mis en pieces, & cinq mal
  soustenus,
Pour le Seigneur & Prelat de Bour-
  boing.

Near unto Parpan, the red ones
  detained,
Those of the middle sunk and carried far away,
Three cut in pieces and five ill sustained,
For the Lord and Prelate of Bur-
  going.

One of the many feuds among the cardinals and lesser clergymen is herein described.

16

De Castel Franco sortira l'assemblee,
L'ambassadeur non plaisant fera
  scisme;
Ceux de Riviere seront en la
  meslee,
Et au grand goulphre desnier ont
  l'entree.

From Spanish Franco shall come
  the assembly,
The Ambassador not pleased, shall
  make a separation,
Those of the Riviera, shall be in
  the melee,
And shall deny entry into the great
  gulf.

This quatrain is remarkable in that it exactly names the protagonist involved. The reference is, of course, to Franco, the Spanish Civil War and its repercussions.

17

Le tiers premier, pis que ne fit
  Neron,
Vuidez vaillant que sang humain
  respandre,
R'edificer fera le Forneron,
Siecle d'or, mort, nouveau Roy
  grand esclandre.

The third first, worse than ever did
  Nero,
Go out of the valiant, he shall
  spill much human blood,
He shall cause the Forneron to be
  rebuilt,
Golden age dead, new King great
  troubles.

This points directly to King Charles IX, third son of Henry II. The most notorious event of his reign was the infamous Massacre of St. Bartholomew.

18

Le lys Dauffois portera dans Nancy,
Jusques en Flandres Electeur de
l'Empire,
Neufve obturee au grand Mont-
morency,
Hors lieux prouvez delivre a clere
peyne.

The Dauphin shall carry the lily
into Nancy,
As far as Flanders the Elector of
the Empire,
New hindrance to great Mont-
morency,
Out of proved places, delivered to
a clear pain.

An incident in the reign of Louis XIII when Nancy was conquered by
the Dauphin.

19

Dans le milieu de la Forest May-
enne,
Sol au Lyon la fourdre tombera,
Le grand bastard issu du grand du
Maine,
Ce jour Fougere pointe en sang en-
trera.

In the middle of the Forest of
Mayenne,
Sol being in Leo, the lightning shall
tumble,
The great bastard, begat by the
great du Main,
That day Fougeres shall enter its
point into blood.

An incident pertaining to one of the noble families of ancient France,
this needs no further interpretation.

20

De nuict viendra par la forest de
Reines,
Deux pars Voltorte Herne, la pierre
blanche,
Le moine noir en gris dedans
Varennes,
Esleu cap. cause tempeste, feu,
sang tranche.

By night shall come through the
forest of Reines,
Two parts Voltorte Herne, the
white stone,
The black monk in gray within
Varennes,
Elected captain, causeth tempest,
fire, blood running.

At Varennes, Louis XVI, disguised in a monk's cloak, was intercepted
as he attempted to escape from the Revolutionists.

21

Au temple haut de Bloys sacre Salonne,	At the high temple of Blois sacred Salon,
Nuict pont de Loyre, Prelat, Roy pernicant;	In the night the bridge of Loire, Prelate, King pernicious,
Cuiseur victoire aux marests de la Lone,	A poignant victory in the marshes of Lone,
D'ou Prelature de blancs abormeant.	Whence Prelature of white shall be abortive.

During the course of one night, both a Prelate and a King will meet their deaths on a bridge, much to the rejoicing of the lesser clergy of the region.

22

Roy & sa court au lieu de langue halbe,	King and his court in the place of half language,
Dedans le temple vis a vis du palais,	Within the church, near the palace,
Dans le jardin Duc de Mantor & d'Albe,	In the garden, Duke of Mantor and of Alba,
Albe & Mantor, poignard, langue & palais.	Alba and Mantor, dagger, tongue in the palace.

This continues the story of the previous quatrain, describing the intrigue and scandal that prevailed in both the church and the palace.

23

Puisnay jouant au fresch dessous la tonne,	The youngest son playing under the tun,
Le haut du toit du millieu sur la teste,	The top of the house shall fall on his head,
Le pere Roy au temple sainct Salonne,	The king, his father, in the temple of Saint Soulaine,
Sacrifiant sacrera fum de feste.	Sacrificing shall make festival smoke.

A young prince shall be injured by the cave-in of a house. No greater significance can be gathered from this obscure verse.

24

Sur le palais au rocher des fenestres
Seront ravis les deux petits royaux,
Passer Aurelle, Lutece, Denis clois-
tres,
Nonnain,   Mallods   avalle   verts
noyaux.

Upon the palace at the rock of the
windows,
Shall be carried the two little royal
ones,
To pass Aurele, Lutece, Denis
cloisters,
Nonnain, Mollods to swallow green
kernels of fruit.

The journey of two children of a royal household is herein described.

25

Passant les Ponts, venir pres des
rosiers,
Tard arrive plustost qu'il cuydera,
Viendront les noves Espagnols a
Besiers,
Qui icelle chasse emprinse cassera.

Going over the bridge, to come
near the rose-trees,
Arriving late, much sooner than he
thought,
Shall come the news of Spaniards
to Beziers,
Who shall chase this hunting undertaking.

In this particular section Nostradamus seems concerned merely with
trivial events of his day; this quatrain continues in that vein, describing
an incident in a hunting expedition.

26

Nice sortie sur nim des lettres
aspres,
La grand cappe fera present non
sien;
Proche de vultry aux murs de vertes
capres
Apres Plombin le vent a bon
escient.

A foolish going out, caused by
sharp letters,
The great cap shall give what is
not his,
Near Vultry by the walls of green
capers,
About Piombino the wind shall be
in good earnest.

The Pope is here referred to as "the great cap," and the meaning is
that he shall be the arbitrator in a dispute between the Italian cities of
Velitrum and Piombino.

27

De bois la garde, vent clos rond
pont sera,
Haut le receu frappera de Dauphin,
Le vieux Teccon bois unis passera,
Passant plus outre du Duc le droict
confin.

The fence being of wood, close
wind, bridge shall be broken,
He that is received high, shall strike
at the Dauphin,
The old Teccon shall pass over
smooth wood,
Going to the right on the side of
the Duke.

Malcontents shall attempt to form a conspiracy against the government, but it shall be put down almost immediately due to the leaders betraying their cause and going over to the side of the Duke.

28

Voille Symacle, Port Massiliolique,
Dans Venise port marcher aux Pannons,
Partir du goulfre & Synus Illyrique,
Vast a Sicille, Ligurs coups de
canons.

Symaclian Sail, Massillion port,
In Venice to march towards the
Hungarians,
To go away from the Gulf and
Illyrian Straits,
Towards Sicily, the Genoese, with
cannon shots.

A great expedition from Marseilles, arriving at Venice, shall march towards the Hungarians. The Genoese will be driven from Sicily by cannon shots.

29

Lors que celuy qu'a nul ne donne
lieu,
Abandonner voudra lieu prins non
pris;
Feu, nef, par saignes, bitument a
Charlieu,
Seront Quintin, Balez reprins.

When he that giveth place to nobody,
Shall forsake the place taken and
not taken,
Fire, ship, by bloody bitumen at
Charlieu,
Then St. Quentin and Calais shall
be taken.

The powerful dictator shall retreat from northern France, and Calais shall be retaken from him.

30

Au port de Puola & de Saincte
Nicolas,
Perir Normandie au Goulfre Phan-
atique,
Cap de Bizance rues crier helas!
Secors de Gaddes & du grand
Philippique.

At the harbor of Puola and St.
Nicolas,
A Norman ship shall perish in the
Fanatic Gulf,
At the Cape of Byzantia, the streets
shall cry "Alas!"
Help from Cadiz and from the
Spanish King.

The reference here is to the port of Malta, which was besieged by the
Turks. Philip II, King of Spain, sent an army to relieve it, which caused
a great commotion among the people of Constantinople.

31

Le tremblement de terre a Mortars,
Cassich, Sainct Georges a demy
perfondrez,
Paix assoupie, la guerre esueillera,
Dans temple a Pasques abysmes
enfondrez.

There shall be an earthquake by
mortars,
Cassich, St. George shall be half
swallowed up,
The war shall awake the sleeping
peace,
On Easter Day, shall be a great
hole sunk in the temple.

Terrific artillery fire shall shake the earth; England (St. George) shall
be almost defeated; the war shall spread to the ends of the earth; and on
Easter Day, a great cathedral will be hit by a bomb.

32

De fin porphire profond collon
trouvee
Dessous la laze escripts capitolin;
Os, poil retors, Romain force
prouvee,
Classe agiter au port de Methelin.

A deep column of fine Porphyry
shall be found,
Under whose base shall be important writings,
Bones, hairs twisted, Roman force
tried,
A fleet about the port of Methelin.

Porphyry (A. D. 233-305), a Neoplatonic philosopher, wrote many
treatises against Christianity.

33

Hercules Roy de Rome & Danne-marc,	Hercules, King of Rome, and Denmark,
De Gaule trois Guion surnomme,	Of France three Guyon surnamed,
Trembler l'Italie & l'un de sainct Marc,	Shall cause Italy to quake and one of Venice,
Premier sur tous Monarque re-nomme.	He shall be above all a famous monarch.

We believe that the "Hercules" referred to indicates the powerful and famous Napoleon, before whom all Europe quaked.

34

La parte solus mary sera mittre.	The separated husband shall wear a mitre,
Retour conflict passera sur la tuille;	Returning, battle, he shall go over the tiles,
Par cinq cens un trahye sera tiltre,	By five hundred, one dignified shall be betrayed,
Narbon & Saulce par coutaux avons d'huille.	Narbon and Saulce shall have oil by Quintal.

Here is one of the most famous and most discussed prophecies of Nostradamus, and the most remarkable for its mention of so many actual names—Narbon (Narbonne), Louis XVI's minister of war; Saulce, oilman and mayor of Varennes; and the reference to "over the tiles" (Tuileries), which was not a palace when Nostradamus was alive, but was the location of kilns for tiles. The interpretation, then, is that the king and queen were arrested at Varennes because Saulce betrayed them to the soldiers when they came to his shop. The five hundred men were the Marseillais who attacked the palace of Tuileries and formally put the king under arrest. At that time the king was wearing the red "miter" of the Revolution.

35

Et Ferdinand blonde sera descorte,	And Ferdinand having a troop of blond men,
Quitter la fleur, suyure le Macedon,	Shall leave the flower to follow the Macedonian,
Au grand Besoing defaillira sa routte,	At his great need his road shall fail him,
Et machera contre le Myrmidon.	And he shall go against the Myrmidon.

King Ferdinand, of Bulgaria, with a German Army at his command, shall campaign against the Greeks and Macedonians, but he shall fail to conquer them.

36

Un grand Roy prins entre les mains d'un jeune,	A great King taken in the hands of a young one,
Non loin de Pasques, confusion, coup cultre,	Not far from Easter, confusion, of a knife,
Perpet. cattif temps, que foudre en la hune,	Shall commit, pitiful time, the fire at the top of the mast,
Trois freres lors se blesseront, & meurtre.	Three brothers then shall wound one another, and murder done.

The reference here is to the execution of Louis XVI, on January 21, 1793; and also indicating the confusing state of affairs in France at that time.

37

Pont & molins en Decembre versez	Bridges and mills in December overturned,
En si hault lieu montera la Garonne;	In so high a place the Garonne shall come,
Murs, edifice, Tholose renversez,	Walls, buildings, Toulouse overturned,
Qu'on ne scaura son lieu autant matronne.	So that no one shall know its place, so much Matrone.

A tremendous overflowing of the Garonne River shall occur in December with disastrous destruction of life and property.

38

L'entree de Blaye par Rochelle & l'Anglois,	The entrance of Blaye, by Rochelle and the English,
Passera outre le grand Aemathien,	Shall go beyond the great Aemathien,
Non loing d'Agen attendra le Gaulois,	Not far from Agen shall expect the French,
Secours Narbonne deceu par entretien.	Help from Narbonne deceived by entertainment.

The English will attempt an invasion of France by way of Bordeaux (Blaye). The French will issue a call for help to the people of Southern France, but, spurred on by traitors in their midst, they shall refuse to aid their countrymen.

39

En Arbissela, Vezema & Crevari
De nuict conduicts par Savone
attraper,
Le vif Gascon, Giury & la Charry.
Derrier mur vieux & neuf palais
gripper.

By Arbisella, Vezema and Crevari,
Being conducted by night to take
Savonna,
The quick Gascon, Giury and the
Charry,
Behind old walls and new palaces
to grapple.

An incident concerning the minor disturbances between the Italians
and Gascons in Nostradamus' day is described.

40

Pres de Quentin dans la forest
Bourlis.
Dans l'Abbaye seront Flamens
tranchez,
Les deux puisnais de coups my
estourdis,
Suitte oppressee & garde tous
haches.

Near St. Quentin in the forest of
Bourlis.
In the Abbey the Flemish shall be
slashed,
The two younger sons half aston-
ished with blows,
The followers oppressed, and the
guards cut to pieces.

An incident during the war in the Flemish lowlands between Flamans
and the Spaniards, this concerns a peculiar accident which caused much
talk at that time.

41

Le grand Chyren soy saisir d'Avignon,
De Rome lettres en miel plein
d'amertume,
Lettre ambassade partir de Chanignon,
Carpentras pris par Duc noir
rouge plume.

The great Henry shall seize upon
Avignon,
Letters from Rome shall come full
of bitterness,
Letters and embassies shall go to
Chanignon,
Carpentras taken by a black Duke
with a red feather.

This prophecy was fulfilled when Avignon, the one time seat of Papal
power, was seized by the French King.

42

De Barcelonne, de Gennes &
  Venise,
De la Sicille pres Monaco unis,
Contre Barbare classe prendront la
  vise,
Barbar poulse bien loing jusqu'a
  Thunis.

From Barcelona, from Genoa and
  Venice,
From Sicily near Monaco united,
Against the Barbarians the fleet
  shall take her aim,
The Barbarian shall be driven back
  as far as Tunis.

Spain and Italy united in war, shall be driven back in Africa as far as
Tunis.

43

Proche a descendre l'armee cru-
  cigere,
Sera guettee par les Ismaelites,
De tous costez batus par nef
  Raviere,
Prompt assaillis de dix galeres
  d'eslites.

The crusading army being about
  the land,
Shall be watched by the Ismaelites,
Being beaten on all sides, the ship
  carried away,
Presently assaulted by ten chosen
  warships.

A crusading (Christian) army shall attempt an incursion against non-
believers. They shall meet with great resistance and will be forced to
withdraw.

44

Migrez, migres de Geneve tres-
  tous,
Saturne d'or en fer se changera,
Le contre Raypoz exterminera tous,
Avant l'advent le Ciel signes fera.

Leave, leave, go forth out of
  Geneva, all
Saturn of gold, shall be changed
  into iron,
The contrary of the positive ray
  shall exterminate all,
Before it happens, the Heavens
  shall show signs.

Startling! Nostradamus here foretells the advent of atomic power.
He indicates clearly that this force can be used for useful or destructive
purposes. But, with terrifying finality, he warns of the eventual destruction
of our civilization by means of the release of atomic energy—holding out
but one ray of hope, "the Heavens shall show signs," meaning that we will
be given one final chance to determine our destiny.

45 - 50

Ne sera soul jamais de demander,
Grand Mendosus obtiendra son
  empire
Loing de la court fera contre·
  mander,
Piedmont, Picart, Paris, Tyrhen le
  pire.

(COMMUNISM)

He shall never be weary of asking,
Great Liar shall obtain his do-
  minion,
Far from the court he shall be
  countermanded,
Piedmont, Picardy, Paris, Tyrhenia
  the worse.

This points to the doctrine of lies and deceit which was the cornerstone of the Nazi philosophy; and indicates the final downfall of the regime.

46

Vuydez, fuyez de Tholose les
  rouges,
Du sacrifice faire expiation,
Le chef du mal dessous l'ombre des
  courges,
Mort estrangler carne omination.

Get you gone, fly from Toulouse,
  ye red ones,
There shall expiation be made of
  the sacrifice,
The chief cause of the evil under
  the shadow of the gourds,
Shall be strangled, a presage to the
  destruction of much flesh.

In Toulouse, the red ones (cardinals) are warned of an imminent on-slaught against members of the clergy.

47

Les soub signez d'indigne deliv-
  rance,
Et de la multe auront contre advis,
Change monarque mis en perille
  pence,
Serrez en cage se verront vis a vis.

The undersigned to a worthless de-
  liverance,
Shall have from the multitude a
  contrary advice,
Changing their monarch and put
  him in peril,
They shall see themselves shut up
  in a cage.

A petition to deliver a monarch from imprisonment shall be against the will of the people; and for this, the petitioners themselves shall be jailed.

48

La grand cite d'ocean maritime,
Environnee de marets en crystal;
Dans le solstice hyemal & la prime,
Sera tentee de vent espouvental.

The great maritime city of the ocean,
Encompassed with marshes of crystal,
In the winter solstice and the spring,
Shall be tempted with a fearful wind.

The people of London are warned of the approach of a great hurricane which will cause much damage to the city.

49

Gand & Bruxles marcheront contre Anvers,
Senat de Londres mettront a mort leur Roy,
Le sel & vin luy seront a l'envers,
Pour aux avoir le regne en desarroy.

Ghent and Brussels shall march against Antwerp,
The Senate of London shall put their King to death,
The salt and wine shall not be able to do him good,
That they may have the kingdom into ruin.

This is a most remarkable prophecy, for here we have a concatenation of circumstances starting with the number of the quatrain itself, 49; and the unmistakable event referred to was the execution of King Charles 1 in the year 1649.

50

Mendosus tost viendra a son haut regne,
Mettant arriere un peuple Norlaris,
Le rouge blesme, le mesle a l'interregne,
Le jeune crainte & frayeur Barbaris.

Mendosus shall soon come to his high government,
Putting aside a little the Norlaris,
The red pale, the male at the inter-reigne
The young fear, and dreadful barbarism.

The great liar (see Quatrain 45) shall gain supremacy, being especially successful in operations among young people.

51

Contre les rouges sectes se ban-
deront,
Feu, eau, fer, corde, par paix se
minera,
Au point mourir ceux qui machi-
neront,
Fors un que monde sur tout ruynera.

Against the reds, sects shall gather
themselves,
Fire, water, iron, rope, by peace it
shall be destroyed,
Those that shall conspire shall be
put to death,
Except one, who above all shall
ruin the world.

Many peoples will join in a coalition against the "reds"; and even
during a so-called period of peace there will be much bloodshed due to
the bitterness of the dissenting groups.

52

La paix s'approche d'un coste & la
guerre,
Oncques ne fut la poursuite si
grande,
Plaindre homme, femme, sang
innocent par terre,
Et ce sera de France a toute bande.

Peace is coming on one side, the
war on the other,
There never was so great a pursuit,
Man, woman, shall bemoan, inno-
cent blood shall be spilt,
It shall be in France at all sides.

The events depicted came to pass during the reign of Charles IX,
when France was embroiled in a series of wars, and was torn internally
by the constant struggles between the Protestant and Catholic factions
of the population.

53

Le Neron jeune dans les trois
cheminees,
Fera de paiges vifs pour ardoir
jetter,
Heureux qui loing sera de tels
menees,
Trois de son sang le feront mort
guetter.

The young Nero in the three chim-
neys,
Shall cause pages to be thrown to
be burnt alive,
Happy shall be he, who shall be far
from this doing.
Three of his own blood shall cause
him to be put to death.

A tyrannical leader (here referred to as a Nero) shall cause much
destruction of life and property. Three men of his own class shall
destroy him.

54

Arrivera au port de Corsibonne,
Pres de Ravenna qui pillera la
dame,
En mer profonde legat de la Ulis-
bonne,
Sous roc cachez raviront septante
ames.

There shall come into the port of
Corsibonne
Near Ravenna, those that shall
plunder the lady,
In the deep sea shall be the Am-
bassador of Lisbon,
The hidden under the rock, shall
carry away seventy souls.

Corsica shall be the birthplace of one (Napoleon) who shall plunder
Italy and cause great damage to the whole of Europe.

55

L'horrible guerre qu'en occident
s'appreste;
L'an ensuivant viendra la pesti-
lence,
Si fort terrible, que jeune, vieil, ne
beste,
Sang, feu, Mercu, Mars, Jupiter en
France.

The horrible war is in preparation
in the west,
The year following shall come the
plague,
So strangely terrible, that young,
old, nor beast shall escape.
Blood, fire, Mercury, Mars, Jupiter in France.

In the western area, a horrible war is in preparation; following this will
come a terrible plague, such as the world has never seen before.

56

Camp pres de Noudam passera
Goussanville,
Et a Maiotes laissera son enseigne,
Convertira en instant plus de mille,
Cherchant les deux remettre en
chaine & legne.

A camp shall by Noudam pass
Goussanville,
And shall leave its flag at Maiotes,
And shall in an instant convert
more than a thousand,
Seeking to put the two parties in
good understanding.

Events and towns related here are of no importance now, but had local
significance in Nostradamus' dav.

57

Au lieu de Drux un roy reposera,
Et cherchera loy changeant d'an-
  atheme,
Pendant le ciel si tresfort tonnera,
Portee neufue Roy tuera soy-
  mesme.

In the place of Drux a king shall
  repose,
And shall seek a law changing
  anathema,
In the meanwhile the heaven shall
  thunder so strongly,
That a new gate shall kill the King
  himself.

Drux is a city in Normandy; and in this region the King shall attempt
to alter the local religious customs, without success.

58

Au coste gauche a l'endroit de
  Vitri,
Seront guettez les trois rouges de
  France,
Tous assoumez rouge, noir non
  meurdry,
Par les Bretons remis en asseurance.

On the left coast over against
  Vitry,
The three red ones of France shall
  be watched for,
All the red shall be beaten to death,
  the black not murdered,
By the Britons set up again in secu-
  rity.

The British shall re-establish a government in France; radicals shall
be eliminated from any participation in it.

59

A la Ferte prendra la Vidame,
Nicol tenu rouge qu'avoit produit
  la vie,
La grand Loyse naistra que fera
  clame,
Donnant Bougongne a Bretons par
  envie.

In the Ferte the Vidame shall take,
Nicol, reputed red, who is the
  product of life,
The great Louis shall be born, who
  shall lay claim,
Giving Burgundy to the Britons
  through envy.

The reds shall be beaten by the opposite party, with the aid of a British
leader named Louis, who will ask for payment in the form of an alliance
between France and England.

60

Conflict barbare, en la cornere noire,
Sang espandu trembler la Dalamatie,
Grand Ismael mettra son promontoire,
Ranes trembler, secours Lusitanie.

A barbarous fight in the black corner,
Blood shall be spilt, Dalamatia shall tremble for fear,
Great Ishmael shall set up his promontory,
Frogs shall tremble, Portugal shall bring succour.

Inter-sectional warfare among the Mohammedans is here predicted.

61

La pille faite a la coste marine,
Incite nova & parens amenez,
Plusieurs de Malte par le fait de Messine,
Estroit serrez seront mal guerdonnez.

The plunder shall be made on the sea coast,
Incited by new people and friends brought up,
Many of Malta, for the fact of Messina,
Being kept close, shall be ill rewarded.

A coalition of small nations, hitherto considered peaceful and harmless, shall attempt to gain control of Europe.

62

Au grand de Cheramonagora,
Seront croisez par rangs tous attachez,
Le Pertinax Oppi, & Mandragora,
Raugon d'Octobre le tiers seront laschez.

To the great one of Cheramonagora,
Shall be crossed by ranges, all tied up.
The Pertinax Oppi, and Mandragora,
Raugon the third of October shall be set loose.

There is a warning implicit in the words of this quatrain, of a world-shaking event that will take place on October third.

63

Plainctes & pleurs, cris & grands hurlements,	Complaints and tears, cries and great howlings,
Pres de Narbon a Bayonne & en Foix,	Near Narbonne, Bayonne and in Foix,
O quel horribles, calamitez, changemens,	O what horrid calamities and changes,
Avant que Mars revolu quelquefois.	Before Mars has made somewhat his revolution.

Much disturbance in France is foreseen, with many changes taking place, leading to a completely reorganized government.

64

L'Aemathion passer monts Pyrenees,	The invader shall pass the Pyrenean Mountains,
En Mars Narbon ne fera resistance,	In March Narbonne shall make no resistance,
Par mer & terre fera si grand menee,	By sea and land he shall make so much ado,
Cap. n'ayant terre seure pour demeurance.	Cap. shall not have safe ground to live in.

An invasion shall come to France, by way of the Spanish Frontier.

65

Dedans le coing de Luna viendra rendre,	He shall come into the corner of Luna,
Ou sera prins & mis en terre estrange,	Where he shall be taken and put in a strange land,
Les fruicts immeurs seront a grand esclandre,	The green fruits shall be in great disorder,
Grand vitupere, a l'un grande louange.	A great shame, to one shall be great praise.

This stanza has a relation to the preceding one, in that the invaded land shall be despoiled.

66

Paix, union sera & changement, Estats, Offices, bas hault, & hault bien bas, Dresser voyage, le fruict premier, torment, Guerre cesser, civils proces, debats.	Peace, union, shall be and profound changes, Estates, offices, the low high and the high very low, A journey shall be prepared for, the first fruit, pains, War shall cease, also civil processes and strife.

A Utopian age shall come into being in the course of time, but not without pain.

67

Du hault des monts a l'entour de Dizere, Port a la roche Valent, cent assemblez, De Chasteau-Neuf, Pierrelate, en Douzere, Contre le Crest, Romains for assemblez.	From the top of the mountains about Dizere, Gate at the rock Valence, a hundred gathered together, From Chateau Neuf, Pierrelate, in Douzere, Against the Crest, Romans shall be assembled.

This prophecy, obscure and meaningless to us, was directed to the people in the provinces of Dauphine and Languedoc, in which all the towns and rivers mentioned were situated.

68

Du mont Aymar sera noble obscurcie, Le mal viendra au joinct de Saone & Rhosne, Dans bois cachez soldats jour de Lucia, Que ne fut onc un si horrible throsne.	From Mount Aymar shall proceed a noble obscurity, The evil shall come to the joining of the Saone and Rhone, Soldiers shall be hid in the wood on St. Lucia's Day, So that there was never such a horrible throne.

A group of men, banded together in a conspiracy to overthrow the local government, shall attempt a march on the city of Lyons, but shall be overcome by soldiers during a battle in the forest just outside the city.

69

Sur le mont de Bailly & la Bresse,
Seront cachez de Grenoble les fiers,
Outre Lyon, Vien, eulx si grand
    gresle,
Langoult en terre n'en restera un
    tiers.

Upon the Mount of Bailly and the
    country at Bresse,
Shall be hidden the fierce ones of
    Grenoble,
Beyond Lyons, Vienna, upon them
    shall fall such a hail,
That languishing on the ground,
    not even a third shall be left.

A fearful hail (bombardment) shall fall on parts of Italy and Austria, destroying two-thirds of the population.

70

Harnois trenchans dans les flam-
    beaux cachez
Dedans Lyon le jour de Sacrement,
Ceux de Vienne seront trestour
    hachez,
Par les Cantons Latins, Mascon
    eront.

Sharp weapons shall be hidden in
    burning weapons,
In Lyons the day of the Sacrament,
Those of Vienna shall be cut to
    pieces,
By the Latin Cantons, after the ex-
    ample of Mascon.

This foretells the advent of terrible incendiary weapons; and deplores the rise of a science that may lead mankind to ultimate destruction.

71

Aux lieux sacrez, animaux veu a
    Trixe,
Avec celuy qui n'osera le jour,
A Carcassonne pour disgrace pro-
    pice,
Sera pose pour plus ample sejour.

The place of sacred objects shall be
    seen at Trixe,
With him that shall not dare in
    the day,
In Carcassone for a favourable dis-
    grace,
He shall be set to make a longer
    stay.

Holy objects in France shall be defiled, by temporary invaders.

72

Encor seront les saincts temples pollus,	Once more shall the Holy Temple be polluted,
Et expillez par Senat Tholosain,	And depredated by the Senate of Toulouse,
Saturne deux trois siecles revollus,	Saturn two, three cycles revolving,
Dans Avril, May, gens de nouveau levain.	In April, May, people of a new leaven.

According to this prophecy, there will be a complete revision of the basic concepts of religion about the year 2150 (600 years after it was written), and a new world order will arise (possibly one religion for all).

73

Dans Fois entrez Roy cerule Turban,	In Foix shall come a King with a blue Turban,
Et regnera moins evolu Saturne,	And shall reign before Saturn is revolved,
Roy turban blanc, Bizance coeur ban,	Then a King with a white turban shall make Turkey quake,
Sol, Mars, Mercure, pres la hurne.	Sol, Mars, Mercury being near the top of the mast.

Foix, a city in southern France, shall be the center of military disturbances, culminating in the selection of a ruler who will bring great prosperity.

74

Dans la cite de Fertsod homicide,	In the city of Fertsod, murder shall be done,
Fait & fait multe beuf arant ne macter,	Causing a fine to be laid for killing a plow ox,
Retours encores aux honneurs d'Artemide,	There shall be a return of the honors due to Artemide,
Et a Vulcan corps morts sepulturer.	And Vulcan shall bury dead bodies.

In this quatrain, Nostradamus pays honor to a spiritual "contemporary," the writer Artemidorus (100 B.C.), who was widely known in his day for his writings on augurs, and whose books on dream interpretation are still extant.

75

| De l'Ambraxie & du pays de Thrace, | From Ambraxia, and from the country of Thracia, |

De l'Ambraxie & du pays de
Thrace,
Peuple par mer, mal & secours
Gaulois,
Perpetuelle en Provence la trace,
Avec vestiges de leur coustumes &
loix.

From Ambraxia, and from the
country of Thracia,
People by sea, evil and French as-
sistance,
The trace of it shall be perpetual in
Provence,
The footsteps of their customs and
laws remaining.

Provence is shown here by Nostradamus, to have been settled originally
by Thracians, with vestiges of the original laws and customs still remaining.

76

Avec le noir rapax & sanguinaire,
Yssu de peaultre de l'inhumain
Neron,
Emmy deux fleuves main gauche
militaire,
Sera meurtry par Joyne Chaul-
veron.

With the black and rapacious near
a bloody peace,
Descended from the hide of the in-
human Nero,
Between two rivers, by the left
military hand,
He shall be murdered by Joyn
Caulveron.

One of a like character to Nero, black and rapacious, shall meet a violent
death at the hands of revolutionaries.

77

Le regne prins le Roy conviera,
La dame prinse a mort jurez a sort,
La vie a Royne fils on desniera,
Et la pillex au fort de la consort.

The Kingdom being taken the King
shall invite,
The lady taken to death,
The life shall be denied unto the
Queen's son,
And the Pellex shall be at the
height of her ease.

The Latin word Pellex means a concubine. The signification here is
that a King, having taken another country, puts his Queen and her son
to death, taking his concubine as wife and crowning her Queen of his
enlarged kingdom.

78

La Dame Greque de beaute laydique,	The Grecian Lady of exquisite beauty,
Heureuse faicte de proces innumerable,	Made happy from innumerable quarrels,
Hors translatee au Regne Hispanique,	Being translated into the Spanish Kingdom,
Captive prinse mourir mort miserable.	Shall be made a prisoner, and die a miserable death.

The reference here is to Elizabeth of Valois who was married to King Philip II of Spain. According to historical gossip she was in love with another and never found any happiness in her royal liaison.

79

Le chef de classe, par fraude stratageme,	The commander of the fleet by fraud and stratagem
Fera timides sortir de leurs galleres,	Shall cause the timid ones to come out of their galleys,
Sortis meurtris chef renieux de cresme,	Come out murdered, chief renouncer of baptism,
Puis par l'embusche luy rendront les saleres.	After that, by an ambush, they shall give him his salary.

The story of a mutiny on board ship is here related. The commander of the fleet, promising clemency to the mutineers, persuades them to give up the ship over which they have won control; but, reneging on his promise, he attacks and kills many of them. The survivors, enraged at this treatment, turn on and kill him.

80

Le Duc voudra les siens exterminer,	The Duke shall endeavor to exterminate his own,
Envoyera les plus forts, lieux estranges,	And shall send away the strongest of them into strange places,
Par tyrannie Bize & Luc ruyner,	By tyranny Pisa and Lucca will be ruined,
Puis le Barbares sans vin feront vendanges.	The Barbarians shall make vintage without wine.

The ruthless plans for conquest of an Italian Duke are here described.

81

Le Roy ruse entendra ses em-
  busches,
De trois quartiers ennemis assaillir,
Un nombre estrange larmes de
  coqueluches,
Viendra Lamprin de tracteur faillir.

The King by a ruse, shall hear of
  the ambushes,
And shall assail his enemies on
  three sides,
A strange number of friars, tears,
Shall cause Lamprin to desert the
  traitor.

The King shall use strategy to defend himself, and the influence of the
clergy shall cause the "Light Prince" to come to the King's aid.

82

Par le duluge & pestilence forte,
La cite grande de long temps as-
  siegee,
La sentinelle & garde de main
  morte,
Subite prinse, mais de nul outragee.

By the deluge and violent plague,
The great city having been long
  besieged,
The sentinal and watch being surprised,
Shall be taken suddenly, but hurt
  by nobody.

Paris shall be taken over by an alien company by means of a bloodless
invasion.

83

Sol vingt de Taurus si fort terre
  trembler,
Le grand theatre remply ruinera,
L'air, ciel & terre, obscurcir &
  troubler,
Lors l'infidele Dieu, & saincts
  voguera.

The sun being in the 20th of
  Taurus, the earth shall so quake,
That it shall fill and ruin the great
  theatre,
The air, the heaven and the earth
  shall be so obscured and
  troubled,
That unbelievers shall call upon
  God, and his saints.

The tenth of May is foretold as the exact day of the great Cataclysm.

84

Roy espose parfaira l'Hecatombe,
Apres avoir trouve son origine,
Torrent ouvrir de marbre & plomb
la tombe,
D'un grand Romain d'enseigne
Medusine.

The King exposed shall fulfill the
Hecatomb,
After he has found out his off-
spring,
A torrent shall open the sepulchre,
made of marble and lead,
Of a great Roman, with a Medusian
design.

A so-called revolutionary movement, based on the ideas advocated in
Ancient Rome, is here compared to the Medusa's head, in that it turns
the beholders thereof into stone, meaning that its concepts will lead to
a static and unprogressive society.

85

Passer Guienne, Languedoc & le
Rhosne,
D'Agen tenans de Marmande & la
Reole,
D'ouvrir par for parroy, Phocen
tiendra son throsne,
Conflict aupres sainct Pol de Man-
seole.

They shall pass over Gascony, Lan-
guedoc, and the Rhone,
From Agen keeping Marmande,
and the Reale,
To open the wall by faith Phocen
shall keep his throne,
A battle shall be by St. Paul of
Manseole.

Armies shall pass through all the above-mentioned French towns, dur
ing the course of a great war.

86

Du bourg Lareyne parviedrot droit
a Chartes
Et feront pres du Pont Anthony
pause,
Sept pour la paix cauteleux comme
Martres
Feront entree d'armes a Paris
clause.

From Bourge, La Reyne they shall
come straight to Chartres,
And shall make a stand near Anthony's Bridge,
Seven for peace as crafty as Martres
They shall enter in Paris besieged
with an army.

This continues the story in the preceding stanza, and foretells a march
on Paris, culminating in its taking.

87

Par la forest de Touphon essartee	By the forest of Touphon cut off,
Par hermitage sera pose le temple,	At the hermitage shall the temple be set,
De Duc d'Estampes par sa ruse inventee,	The Duke of Prints by his invented ruse,
De Montleheri prelat donra exemple.	Shall give an example to the prelate of Montleheri.

By the ruse of inflated money, the temporal governments shall overcome the authority of the Church.

88

Calais, Arras secours a Theroanne,	Calais, Arras shall give help to the Theroanne,
Paix & semblant simulera l'escoute,	Peace or the like, shall dissemble the hearing,
Soul de d'Alobrox descendre par Roane,	Soldiers of Allobrox shall descend by Roanne,
Destornay peuple qui defera la routte.	People persuaded, shall spoil the march.

An incident in a war between France and Spain, concerning the Netherlands.

89

Sept ans sera Philip, fortune prospere,	Seven years of prosperous fortune shall Philip have,
Rabaissera des Barbares l'effort,	And shall beat down the attempt of the Barbarians,
Puis son midi perplex, revours affaire,	Then in his heyday, perplexed with misdirections,
Jeune Ogmion abysmera son fort.	Young Ogmion shall pull down his strength.

The story here is clearly that of the career of Philip II of Spain.

90

William II

Un grand Capitaine de la grand
  Germanie,
Se viendra rendre par simule
  secours,
A Roy des Roys, ayde de Pannonie,
Que sa revolte fera de sang grand
  cours.

A Captain of great Germany,
Shall come to yield himself by
  simulating help,
To the Kings of Kings, with the
  help of Hungary,
So that his revolt shall cause great
  bloodshed.

Hitler, offering help to Hungary, shall involve her in the general ruin
that follows.

91

L'horrible peste Perynthe & Nico-
  polle,
Le Chersonnez tiendra & Marce-
  loune,
La Thessalie vestera l'Amphipolle,
Mal incogneu, & le refus d'Anthoine.

The horrid pestilence shall be in
  Corinth and Nicopol,
The Crimeans and the Mace-
  donians also,
It shall waste Thessaly and Amphi-
  polis,
An unknown evil and the refusal
  of Anthony.

A great plague shall befall the places mentioned.

92

Le Roy voudra dans cite neufve
  entrer,
Par ennemis expugner l'on viendra,
Captif libere faulx dire & perpetrer,
Roy dehors estre, loin d'ennemis
  tiendra.

The King shall desire to enter into
  the New City,
With foes they shall come to overcome it,
The prisoner being freed, shall
  speak and act falsely,
The King being gotten out, shall
  keep far from enemies.

The New City shall be besieged by a powerful person helped by spies
within.

93

Les ennemis du fort bien esloig- nez, Par chariots conduict le Bastion, Par sur les murs de Bourges esgrongnez Quand Hercules battra l'Haema- thion.	The enemies being a good way from the fort, By chariots shall be conducted to the Bastion, From the top of Bourges' walls they shall be cut less, When Hercules shall beat the Bloody One.

Bourges, a city in France, south of Paris, shall be in the direct path of a march on Paris, and shall be devastated by the invading army.

94

Foibles galeres seront unis ensem- ble, Ennemis faux, le plus fort en rem- part, Foible assaillies Vratislave tremble, Lubecq & Mysne tiendront Bar- bare part.	Weak ships shall be united to- gether False enemies, the strongest shall be fortified, Weak assaults, and yet Bratislava quakes for fear. Lubeck and Misne shall take the part of the Barbarians.

Weak nations, although not trusting each other, shall be forced to unite. Bratislava, a Czecho-Slovakian city, Lubeck and Misne shall be in the hands of the Germans.

95

Le nouveau faict conduira l'exer- cite, Proche Apame jusqu'aupres du rivage, Tendant secours de Milanoise eslite, Duc yeux prive, a Milan fer de cage.	The New Man shall lead up the Army, Near Apame, till near the bank, Carrying aid of elite forces from Milan, The Duke deprived of his eyes, and an iron cage at Milan.

A mob of rebellious soldiers aided by civilians captured and lynched Mussolini and his paramour at Milan in April, 1945.

96

Dans cite entrer exercit desniee,	Being denied entrance into the city,
Duc entrera par persuasion,	The Duke shall enter by persuasion,
Aux foibles portes clam armee amenee,	To the weak gates, secretly the army being brought,
Mettront feu, mort, de sang effusion.	Shall put all to fire and sword.

Because of the clarity of the English verse, we feel that this needs no further interpretation.

97

De mer copies en trois parts divisees,	A fleet being divided into three parts,
A la seconde les vivres failleront,	The living shall fail the second part,
Desesperez cherchant Champs Elisees,	Being in despair, they shall seek the Champs Elysées,
Premiers en breches entrez victoire auront.	And entering the breach first, shall obtain victory.

Three armies shall converge at Paris; the second one will enter it first, and parade on the Champs Élysées.

98

Les affligez par faut d'un seul taint,	The afflicted by fault of one, only died,
Contremanant a partie opposite,	Carrying against the opposite part,
Aux Lygonnois mandera que contraint,	Shall send word to those of Lyons, they shall be compelled,
Seront de rendre le grand chef de Molite.	To surrender the great chief of Molite.

The reference here, we believe, is to Laval and the role he played in the betrayal of France.

99

Vent Aquilon fera partir le siege,
Par murs jetter cendres, chaulx, &
  poussiere,
Par pluye apres qui leur fera bien
  piege,
Dernier secours encontre leur frontiere.

The North Wind shall cause the
  siege to be raised
They shall throw ashes, lime and
  dust,
By a rain after they shall be a trap
  to them,
It shall be the last help against the
  frontier.

The siege of a city will be lifted and an enemy driven back by a wind
storm of such ferocity as to make it impossible for the armies to make
use of their weapons.

100

Navalle pugne nuict sera superee,
Le feu, aux naves a l'Occident
  ruine;
Rubriche neuve, la grand nef
  coloree,
Ire a vaincu, & victoire en bruine.

In a sea fight night shall be overcome,
By fire, to the ship of the west,
  ruin shall happen,
A new stratagem, the great ship
  coloured,
Anger to the vanquished, and victory in a fog.

This tells of a naval battle which took place at night, in which the
firing from both sides was so constant and fierce, that it literally turned
night into day.

CENTURY X

1

A l'ennemy, l'ennemy foy promise,
Ne se tiendra, les captifs retenus;
Prins preme mort, & le reste en chemise,
Donnant le reste pour estre secourus.

To the enemy, the enemy faith promised,
Shall not be kept, the captives will be detained,
The first taken, put to death, and the rest stripped,
Giving the rest that they may be rescued.

The enemy, capturing many by the promise of fair treatment, shall violate his pledge.

2

Voile gallere voil de net cachera,
La grande classe viendra sortir la moindre,
Dix naves proches le tourneront poulser,
Grand vaincue, unies a soy joindre.

The galley and the ship shall hide their sails,
The great fleet shall make the little ones come out,
Ten ships approaching shall turn and push it,
The great being vanquished, they shall unite together.

This is a prophetic description by Nostradamus of the defeat of the Spanish Armada, August, 1588.

3

En apres cinq troupeau ne mettra hors,	After five he shall not put out his flock,
Un fuytif pour Penelon laschera,	He will let loose a runaway for Penelon,
Faux murmurer secours venir par lors,	There shall be a false rumor, help shall then come,
Le chef, le siege lors abandonnera.	The commander shall forsake the siege.

A small group of men, defending their city against a large enemy army, sends out a scout who succeeds in getting through the enemy lines and in bringing back enough reinforcements to drive back the enemy and lift the siege.

4

Sur la minuict conducteur de l'armee.	About midnight the leader of the army,
Se sauvera subit esvanovy,	Shall save himself, vanishing suddenly,
Sept ans apres la fame non blasmee,	Seven years after his fame shall not be blamed,
A son retour ne dira oncq ouy.	And at his return he shall never say yes.

This puts forth the prophecy that Hitler will return alive seven years after his supposed death in 1945.

5

Albi & Castres seront nouvelle ligue,	Albi and Castres shall make a new league,
Neuf Arriens, Lisbon & Portuges.	Nine Aryans, Lisbon and Portuguese,
Carcas, Tholose consurmeront leur brigue.	Carcasonne, Thoulouse, shall make an end of their confederacy,
Quand chef neuf monstre de Lauragues.	When the new chief shall come from Lauragais.

Although this verse is most obscurely worded and weighted down with many seemingly unconnected names, we gather from it the prognostication of the rise of the theory of Aryan supremacy which was one of the basic concepts of the Hitler regime.

6

Gardon a Nemans, eaux si hault
  desborderont,
Qu'on coidera Deucalion renaistre,
Dans le colosse la plus part fuyront,
Vesta sepulchre feu estaint apparo-
  istre.

Gardon at Nismes, waters shall
  overflow so high,
That they think Deucalion be born
  again,
Most of them will run into the
  colossus,
And a sepulchre, and fire extinguished, shall appear.

The description here is of the great flood of the River Gardon, in 1557, which Nostradamus likens to that which was sent upon the world by Zeus and of which Deucalion and his wife were the sole survivors.

7

Le grand conflit qu'on apreste a
  Nancy,
L'Aemathien dira tout le soubmets,
L'Isle Britanne par vin, sel en
  soley,
Hem. mi. deux Phi. long temps ne
  tiendra Mets.

A great war is in preparation at
  Nancy,
The Aemathien shall say, submit to
  all, to me,
The British Isle shall be put in
  want for salt and wine,
The two bloody friends shall keep
  Metz long.

A war between France and Germany, instigated by the arrogant demands on the part of the rulers of Germany, is forecast. The British Isles will be involved much to the distress and suffering of the English people. France will be occupied for some years by the "two bloody friends," but will finally be liberated by the joint efforts of her allies.

8

Index & Poulse parfondera le front,
De Senegalia le Compte a son fils
  propre,
La Myrnamee par plusieurs de
  plain front,
Trois dans sept jour blessez more.

Index and Poulse shall break the
  forehead,
Of the son of the Earl of Senegal,
The Myrnamee by many at a full
  bout,
Three within seven days shall be
  wounded to death.

The reference here seems to be almost purposely obscured by apparently meaningless names; nevertheless, it seems clear to me that it points directly to the situation in North Africa during the early days of World War II, especially pertaining to the death of Admiral Darlan.

9

De Castillon figuires jour de brune,
De femme infame naistra sou-
  verain prince,
Surnom de chausses per hume luy
  posthume,
Onc Roy ne fut si pire en sa
  province.

Out of Castilon, signalized on a
  misty day,
From an infamous woman shall be
  born a sovereign Prince,
His surname shall be from
  breeches, born after his father's
  death,
Never a King was worse in his
  province.

The story told in this and the following two stanzas concerns the
illegitimate son of a woman of ill repute, born after the death of his
father, who grows up to be a powerful and tyrannical figure in the politics
of his day.

10

Tasche de murdre, enormes adul-
  tres,
Grand ennemy de tout le genre
  humain,
Que sera pire qu'ayeuls, oncles, ne
  peres.
En fer, feu, sanguin & inhumain.

Endeavor of murder, enormous
  adulteries,
A great enemy of all humanity,
That never saw worse grandfathers,
  uncles, or fathers,
In iron, water, bloody and inhu-
  mane.

Continuing the story told above, the infamous deeds of this tyrant are
further described.

11

Dessous jonchere du dangereux
  passage,
Fera passer le Posthume sa bande,
Les monts Pyrens passer hors son
  bagage
De Paripignan couvrira Duc a
  Tende.

Below Jonchere a dangerous pas-
  sage,
The Posthume shall cause his army
  to go over,
And his baggage to go over the
  Pyrenean Mountains.
A Duke shall run from Perpignan
  to Tende.

Here we are told that the tyrant becomes the leader of an army, powerful enough to conquer Spain and cause other nations to fear him.

12

Esleu en Pape, d'esleu sera mocque,
Subit soudain, esmeu prompt &
timide,
Par trop bon doux a mourir pro-
voque,
Crainte estainte la nuit de sa mort
guide.

Elected for a Pope, from elected
shall be baffled,
Upon a sudden, moved promptly
and fearful,
By too much sweetness provoked
to die,
His fear being out in the night,
shall make a guide.

After the death of Pope Innocent IX, Cardinal Santa Severina was
elected Pope. However, his election was declared illegal and Clement VIII
was chosen in his place, for which shortly after the deposed one died of
grief.

13

Soubs la pasture d'animaux rumi-
nants,
Par eux conduicts au ventre Herbi-
polique,
Soldats cachez, les armes bruit
menants,
Non loing temptez de cite Anti-
polique.

Under the pasture of cud-chewing
animals,
Conducted by them to the Herbi-
polique belly
Soldiers hidden, the weapons making a noise,
Shall be attempted not far from
the Free City.

Soldiers, disguised as shepherds, shall attempt a surprise attack upon
an enemy town. Betrayed by the clanging of their weapons beneath their
cloaks, they shall be exposed and routed.

14

Urnel Vaucile sans conseil de soy
mesmes,
Hardit timide, par crainte prins
vaincu,
Accompagne de plusieurs putains
blesmes,
A Barcellone aux Chartreux con-
naincu.

Urnel-Vaucile, without advice of
his own,
Stout and fearful, by fear taken and
overcome,
Pale and in company of many
whores,
Shall be convicted at Barcelona by
the Charterhouse.

This stanza is a reading of the horoscope of a contemporary of Nostradamus, Urnel Vaucile.

15

Pere Duc vieux d'ans & de soif charge,	A Father Duke aged and very thrifty,
Au jour extreme fils desniant les guiere,	In his extremity his son denying him the pail,
Dedans le puis vif mort viendra plonge,	Alive into a well, where he shall be drowned,
Senat au fil la mort longue & legere.	The Senate shall give to the son a death sentence.

An ungrateful son shall lead his father to a well and drown him; he is later put to death for the crime.

16

Heureux au Regne de France heureux de vie,	Happy in the Kingdom of France in his life,
Ignorant sang, mort fureur, & rapine,	Ignorant of blood, death, fury of taking by force,
Par non flateurs seras mis en envie,	By no flatterers shall be envied,
Roy desrobe, trop de foy en cuisine.	King robbed, too much faith in kitchens.

This prognostication concerns a King of France who, though happy in his reign and given to no great vices, is yet envied and hated by his subjects, and shall be betrayed by those of his own household.

17

La Reyne Ergaste voyant sa fille blesme,	Queen Ergast seeing her daughter pale,
Par un regret dans l'estomach enclos.	By a regret contained in her breast,
Crys lamentables seront lors d'Angolesme,	Then shall lamentable cries come out of Angolesme,
Et au germain mariage forclos.	And the marriage shall be denied to the German.

The French patriots shall lament and fight against the attempted union with the Germans by the collaborationists.

18

Le rang Lorrain fera place a Van-dosme,	The house of Lorraine shall give place to Vendome,
Le haut mis bas, & le bas mis en haut,	The high pulled down, the low raised up,
Le fils d'Hamon sera esleu dans Rome,	The sons of Haman shall be elected in Rome,
Et les deux grands seront mis en defaut.	And the two great ones shall not appear.

The reference here is to the downfall and subsequent triumph of two rival ruling Houses of France.

19

Jour que sera par Royne saluee,	The day that she shall be saluted Queen,
Le jour apres le salut, la priere;	The next day after the evening prayer,
Le compte fait raison & valbuee,	The account being settled and paid,
Par avant humble oncques ne fut si fiere.	She that was humble before, never was so proud.

A woman of lowly birth shall become a Queen; and as soon as the crown is placed upon her head she shall assume a regal and arrogant manner.

20

Tous les amys qu'auront tenu party,	All the friends that shall have taken the part,
Pour rude en lettres mis mort & saccage	Of the unlearned, put to death and robbed,
Biens publiez par fixe, grand neanty,	Goods sold at public auction, great emptiness,
Onc Romain peuple ne fut tant outrage.	Never Roman people were so much outraged.

A period of oppression of liberals shall occur, accompanied by general confiscation of their property.

21

Par le despit du Roy soustenant
moindre
Sera meurdry luy presentant les
bagues,
Le pere & fils voulant noblesse
poindre,
Fait comme a Perce jadis feirent les
Magues.

To spite the King, who took the
part of the weaker,
He shall be murdered, presenting
the jewels,
The father and the son going to
vex the nobility,
It shall be done to them as the
Magi did at Persia.

A King and his son, taking the part of the people against the nobility,
shall be murdered by a method once used by the ancient Persians when
they desired to dispose of their rulers.

22

Pour ne vouloir consentir au
divorce,
Qui puis apres sera cogneu indigne,
Le Roy des Isles sera chasse par
force,
Mis a son lieu que de Roy n'aura
signe.

For not consenting to the divorce,
Which afterwards shall be acknowledged unworthy,
The King of the Island shall be
expelled by force,
And another subrogated, who shall
have no mark of the King.

On the occasion of King Charles I being beheaded, and Oliver Cromwell being raised in his place, this prophecy of Nostradamus was fulfilled.

23

Au peuple ingrat faictes les remonstrances,
Par lors l'armee se saisira d'Antibe,
Dans l'arc Monech feront les
dolesances,
Et a Freius l'un l'autre prendra
ribe.

The remonstrances being made to
ingrates,
At the time the army shall seize
Antibes,
In the vault of Monaco, they shall
make their complaints,
And at Freius both of them shall
take their share.

A period of unrest and inter-city warfare in Southern France is here
described.

24

Le captif prince aux Itales vaincu,
Passera Gennes par mer jusqu'a
Marseilles.
Par grand effort des forens sur-
vaincu,
Sauf coup de feu, barril liqueur
d'abielle.

The captive prince captured in
Italy,
Shall pass by sea through Genoa to
Marseilles,
By great efforts of foreign forces
overcome,
A barrel of honey shall save him
from fire.

A prince, captured in Italy, shall be brought back to France for trial
in Marseilles. His friends shall obtain his release by bribing the city
officials.

25

Par Nebro ouvrir de Brisanne passage,
Bien esloignez el tago fara muestra,
Dans Pelligouxe sera commis l'outrage,
De la grand dame assise sur
l'orchestra.

By Nebro to open the passage of
Brisanne,
A great way off, el tago fara
muestra,
In Pelligouxe the wrong shall be
done,
On the great lady sitting in the
orchestra.

The only clear reference here is to the "great lady sitting in the
orchestra," which means a woman of noble birth. The interpretation of
the rest of the verse is hard to come by, but we believe there is no greater
significance than that some harm shall befall this woman.

26

Le successeur vengera son beau
frere,
Occuper regne soubs ombre de vengeance,
Occis ostacle son sang mort vitu-
pere,
Long temps Bretagne tiendra avec
la France.

The successor shall avenge his
brother-in-law,
And rule under the pretense of revenge.
That obstacle killed, his dead
blood vituperated,
A long time shall Brittany hold
with France.

The prognosticated event and the fact that it refers to a quarrel between
Brittany and other provinces in France are clearly described in the verse
itself.

27

Charle Cinquiesme & un grand Hercules,	Charles the Fifth and a great Hercules,
Viendront le temple ouvrir de main bellique,	Shall open the temple with a warlike hand,
Un Colonne, Jule & Ascans reculez,	One Colonne Julius and Ascan shall put back,
L'Espagne, clef, aigle, n'eurent onc si grand picque.	Spain, the key, and eagle never at such great pique.

It is here predicted that Charles V of Spain and Henry II of France will split the Church with their quarrels.

28

Second & tiers qui font prime musique	Second and third that make first music,
Sera par Roy en honneur sublimee,	Shall by the King be raised to high honors.
Par grasse & maigre presque a demy eticque,	By a fat one, and a lean one, and one emaciated,
Rapport de Venus faux rendra deprimee.	A false report of Venus shall pull her down.

Here we have a detailed prognostication of events and people involved in the French Revolution. Because of the hostility displayed by the nobility and clergy, two of the most powerful groups in France, toward the Tiers État, this "third estate" constituted itself as a National Assembly and took one of the most active parts in the fomenting of the Revolution. The King (Louis XVI), during this time, was retained as "ruler" of the country. Perhaps the most remarkable part of this prophecy is the clarity of the descriptions of Mirabeau (the fat one), Danton (the lean one), and Marat (the emaciated one), three of the leading figures in the Revolution.

29

De Pol Mansol dans caverne caprine,	From St. Paul's house in a goats' cavern,
Cache & prins extraict hors par la barbe,	Hidden and taken, drawn out by the beard,
Captif mene comme beste mastine,	Captive, like unto an accursed beast,
Par Begourdans amenee pres de Tarbe.	By Begourdane shall be brought near to Tarbe.

One shall seek sanctuary in the Cathedral of St. Paul, but he will be taken prisoner and subjected to great indignities.

30

Nepveu & sang du sainct nouveau venu,	Nephew and blood of the saint newly come,
Par le surnom soustient arc & couvert,	By the surname, upholds arches and covers,
Seront chassez mis a mort chassez nu,	They shall be driven, put to death, and chased out nude,
En rouge & noir convertiront leur vert.	They shall change their red and black to green.

The downfall of the totalitarian groups in Europe is here predicted; but there is also a warning that they will attempt to continue their operations even though they may change their "colors."

31

Le Sainct Empire viendra en Germaine,	The Holy Empire shall come into Germany, _1806_
Ismaelites trouveront lieux ouverts,	The Ismaelites shall find open places, _ISLAM_
Asnes viendront aussie la Carmanie,	Asses shall also come out of Carmania, _KARMATHIAN Mohammedan sect_
Les soustenans de terre tous couverts.	Taking their part, and covering the earth. _BYZANTINE Empire Fell 1529_

The Germans, imbued with the spirit of barbarism, shall embark on a conquest of the world.

32

Le grand Empire chacun en devoit estre,	The great Empire, every one would want it,
Un sur les autres le viendra obtenir.	One above the rest shall obtain it;
Mais peu de temps sera son regne & estre,	But his time and reign shall last little,
Deux ans aux naves se pourra soustenir.	He may maintain himself two years in his shipping.

The struggle for the control of an empire is here described, and the prediction that the successful party will exercise its power for only two years.

33

La faction cruelle a robbe longue,
Viendra cacher souz les pointus
  poignards,
Saisir Florence, le Duc & le
  diphlongue,
Sa descouverte par immeurs &
  flangnards.

The cruel faction of the long robe,
Shall come and hide under the
  points of daggers,
Seize upon Florence, the Duke and
  the long skins,
The discovery of it shall be by vas-
  sals and serfs.

Temporal and spiritual conflict shall ensue in Florence, the city of culture.

34

Gaulois qu'empire par guerre occupera,
Par son beau-frere mineur sera
  trahy;
Par cheval rude voltigeant trainera,
De fait le frere long temps sera
  hay.

A Frenchman who shall occupy an
  empire by war,
Shall be betrayed by his brother-in-
  law, a pupil,
He shall be drawn by a rude
  prancing horse,
For which fact his brother shall
  be long hated.

A true picture, foreseen by Nostradamus, of Napoleon and his numerous relatives, whom he placed on the thrones of Europe.

35

Puisnay royal flagrant d'ardant
  libide,
Pour se jouyr de cousine Germaine,
Habit de femme au temple
  d'Artemide;
Allant murdry par incongeau du
  Marne.

The royal son, heated with ardent
  love,
For to enjoy his German cousin,
Shall in woman's clothes go to the
  temple of Artemis,
Going shall be murdered by an unknown du Marne.

This concerns the son of a King who, very much in love with his German cousin, disguises himself in woman's clothing in order to keep a rendezvous with her in a Church. While going to meet her he is murdered by a person named du Marne.

36

Apres le Roy du Sud guerres parlant,	After the King of the South shall have talked of wars,
L'Isle Harmotique le tiendra a mespris;	The Harmotic Island shall despise him,
Quelques ans bons rongeant un & pillant	Some good years gnawing and pillaging,
Par tyrannie a l'Isle changeant pris.	And tyranny shall change the price of the Island.

The direct implication in this verse concerns King Philip II and the defeat of his Spanish Armada by the English Fleet of Queen Elizabeth. It is further predicted that England will go on to greater glories during the reign of this Queen.

37

Grande asemblee pres du lac de Borget,	A great assembly of people near the lake of Borget,
Se ralleront pres de Montmelian;	Will go and gather themselves near Montmelian,
Passants plus outre pensifs, feront projet,	Going still further, they shall make a project,
Chambary, Moriant, combat Sainct-Julian.	Upon Chambary, Morienne, and shall fight at St. Julian.

Internal struggles shall cause great disturbances in the above-mentioned towns of France.

38

Amour alegre non loin pose le siege,	Cheerful love lays siege not far,
Au Sainct Barbar seront les garnisons.	At St. Barbar shall be the garrisons,
Ursins, Hadrie, pour Gaulois feront plaige,	Ursini, Hadria shall be sureties for the French,
Pour peut rendus de l'Armee, aux Grisons.	And many for fear shall go from the Army to the Grifons.

A general truce shall be declared between the French and Italians; but a period of general conscription, in France, is to follow, because of the large number of army deserters.

39

Premier fils veufve mal'heureux mariage,
Sans nuls enfans deux Isles en discord,
Avant dixhuict incompetant aage,
De l'autre pres plus bas sera l'accord.

The first son will make an unhappy marriage and a widow,
Without any children, two Islands in discord,
Before eighteen, an incompetent age,
Of the other, lower shall be the agreement.

Francis II, King of France, was married to Mary Stuart at the age of fourteen; before he was eighteen he died, leaving her a widow.

40

La jeune nay au regne Britannique,
Qu'aura le pere mourant recommande,
Iceluy mort Londre donra topique,
Et a son fils le Regne demande.

The young man born to the Kingdom of Britain,
Whom his father dying shall have recommended,
After his death, London shall give him a topic,
And shall ask the Kingdom away from his son.

This is a reiteration of a previous prophecy, namely, the abdication of Edward VIII of England, and the accession to the throne of his brother, George VI. This verse, however, enlarges on the subject and hints at the gossip which was directed at Edward VIII and his future wife.

41

En la frontiere de Caussade & Charlus,
Non gueres loing du fond de la valee,
De Ville Franche musique a son de luths,
Environnez combouls & grand myrtee.

On the borders of Caussade and Charlus,
Not far from the bottom of the valley,
Of Ville Franche shall be heard the music of lutes.
Great dancing and company of people met together.

Caussade, Charlus and Ville Franche are towns in Provence, all in the same general vicinity; and the event described is quite obviously a festival.

42

Le regne humain d'Angelique geni-
ture,
Fera son regne, paix union tenir,
Captive guerre demy de sa closture,
Long temps la paix leur fera main-
tenir.

The humane reign of an angelic off-
spring
Shall cause his reign to be in peace
and union,
Shall make war, captive shutting it
half up,
He shall cause them to keep peace
a great while.

A powerful sovereign, of great goodness, shall have a long reign of peace
and prosperity.

43

Le trop bon temps, trop de bonte
royale
Faicts & deffaicts prompt, subit,
negligence,
Leger croira faux, d'espouse loyale,
Luy mis a mort par sa benevolence.

The time too good, too much of
royal bounty,
Feats and prompt defeats, quick
negligence,
Fickle shall believe false of his loyal
spouse,
He shall be put to death for his
benevolence.

By trusting those about him, even believing false rumors about his
wife, a King shall be destroyed.

44

Par lors qu'un Roy sera contre les
siens,
Natif de Bloys subjugeura Ligures,
Mammel, Cordobe & les Dalma-
tiens,
Des sept puis l'ombre a Roy
estrennes & lemures.

At the time that a King shall be
against his own,
One born at Blois shall subdue the
Ligurians,
Mammel, Cordova and the Dal-
matians,
Shadow of the seven, both a Royal
present and spectre.

Many European countries shall be conquered by a great French leader,
but he shall not hold them long.

45

L'ombre du regne de Navarre non vray, Fera la vie de sort illegitime; La veu promis incertain de Cambray, Roy d'Orleans donra mur ligitime.	The shadow of the reign of Navarre not true, Shall make the life of illegitimate chance, The uncertain allowance from Cambrai, King of Orleans shall give a lawful wall.

This deals with the legitimist quarrels of the various contending families for the French throne.

Century VI
49 page 195

46

Vie sort mort de l'or vilaine indigne, Sera de Saxe non nouveau electeur; De Brunsvick mandra d'amour signe, Faux le rendant au peuple seducteur.	The living die of too much gold, an infamous villain, Shall be of Saxony, not the new elector, From Brunswick shall come a sign of love, Rendering a false account, seducing the people.

Industrialists shall seduce the people of Germany, misleading them with many promises, on the strength of which they shall change their government.

47

De Bourze Ville a la Dame Gurlande, L'on mettra sus par la trahison faicte, Le grand prelat de Leon par Formande, Faux pellerins & ravisseurs deffaicte.	From Bourze, City of the Lady Garland, They shall by a set treason, The great prelate of Leon by Formande, False pilgrims and ravishers destroyed.

Paris, City of the Garlands, shall be threatened by a treasonable conspiracy, engineered by a Spanish Prelate.

48

Du plus profond de l'Espagne ancienne,	From the deepest part of old Spain,
Sortant du bout & des fins de l'Europe,	Going out to the extremities of Europe,
Trouble passant aupres du pont de Laigne,	He that troubled the travelers by the bridge of Laigne,
Sera deffaicte par bande sa grand troppe.	Shall have his great troop defeated by another.

Nostradamus predicts the equipment by Spain of the Fascist Blue Division to fight alongside the Nazi Armies at the other extreme of Europe, and their defeat and annihilation at the hands of the Russians.

49

Jardin du Monde aupres de cite neufue,	Garden of the World, near the New City,
Dans le chemin des montagnes cavees,	In the way of the man-made mountains,
Sera saisi & plogne dans la cuve,	Shall be seized on and plunged into a ferment,
Beuvant par force eaux soulphre envenimees.	Being forced to drink sulphurous poisoned waters.

This startling prophecy of a catastrophic event at a pleasure resort not far from the great new city, predicts a tremendous tidal wave of poisoned waters that shall sweep in from the resort and overwhelm the man-made mountain-like skyscrapers of the city.

50

La Meuse au jour terre de Luxembourg,	The Meuse by day in the land of Luxembourg,
Descouvrira Saturne & trois en Lurne,	Shall discover Saturn and three in the Lurne,
Montagne & plaine, ville, cite & bourg,	Mountains and plains, town, city and country,
Lorrain deluge, trahison par grand hurne.	A Lorrain flood, treason by a great Heron.

Commerce and learning shall be endangered by a "flood" of wars, affecting all the peoples of the world.

51

Des lieux plus bas du pays de Lor-
raine,
Seront des basses Allemagnes unis,
Par ceux du siege Picards Nor-
mans, du Maisne,
Et aux Cantons se seront reunis.

In the place of peace of lower Lorraine,
Shall be a basis of a German unity,
By reason of the siege of Picards
and Normans from Maisne,
And in the Cantons they shall be
reunited.

Germany shall endeavor to unify all Europe under her banners, but
shall meet with resistance from all the nations.

52

Au lieu ou Laye & Scelde se
marient,
Seront les nopces de long temps
mainees,
Au lieu d'Anvers ou la grappe
charient.
Jeune vieillesse conforte intaminee.

In the place where the rivers Laye
and Scelde unite,
Shall the nuptials be, that were
long a doing,
In the place of Antwerp where they
draw the grape,
The young unsullied will comfort
old age.

An era of peace in Belgium is foreshadowed.

53

Les trois pellices de loing s'entre-
batron,
La plus grand moindre demeurera
a l'escoute;
Le grand Selin n'en sera plus
patron,
Le nommera feu, pelte, blanche,
routte.

The three harlots shall be long embattled,
The greatest less shall remain
watching
The great Selin shall be no more
their patron,
And shall call it fire, pelt, white,
route.

Three corrupt nations shall be defeated; only the weakest of them shall
survive even though it will suffer much privation.

54

William II

Nee en ce monde par concubine furtive,
A deux halt mise par les tristes nouvelles.
Entre ennemis sera prinse captive,
Et amenee a Malines & Bruxelles.

Born in this world from a furtive concubine,
Set up at two heights by the sad news,
Shall be taken prisoner among the enemies,
And brought to Malines and Brussels.

This is the story of a noblewoman, born of a concubine, who, by the pretext of sad news, is brought to Brussels and there made captive by those who envied and resented her high position.

55

Les mal'heureuses nopces celebreront
En grande joye mais la fin mal'heureuse;
Mary & mere Nore desdaigneront,
Le Phybe mort, & Nore plus piteuse.

The unhappy nuptials shall be celebrated,
With great joy, but the end shall be unhappy,
Husband and wife shall disdain Nore,
The Phybe dead, and Nore most piteous.

This predicts the marriage, in 1572, of Henry IV, then King of Navarre, and Margaret of Valois. The tragedy of the Massacre of St. Bartholomew, in the same year, is also foreseen.

56

Prelat Royal son baissant trop tire,
Grand flux de sang sortis par sa bouche,
Le regne Anglique par regne respire,
Long temps mort vif en Tunis comme souche.

Royal Prelate bowing himself too much,
A great flood of blood shall come out of his mouth,
The English reign by reign restored,
A great while dead, alive in Tunis like a log.

Two separate and completely unrelated prophecies are contained in this stanza. One deals with the death of a dignitary of the Church by a hemorrhage of the throat. The other predicts the saving of the British Isles by the interference in their behalf of a distant nation.

57

Le subleve ne cognoistra son
   sceptre,
Les enfans jeunes des plus grands
   honnira,
Oncques ne fut un plus ort cruel
   estre,
Pour leurs espouses a mort noir
   bannira.

The exalted shall not know his
   sceptre,
He shall put to shame two young
   children of the greatest,
Never was one more dirty or cruel,
He shall put their spouses to the
   black death.

A great tyrant, raised to the dignity of King, shall misgovern greatly, being especially harsh in his treatment of the poor.

58

Au temps du dueil que le Selin
   monarque,
Guerroyera le jeune Aemathien;
Gaule bransler, perecliter la barque,
Tenter Phossens au ponant entre-
   tien.

In the time of mourning, when
   the monarch Selin, *KING of GREECE*
Shall make war against the young
   Aemathien,   *The church*
France shall quake, the ship being
   in danger,
Phocens shall be tempted, the real
   danger in the west.

In the West the Germans shall make their strongest stand; France shall be occupied by enemy forces.

59

Dedans Lyon vingt & cinq d'une
   haleine,
Cinq citoyens Germains, Bressans,
   Latins,
Par dessous noble conduiront
   longue traine,
Et descouvers par abbois de mas-
   tins.

In Lyons, five and twenty of one
   breadth,
Five citizens, Germains, [Brescians
   and Latins,   *CAPITOL LOMBARD ITALY*
Under noblemen shall conduct a
   long trail,
And shall be discovered by a bark-
   ing of mastiffs.

In a time of war, an underground conspiracy against France, fostered by Germans and Italians, shall be shown to be in existence.

60

Je pleure Nisse, Monaco, Pise,
  Gennes,
Savone, Sienne, Capue, Modene,
  Malte,
Les dessus sang & glaive par
  estrennes,
Feu, trembler terre, eau, mal'heu-
  reusse nolte.

I bewail Nice, Monaco, Pisa,
  Genoa,
Savona, Sienna, Copua, Modena,
  Malta,
Upon them blood and sword for a
  new year's gift,
Fire, earthquake, water, unhappy
  ending.

All places mentioned are cities on the Mediterranean; great disasters
to befall them are foreseen.

61

Betta, Vienne, Comorre, Sacar-
  bance,
Voudront livrer aux Barbares Pan-
  none,
Par pique & feu, enorme violance,
Les conjurez descouverts par
  matrone.

Betta, Vienna, Comorre, Sacar-
  bance,
Shall endeavor to deliver Hungary
  to the Barbarians,
By pike and fire, enormous violence,
The conspirators discovered by a
  matron.

(communism)

A conspiracy to betray and surrender Hungary to "barbarians" shall be
uncovered by an elderly woman.

62

Pres de Sorbin pour assaillir Hongrie,
L'herauld de Budes les viendra
  advertir,
Chef Bizantin, Sallon de Sclavonie,
A loy d'Arabes les viendra con-
  vertir.

Near Sorbin, to invade Hungary,
The herald of Buda, shall give
  notice,   *China*
The chief Easterner, Sallon of
  Sclavonia,   *commun-*
Shall convert them to the Asiatic
  law.

(communism)

This stanza has some bearing on the preceding one, inasmuch as it
portends the eventual surrender of Hungary to a "barbarian" form of
government.

63

Cydron, Raguse, la cite au Sainct
    Hieron,
Reveidira le medicant secours,
Mort fils de Roy par mort de deux
    heron,
L'Arabe, Hongrie, feront un mesme
    cours.

Cydron, Ragusa, the city of St.
    Jerome,
Shall revive again the medical help,
The King's son dead, by the death
    of two herons,
Oriental Hungary shall go the same
    way.

This predicts a plague that will fall on Hungary and which, because of the lack of doctors and medical supplies, will kill off great numbers of people, including the son of the King.

64

Pleure Milan, pleure Lucques,
    Florence,
Que ton grand Duc sur le Char
    montera,
Changer le siege pres de Venice
    s'advance,
Lors que Colonee a Rome chan-
    gera.

Weep Milan, weep Lucques, and
    Florence,
When the great Duke shall go
    upon the Chariot,
To change the siege near Venice he
    advances,
When Colonee shall change at
    Rome.

An attempt to change the residence of the Pope from Rome to some place near Venice is predicted.

65

O vaste Rome ta ruyne s'approche,
Non de tes murs, de ton sang &
    substance;
L'aspre par lettres fera si horrible
    coche,
Fer poinctu mis a tous jusques au
    manche.

Oh mighty Rome, thy ruin ap-
    proaches,
Not of thy walls, but of thy blood
    and substance,
The sharp by letters, shall make so
    horrid a notch,
Sharp iron thrust in all the way
    to the shaft.

Rome is doomed to destruction, not actually, but metaphorically by verbal and literary assault.

66

Le chef de Londres par regne l'Americh,	The chief of London by rule of America,
L'Isle d'Escosse t'empiera par gelee;	The Island of Scotland shall be tempered by frost,
Roy Reb auront un si faux Antechrist,	Kings and Priests shall have one, who is a false Anti-Christ
Que les mettra trestous dans la meslee.	Who will put them altogether in discord.

British and American leaders, united in a political venture, shall set up a dictator, who shall in the end betray both leaders and common people.

67

Le tremblement si fort au mois de May,	The earthquake shall be so great in the month of May,
Saturne, Caper, Jupiter, Mercure au Boeuf;	Saturn, Caper, Jupiter, Mercury in Taurus,
Venus aussi, Cancer, Mars en Nonnay,	Venus also, Cancer, Mars in Zero,
Tombera gresle lors plus grosse qu'un oeuf.	Then shall hail fall bigger than an egg.

Confirmation of a previous prophecy, this again signifies May 10th as a fateful day, when the earth shall tremble violently and be bombarded by hitherto unknown weapons.

68

L'armee de mer devant cite tiendra,	The marines shall stand before the city,
Puis partira sans faire longue allee;	Then shall go away for a little while,
Citoyens grande proye en terre prendra,	A citizen army shall then hold the ground,
Retourner classe reprendre grande emblee.	The fleet returning and recovering a great deal.

France shall be blockaded both on land and sea, but a citizen's army will break through on all lines.

69

Le fait luysant de neuf vieux esleve,	The bright action of new old ex-
Seront si grands par midy Aquilon,	alted,
De sa soeur propre grandes alles	Shall be so great throughout the
leve;	North and South,
Fuyant, meurdry au buisson d'Am-	By his own sister great forces shall
bellon.	be raised,
	Fleeing, murdered near the bush
	of Ambellon.

Political upheavals, following the French Revolution, are prognosticated.

70

L'oeil par object fera telle excrois-	The eye of the object shall make
sance,	such an excrescence,
Tant & ardente que tombera la	Because so much, and so burning
neige,	shall fall the snow,
Champ arrouse viendra en decrois-	The field watered shall come to de-
sance,	cay,
Que le primat succombera a Rhege.	That the primat shall succumb at
	Reggio.

A volcanic-like eruption at Reggio in Italy shall cause widespread destruction.

century I
50   page 25

71

La terre & l'air geleront se grand	The earth and air shall freeze with
eau,	so much water,
Lors qu'on viendra pour Jeudy	When they shall come to worship
venerer;	Thursday,
Ce qui sera jamais ne feut si beau,	That which shall be, never was so
Des quatre parts le viendront hon-	fair,
orer.	From the four parts, they shall
	come to honour him.

Nostradamus here predicts the return of an "Ice Age," in other words, a reversal of mankind to the worship of lowly gods.

Century I
16 page 14

72

L'an mil neuf cens nonante neuf sept mois,	In the year 1999 and seven months,
Du ciel viendra un grand Roy d'ef-frayeur,	From the skies shall come an alarmingly powerful king,
Resusciter le grand Roy d'Angol-mois,	To raise again the great King of the Jacquerie,
Avant apres, Mars regner par bon heur.	Before and after, Mars shall reign at will.

A tremendous world revolution is foretold to take place in the year 1999, with a complete upheaval of existing social orders, preceded by world-wide wars.

Nostradamus shows his mystic knowledge of the great secret of the book of revelations and solves for us the identity of the "Beast of the Apocalypse" and the time of his arrival which John of Patmos (Rev. XIII:18) records "Here is wisdom. Let him that hath understanding count the number of the Beast: for it is the number of a man; and his number is 666." By a simple reversal of the numbers and turning 999 upside down we obtain 666.

Also in agreement with the prophetic vision of H. G. Wells and other gifted History and Science-Fiction writers, Nostradamus actually ties in the date 1999 when "from the skies shall come an invasion . . . and Mars shall reign at will." Time alone will tell whether this "War of the Worlds" is to be accepted literally or metaphorically.

Century I
48 page 25

74

Au revolu du grand nombre sep-tiesme,	The year seven of the great number being past,
Apparoistra au temps ieux d'Heca-tombe,	There shall be seen the sports of the ghostly sacrifice,
Non esloingne du grand age mil-liesme,	Not far from the great age of the millennium,
Que les entrez sortiront de leur tombe.	That the buried shall come out of their graves.

When the year 7000 is reached, then Judgment Day shall be pronounced, and the dead shall rise out of their graves.

75

Tant attendu ne reviendra jamais,
Dedans l'Europe, en Asie apparo-
istra,
Un de la ligue yssu du grand Her-
mes,
Et sur tous Roy des Orients cois-
tra.

So long expected shall never come,
Into Europe, in Asia shall appear,
One issued of the line of the great
Hermes,
And shall be over all the Kings of
the Orient.

A consolidation of nations of the East is forecast, under the leadership of a notable scientist.

76

Le grand Senat decernera la
pompe,
A un qu'apres sera vaincu, chasse;
Des adherans seront a son de
trompe,
Biens publiez, ennemy dechasse.

The great Senate will bestow a
great honour,
To one who afterwards shall be
vanquished and expelled,
The goods of his partners shall be,
Publicly sold, and the enemy shall
be driven away.

A man, once held in high esteem by his countrymen, shall betray their interests and shall be exiled for his misdeeds.

77

Trente adherans de l'ordre des Qui-
rettes,
Bannis, leurs biens donnez ses ad-
versaires,
Tous leurs bienfaits seront pour
demerites,
Classe espargie, delivrez aux cor-
saires.

Thirty adherents of the order of
the Quirettes,
Banished, their goods shall be
given to their adversaries,
All their good deeds shall be reputed to them as crimes,
The feet scattered, they shall fall
in the hands of the corsairs.

This continues the preceding stanza, going on to relate the similar fate that was meted out to the followers of the above-mentioned traitor.

78

Subite joye en subite tristesse,	Sudden joy shall turn to sudden sadness,
Sera a Rome aux graces embras-sees,	At Rome to the embraced graces,
Dueil, cris, pleurs, larm, sang, ex-celent liesse,	Mourning, cries, weeping, tears, blood, excellent mirth,
Contraires bandes surprinses & troulsees.	Contrary troops surprised and carried away.

Some newly married couples shall be surprised by a great disaster in the midst of their jollity.

79

Les vieux chemins seront tous em-bellis,	The old roads shall be made more beautiful,
L'on passera a Memphis somen-trees,	There shall be a passage to Memphis summarily,
Le grand Mercure d'Hercules fleur de lys,	The great Mercury of Hercules, fleur de lys,
Faisant trembler terre, mer, & con-trees.	Making the earth, the sea and the countries to quake.

This foretells the time of increased and varied means of communication between the countries of the world.

80

Au regne grand, du grand regne regnant,	In the great reign, of the great reign reigning,
Par force d'armes les grands portes d'arian,	By force of arms the great brass gates,
Fera ouvrir, le Roy & Duc joignant,	He shall cause to be open, the King being joined with the Duke.
Port demoly, nef a fons, jour serain.	Port demolished, ship sunk on a fair day.

This relates the story of a great naval victory that shall take place when a King and a Duke join forces.

81

Mis thresor temple, citadins Hes-
periques,
Dans iceluy retire en secret lieu
Le temple ouvrir les liens famil-
iques,
Reprens, ravis, proue horrible au
milieu.

A treasure put in a temple by Hes-
perian citizens,
In the same hid in a secret place,
The hungry serfs shall cause the
temple to be open,
And take again and ravish, a fearful
prey in the middle.

The Spanish shall put their trust in the Church, taking refuge within
it, but a fearful revolution shall make the temple a ravished place.

82

Cries, pleurs, larmes viendront avec
coteaux,
Semblanyt faux donront dernier as-
sault,
L'entour parques planter profons
plateaux,
Vifs repoussez & meurdris de prin-
sault.

Cries, weeping, tears, shall come
with daggers,
With a false semblance they shall
give the last assault,
Set around they shall plant deep,
Beaten back alive, and murdered
upon a sudden.

This has a relation to the preceding stanza, with reference to a Spanish
revolution.

83

De batailler ne sera donne signe,
Du parc seront contraints de sortir
hors,
De Gand lantour sera cogneu l'en-
seigne,
Qui fera mettre de tous les siens a
mors.

Of battle there shall be no sign
given,
Out of the park they shall be compelled to come,
Round about Gand, shall be known
to the ensign,
That shall cause all his own to be
put to death.

A massacre of a surrendered garrison shall take place in a civil war, between two opposing armies of the same blood.

84

Le naturelle a si haut, haut non bas,	The natural to one so high, high not low,
Le tard retour fera marris contens,	The late return shall make the sad contented.
Le Recloing ne sera sans debats,	The Recloing shall not be without strife,
En emploiant & perdant tout son temps.	In employing and loosing all the time.

A person in high office shall give birth to a natural child, which event shall cause her opponents to rejoice.

85

Le vieil Tribun au point de la Trehemide,	The old Tribune, at the end of the Trehemide,
Sera pressee captif ne delivrer,	Shall be much entreated not to deliver the captain,
Le vueil non vueil, le mal parlant timide,	They will not will, the evil speaking timidly,
Par ligitime a ses amis livrer.	By legitimate to his friends shall deliver.

After three months of imprisonment, an old judge shall deliver the captive safely to his friends, in spite of contrary influences.

centoury VI
49 page 195

86

Comme un Gryphon viendra le Roy d'Europe,	As a Griffon shall come the King of Europe,
Accompagne de ceux d'Aquilon,	Accompanied by those of the North,
De rouges & blancs conduira grande troupe	Of reds and whites shall conduct a great troop,
Et iront contre le Roy de Babylon.	And then, shall go against the King of Babylon.

The Griffon, a mythical monster, half lion and half man, was supposed to keep watch over the gold of Russia. Nostradamus foretells a United States of Europe, under the leadership of Russia, opposing the forces of Mammon.

87

Grand roy viendra prendre port pres de Nice,	A great king shall land at Nice,
Le grand empire de la mort si en fera,	The great empire of death shall interpose with it,
Aux Antipodes posera son genisse,	In the Antipodes, he shall put his horse,
Par mer la Pille tout esvanoistra.	By sea all the pillage shall vanish.

An invasion of the southern coast of France shall take place. In the Antipodes (Japan), they shall put their trust in conquest, but they shall be defeated decisively by sea power and lose their ill-gotten empire.

88

Pieds & Cheval a la seconde veille,	Foot and Horse upon the old watch,
Feront entree vastiant tout par la mer,	Shall come in destroying all by sea,
Dedans le port entrera de Marseille,	They shall come into the harbor of Marseilles,
Pleurs, crys, & sang, onc nul temps si amer.	Tears, cries, and blood, never was so bitter a time.

An invasion of Marseilles by a great armada is indicated.

CENTURY I
63 PAGE 30

89

De brique en marbre serot les murs reduicts,	The walls shall be turned from brick into marble,
Sept & cinquante annees pacifique,	There shall be peace for seven and fifty years,
Joye aux humains, renove l'aqueduct,	Joy to mankind; the aqueduct shall be rebuilt,
Sante, grands fruits, joye & temps melifique.	Health, abundance of fruits, joys and a mellifluous time.

Nostradamus predicts a golden age for humanity after a great calamitous war among nations.

90

Cent fois mourra le tyran inhu-
main,
Mis a son lieu scavant & debon-
naire,
Tout le senat sera dessoubs sa main,
Fasche sera par malin temeraire.

The inhuman tyrant shall die a
hundred times,
In his place shall be put a savant,
a kindly disposed man,
All the senate shall be at his command,
He shall be made angry by a rash
malicious person.

After the death of one of the world's greatest tyrants, a wise and kindly
man shall take his place, and shall fight against the evil laws laid down
by his predecessor.

91

Clerge Romain l'an mil six cens &
neuf,
Au chef de l'an fera election,
D'un gris & noir de la Compagne
yssu,
Qui onc ne fut si malin.

The Roman clergy in the year 1609,
In the beginning of the year shall
make a choice,
Of gray and black, come out of the
country,
Such a one never a worse was.

As stated before, Nostradamus dates all events from the Council of
Nicaea, A.D. 325. By adding 1609 to this date we have 1934, the year
Hitler was granted full power.

92

Devant le pere l'enfant sera tue,
Le pere apres entre cordes de jonc,
Genevois peuple sera esvertu,
Cisant le chef au milieu comme un
tronc.

The child shall be killed before the
father's eyes,
The father shall enter into ropes
of rushes,
The people of Geneva shall not-
ably stir themselves,
The chief lying in the middle like
a log.

The League of Nations, its headquarters at Geneva, and its unhappy
career, are clearly foreshadowed by Nostradamus.

93

La barque neufue rescuera les voyages,
La & aupres transfereront l'empire,
Beaucaire, Arles, retiendront les hostages,
Pres deux colomnes trouvees de porphire.

The new ship shall make a voyage,
Into the place, and thereby transfer the empire,
Beaucaire, Arles, shall keep the hostages,
Near them shall be found two columns of porphyry.

A government shall change not only its political and economic structure, but shall move to a new city and establish new headquarters there.

94

De Nismes, d'Arles, & Vienne contemner,
N'obey tout a l'edict Hesperique;
Aux labouriez pour le grand condamner,
Six eschappez en habit seraphicque.

From Nismes, from Arles, and Vienna contempt,
They shall not obey the Spanish proclamation,
To the laboratories to condemn the great one,
Six escaped in a seraphical habit.

This predicts a rebellion of the cities mentioned against an edict issued by a tyrannical leader of the Spanish nation.

95

Dans les Espagnes viedra Roy trespuissant,
Par mer & terre subjugant au midy;
Ce mal sera, rabaissant le croisant,
Baisser les aesles a ceux du Vendredy.

A most potent King shall come into Spain,
Who by sea and land shall subjugate the south,
This evil shall beat down the horns of the crescent,
And lower the wings of those of Friday.

A powerful ruler shall embark from Spain to crush an Arab confederation.

96

Religion du nom des mers viendra,
Contre la secte fils Adaluncatif,
Secte obstinee deploree craindra,
Des deux blessez par Aleph &
Aleph.

Religion of the name of the seas
shall come,
Against the Sect of Caitifs of the
Moon,
The deplorably obstinate sect, shall
be afraid,
Of the two wounded by A. and A.

One must delve deeply into these cryptic words in order to grasp their full meaning. The "Caitifs of the Moon" indicates the Arab nation. The phrase "A. and A." means America. The sense then is that there will be a struggle between the opposing philosophies of the two groups.

97

Triremes pleines tout aage captifs,
Temps bon a mal, le doux pour
amertume,
Proye a Barbares trop tost seront
hastifs,
Cupide de voir plaindre au vent la
plume.

Triremes full of captives of all ages,
Time good for evil, the sweet for
the bitter,
Prey to the Barbarians, they shall
be too hasty,
Desirous to see the feather com-
plain in the wind.

A continuation of the preceding stanza, this relates the bitter struggles that will ensue.

98

La splendeur claire a pucelle jou-
euse
Ne luyra plus long temps sera sans
sel;
Avec marchans, ruffians, loups odi-
euse,
Tous pesle mesle monstre universal.

The clear splendour of the joyous
maid,
Shall shine no more, she shall be
a great time without salt,
With merchants, ruffians, wolves,
odious,
All promiscuously, she shall see a
universal monster.

France shall be closely associated for a while with nations of hitherto enemy status.

99

La fin le loup, le lyon, boeuf &
l'asne,
Timide dama seront avec mastins,
Plus ne charra a eux la douce
manne,
Plus vigilance & custode aux mastins.

At last the wolf, the lion, ox and
ass,
The gentle doe, shall lie down
with the mastiffs.
The manna shall no more fall to
them,
There shall be no more watching
and keeping of mastiffs.

This reiterates previous prognostications of a period of peace and plenty and elimination of war.

100

Le grand empire sera par Angle-
terre,
Le Pampotam des ans plus de trois
cens,
Grandes copies passer par mer &
terre,
Les Lusitains n'en seront pas contens.

The great empire shall be in England,
The Pempotan for more than three
hundred years,
Great armies shall pass through
land and sea,
The Lusitainians shall not be content therewith.

A period of great power for England, during which time her empire will reach to the far ends of the earth, is here predicted.

73

Le temps present avec ques le
passe,
Sera juge par grand jovialiste,
Le monde tard luy sera lasse,
Et desloyal par le clerge juriste.

The present time together with the
past,
Shall be judged by a great jovialist,
The world shall at last be weary of
him,
And shall be thought without faith
by churchly critics.

This describes the influence of Rabelais on customs and manners during the time of Nostradamus.

CENTURY XI

[There follow fragments of Centuries XI and XII, the remainder of which have been lost. The original numbering of the verses has been retained.]

91

Meysinier, Manthis & le tiers qui viendra,
Peste & nouveau insult, enclos troubler,
Aix & les lieux fureur dedans mordra,
Puis le Phocens viendrot leur mal doubler.

Meysinier, Manthi and the third that shall come,
Plague and new insult shall trouble them,
The fury of it shall bite in Aix and places nearby,
Then the Phocens shall come and double their misery.

This prognosticates not only the coming of a plague to the city of Aix, in Provence, but also implies that they will have trouble with the inhabitants of Marseilles (Phocens).

97

Par Ville-franche, mascon en desarroy,
Dans les fagots, seront soldats cachez,
Changer de temps enprime pour le Roy,
Par de chalon & moulins tous hachez.

By the Ville Franche, Mascon shall be in disorder,
In the fagots shall soldiers be hidden.
The time shall change in prime for the King,
By dragnets and mills they shall be hewed to pieces.

Civil war will bedevil France in a struggle between the rulers and the people.

5

Feu, flamme, faim, furt, farouche,
fumee,
Fera faillir, froissant fort, foy
faucher;
Fils de Deite! toute Provence hu-
mee,
Chasse de Regne, enrage sans
crocher.

Fire, flame, hunger, theft, wild
smoke,
Shall cause to fail, bruising hard to
move faith,
Son of God! All Provence swallowed up,
Driven from the Kingdom, raging
and without spitting.

Religious wars, having to do with the struggle for supremacy between faiths, are visualized by Nostradamus.

24

Le grand secours venu de la Guen-
ne,
S'arrestera tout aupres de Poitiers.
Lyon rendu par Montluel & Vienne,
Et saccagez par tout gens de mes-
tiers.

The great help that came from
Gascony,
Shall stop suddenly at Poitiers,
Lyon surrendered by Montluel and
Vienna,
And ransacked by all kinds of
tradesmen.

Help for oppressed France shall be delayed; meanwhile German industrialists shall entrench themselves in the economic life of the nation.

CENTURY VI
45 · 80

36

Assault farouche en Cypre se prepare,
Larme a l'oeil, de ta ruine proche;
Byzance classe, Morisque, si grand
tare,
Deux differente, le grand vast par
la roche.

A savage assault is preparing in
Cyprus,
Tears in my eye, thy ruin ap-
proaches,
The fleet of Turkey and the Moors
so great damage,
Two opposing, the great waste by
the rock.

Many battles between Moslems and Christians are envisaged by Nostradamus.

52

Deux corps un chef, champs divisez
en deux,
Et puis respondre a quatre ouys,
Petits pour grands, a pertuis mal
pour eux,
Tour d'Aigues foudre, pire pour
Eussovis.

Two bodies, one head, fields divided into two,
And then answer to four unheard
ones,
Small for great ones, open evil for
them,
The tower of Aigues struck by
lightning, worse for Euffovis.

Two nations shall amalgamate, electing one ruler; they shall then be
challenged by four other nations, and shall prove their united strength.

55

Tristes consiels, desloyaux, cauteleux,
Aduis meschant, la loy sera trahie,
Le peuple esmeu, farouche, querel-
leux;
Tant bourg que ville, toute la paix
haye.

Sad councils, unfaithful and malicious,
By ill advice the law shall be betrayed,
The people shall be moved, wild
and quarrelsome,
Both in country and city the place
shall be hated.

Here is a picture of the consequences of bad laws and government,
and the ills that befall the people thereby.

56

Roy contre Roy & le Duc contre
Prince,
Haine entre iceux, dissension hor-
rible,
Rage & fureur sera tout province,
France grande guerre & change-
ment terrible.

King against King, and Duke
against Prince,
Hatred between them, horrid dissension,
Rage and fury shall be in every
province,
Great wars in France and horrid
changes.

Civil war in France is repeatedly predicted by Nostradamus.

59

L'accord & pache sera tu tout rompue;
Les amitiez polues par discorde,
L'haine euvieillie, tout foy corrom-
pue,
Et l'esperance, Marseille sans concorde.

The accord and pact shall be
broken to pieces,
The friendship polluted by discord
The hatred shall be old, all faith
corrupted,
And hope also, Marseilles without
concord.

A continuation of the preceding stanza this goes on to give the evil
consequences of such debacles.

62

Guerres, debats, a Blois guerre &
tumulte,
Divers aguets, adveux inopinables,
Entrer dedans Chasteau Trompette, insulte,
Chasteau du Ha, qui en seront
coulpables.

War and debates, at Blois fighting
and tumult,
Several lying in wait acknowledg-
ment unexpected,
They shall get into the Chateau
Trompette, by abuse,
And into the Chateau du Ha, who
shall be culpable.

These last few verses show the concern and uneasiness with which
Nostradamus viewed the France of his day, and the France which he foresaw. Here again he warns of the horror of internecine warfare.

65

A tenir fort par fureur contraindra,
Tout coeur trembler, Langon advent terrible,
Le coup de pied mille pied se rendra,
Guiront, Garon, ne furent plus horribles.

He shall by fury compel them to hold out,
Every heart shall tremble, Langon shall have a terrible event
The kick shall return to thee a thousand kicks,
Gironde, and Garonne rivers are no more horrible.

The confusion within the League of Nations, and the role of France in its final dissolution, is foretold.

69

Eiovas proche, esloigner Lac Leman,
Fort grands appreste, retour confusion,
Loin des nepeuex, du feu grand Supelman,
Tous de leur suyte.

Eiovas is near, yet seemeth far from Lake Geneva,
Very great preparations, return confusion,
Far from the nephews of the late Supelman,
And all of their suite.

And in this stanza, Nostradamus looks far into the future to predict the coming of a French leader, stern and unyielding, who shall lead his people out of bondage.

71

Fleuves, rivieres de mal seront obstacles,
La vieille flame d'ire non appaisee,
Courir en France, cecy comme d'oracles,
Maisons, manoirs, palais, secte rasee.

Brooks and rivers, shall be a stopping to evil,
The old flame of anger being not yet appeased,
Shall run through France, take this as an oracle,
Houses, manors, palaces, sects shall be razed.

This final prediction by Nostradamus points to the fact that not until complete political and economic equality is realized in France, shall there be an end to the spirit of unrest.